Hens, Hooves, Woollies and Wellies

The Diary of a Farmer's Wife

Bobbi Mothersdale

Old Pond
PUBLISHING

Hens, Hooves, Woollies and Wellies

The Diary of a Farmer's Wife

Bobbi Mothersdale

Old Pond
PUBLISHING

First published 2016

Published by
Old Pond Publishing
an imprint of
5M Publishing Ltd,
Benchmark House,
8 Smithy Wood Drive,
Sheffield, S35 1QN, UK
Tel: +44 (0) 1234 81 81 80
www.5mpublishing.com
www.oldpond.com

A catalogue record for this book is available from the British Library

ISBN 978-1-910456-27-9

Book layout by Servis Filmsetting Ltd, Stockport
Printed and bound in India by Replika Press Pvt. Ltd.
Illustrations by Jacqueline Sinclair
Photos by Bobbi Mothersdale unless otherwise credited

Contents

Acknowledgements

All my love and thanks to John, my wonderful husband, without whose cajoling and encouragement I would never have managed to organise myself enough to put this diary together. And also to my daughters Bryony and Joanna, and their husbands Chris and Matt, who have had such faith in me finally managing to do it. Not forgetting our grandchildren, Jessica, Oliver and Sophie for the joy they have brought to our life. Or the dogs, poultry, cows and sheep, who may not always bring joy, but certainly provide inspiration, occasionally an income, and always fulfil our lives. Many apologies and thanks, too, to the wide circle of friends I have unscrupulously drawn on when they unwittingly provide me with material. Thanks too to Rachel, of 5m/Old Pond Publishing, who found my email wondering if they would be interested in a book and acted on it so swiftly. Finally, last but certainly not least, my fantastic and loyal friend of many many years, Jacqueline Sinclair, for the fun that her witty and clever illustrations bring to this diary.

Introduction

It was the incongruity of the scene that amused me. A dozen men, each wearing a sartorial blend of green, green or green, sat on straw bales in the back of our livestock trailer. Add to this a pack of yapping dogs either entranced by the possibility of a close encounter with a fresh bitch or a punch-up with that snarly spaniel, and the comedy mix was irresistible. Only the fact that each man was hanging on grimly to a shotgun as they tried to quell their overexcited dogs, sobered the scenario up.

And it was this image that stayed with me as I retired to the kitchen to clear up coffee cups, sweep away dog hairs and retrieve a terrified cat from where she had been hiding upstairs on our daughter's bed. Computers in any shape or form were unknown then on this farm. In fact the farm accounts and records are still inscribed long hand. Only the fact that we have to do the VAT each month on the government portal has forced us online. So, with the image of men standing in the yard waiting to be divided into teams, just as if they were still in the infants' playground, despite guns slung casually over arms and cartridge belts and gun bags rather distracting from that image, I set pen to paper to record it. I still do. Every week. Keeping a diary of the farms highs and lows, changes in agricultural policy from changing government departments, comings and goings in farm pets, family, visitors, officials, crops, friends and tackle. The most life changing was ceasing to milk. But we were spared the trauma of herd dispersal by introducing a bull to our ladies instead of a visit by your friendly artificial inseminator operator. Now we have a beef herd. And contented cows and a very lucky bull.

My husband John has always farmed. His parents farmed. His mum was a Land Army girl in the war. His father, as farm manager, managed a pedigree Jersey herd and ran a large arable farm in Nottinghamshire. It was only on the retirement of his father and recognition that their sons John and Geoff, and especially John who had been to Brackenhurst agricultural college, saw their future in farming, that the family sank their combined savings into a small farm in Yorkshire in 1970. And nine milking cows. One of which died in the first week.

For the first years life was a struggle. Geoff, a qualified joiner, supplemented the farm income by working off the farm in between milking cows. John spent the summers as part of a sheep-clipping gang. Where, according to him, you have to be 'strong in the back, but not in the head'. Both of them, as keen shots, provided their mother Rose with a plentiful supply of game, whilst Pop, a keen gardener, tilled the kitchen garden.

Now settled in farm life, John married his college girlfriend Kath. Who, tragically, died only a few years later from cancer. So it was by chance, lucky for me, questionable for him, that we met. And married in 1986. Not being brought up on a farm, I found the whole lifestyle wonderful. Funny. Frustrating. Rich, and here I mean in experiences. Tragic at times. Uplifting, others.

After splitting the farm with John's brother in 2007, we now farm two hundred acres of mixed grassland and arable. A suckler herd and flock of sheep are the livestock enterprises. My poultry and the dogs, Fizz, Pip and Millie, grace the farmyard. Bryony and Jo, our daughters, and three grandchildren, Jessica, Ollie and Sophie, emotionally enrich and financially impoverish our lives. As they do most families.

I have tried to write an account of a year on the farm. It gives I hope a flavour of the fun, friends, family, failures and fortunes we have. I just love it. And those men and their dogs still keep turning up in the yard. Think it's the coffee they like.

January

1st

Five new calves in five days. The New Year is starting well. Few of the cows have required assistance with calving. This was fortunate as nearly all the calves have arrived in the wee small hours, midway between the midnight check and the six o'clock look in. The calves are all smaller than the average and John attributes this to the fact that neither the grazing nor the silage the cows have been on since bringing the herd in, is as nutritious as in previous years. The culprit? The weather. More particularly the excess rain and low temperatures of last year's summer. But the positive side is the fact that calving has undoubtedly been easier for the cows. Variability in weather temperatures is creating its own set of problems – a threat of pneumonia for the calves. The cows themselves regularly leave the main foldyard to visit the silage clamp, which enjoys, although under cover, good access to fresh air and through draughts. The foldyard, which is where the calves tend to stay, bedded up cosily in the straw, is much muggier and provides an ideal environment for respiratory infections to thrive. John is keeping the outside gates open to ensure fresh air can blow through, but it is still a steamy hothouse with all those plops of cow poo emerging at frequent intervals.

This morning another set of twins arrived. John was off out early on farm business despite it being New Year's Day, but had time to give them a quick squirt of iodine on their umbilical cords at breakfast time. This evening I helped him dip their navels and put some ear tags in for identification. Tricky with an increasingly crowded foldyard. We noticed, however, a previously healthy calf, now a fortnight old, looked decidedly poorly and off colour. 'If it was a lamb I would say it had watery mouth,' John said. He was not sure so rang the vet. I had seen the calf drink from its mum this morning but its breathing was now laboured. The vet came quickly and gave the calf an antibiotic jab as it appeared to have a bacterial infection. Within an hour the calf looked even worse. Had gone down completely. We rang the vet again, who thought it might have had a severe reaction to the injection and was very distressed. The vet diagnosed it as an anaphylactic response with the only treatment he recommended being a steroid jab. Unhappily it did not work and we lost the calf within a short time just before midnight. A very long New Year's Day.

2nd

Fizz, our young sheepdog, has had a meaningful encounter with the sheep. We took her with us on a lead when we were moving the ewes from one field, along the lane, to another pasture. Around the yard she is quite brave with the guinea fowl and hens, but I am afraid that my plans for training her with the Aylesbury ducks came to nothing. There is not much rounding up a dog can do with a freezer full of frozen ducks. Which was their fate yesterday. Amazingly the ewes responded to the sight of Fizz. She may only just be full grown, but that silhouette/ shape/outline of a black and white border collie is clearly imprinted on the ewes' minds as one to be wary of. There was no way they were going to come to the gate, despite the alluring shake of a feed bag, whilst I had her on the lead. So I backed off. John then decided to take her with him to get behind the sheep and drive them to the gate. Fizz wriggled out of her collar and ran to me, scattering sheep. Finally when they left the field I walked ahead of the flock with her, and led them to the fresh grazing. Normally the sheep belt past at this stage, overwhelming you in a fetlock, fleck, flick and frock (I hope you are impressed) of sheep. Not so this time. Fizz may still be only young, but it was enough to keep that headstrong, rampant flock in order. Bodes well for the future.

3rd

After fifteen minutes of frantic barking I decided I had better investigate what our Jack Russell, Millie, was up to. I traced the call to the main grain shed. John had been loading wheat onto an articulated lorry and Millie had seized her chance to investigate in forbidden territory. We try to keep Millie out of this shed, as she is addicted to ripping down the plastic sheeting that lines the walls. The sheeting is to prevent any damp coming through the breeze blocks but unfortunately it also provides an insulated and protected environment for mice to breed in. There are mouse traps galore but it is difficult to keep the shed totally vermin free, especially when the doors are left open at times for vehicles to access the corn heaps. The intensity of yapping increased as I walked up to the combine harvester that is stored over winter in this grain shed. Beside the combine a rat breathed its last. Shaken to death by a killer terrier. Millie's frenzied barking now had an echoing ring. She had accessed the bowels of the combine, tracking down yet another rat, and the crescendo of yips and yaps did not cease until a muffled banging indicated she had cornered her quarry and was shaking it from side to side against the combine walls. Two minutes later a triumphant Millie appeared. Rat in jaws. One last crunch and she dropped her trophy at my feet, ready to return to her bed in front of the cooker and a well-deserved kip.

Millie's best trick, however, is discovering mice hiding inside the tread of tractor tyres. She waits beside the huge wheels occasionally scratching impotently at the tyres in a doomed attempt to persuade the mice to commit suicide by venturing out from the safety of the tread. Then after a few minutes of fruitless barking at the wheel, she turns her attention to anyone in the vicinity and barks at them. This is a sign/instruction/demand to drive the tractor forward an inch or two to frighten the mouse into making a bolt for it. Its last one. I am amazed at her transformation from lapdog to killer mode. She is wonderful with little children, fawns over visiting adults, dotes on John, and tolerates me. Because I feed her. To add to her virtues, she joyfully accepts endless stroking, never objects to the other dogs thieving her titbits and uncomplainingly shares her pile of squeaky toys. The perpetual perfume of cow muck or sheep poo does not always endear us to her on the sofa. Plus the enticing licks and kisses she gives us after having chewed on a tasty morsel of a cow's afterbirth are best avoided. But say 'Rats, rats, Millie' to her, and she is instantly on the alert, bouncing up and down ready to assassinate at the drop of a dog biscuit. We have friends (just a few) whose Jack Russell was a distant relation to Millie. Fly, a very pretty, intelligent bitch went manic when told 'Cyril squirrel' is in the garden. Must be in the genes. Fly too was a brilliant ratter, and particularly adept at tracking down anything at all that was vaguely edible, including, I remember, salted peanuts. Unusual, as all our Jack Russells have been very fussy eaters. But Millie is especially keen to hang around the foldyards when they are being cleaned out. Her moment of glory is when feed troughs are moved and the population of mice or rats that have set up house near a regular meal of barley, leave it till the last minute to run. Straight into the jaws of an eager Jack Russell.

4th

It is a relief to be getting back to normal after the hustle and bustle of festive occasions. I love Christmas and New Year but there is no doubt that it's hard work feeding and cleaning and washing and changing beds, and clearing up toys and entertaining for nearly a fortnight. You get out of the habit. Our youngest grandchild Sophie, aged two, was born on Christmas Day, so that is always a happy mix of Christmas and birthday cakes, more presents than can be reasonably opened on one day and clear space between Christmas lunch and birthday tea. This double celebration is enjoyed by the whole family, especially her cousins Jessica, aged twelve, and Ollie, ten.

This morning the house was empty except for we two and the dogs. I read in bed until summoned to help with the sheep, knowing that we are having a clean-up day of food and not much to do except crush the odd discarded decoration underfoot. Come the end of the week they will all be back in boxes up in the loft and the house will not look half so cheerful, colourful and fun. My singing Santas in assorted aeroplanes, sleds, seesaws, climbing up ropes, doing exotic dances and whizzing round in circles, may be naff, but the kids love 'em. Nothing tasteful in this house.

A slight error in sheep management has presented itself today. When we want to move any part of the flock, a simple flirtatious wave of a feed bag, plus enticing rattle of sheep pellets, is all that usually suffices to bring the whole lot of them racing towards the possibility of food.

The lambs were weaned from their dams at the end of summer. Since then they been moved around inland gated fields, and not needed encouragement in the way of sheep pellets to move from one fresh patch of grazing to the next. Therefore their short-term memory has deleted any recall of what is in that brown bag that woman is waving. This morning that woman, and that man with her, needed to move about 120 of these lambs across fields, along the lane, through the village (with all those tasty festive garlands on doorways) and out into fields on the other side of the farm. Not a glimmer of interest when I flapped a bag at them, just a huddle at the other end of the field and mini conference on the sinister motives John and I presented. So it has been back to the drawing board, or in this case, set of stack bars. We last used them to erect a corral for the sheep in a field John now rents out to another farmer. So Plan B was to re-erect it in the lambs' field and Plan C was that after lunch we would take a trailer down, get the lambs into the corral (sounds so simple on paper) and bring them back twenty at a time to pastures new. Fortunately it worked.

5th

You know when you get that prickly feeling at the back of your neck and suddenly think, 'I'm being watched.' Well, I was. By John. Just as I had clicked on Pay Now for a highly desirable (to me) item on eBay. 'I thought you were hard up and didn't need anything,' he said. Well, I am. And I do not really need anything. But that's not the point. A bargain is a bargain. But why, when I never query anything that John buys or spends, am I always accused of extravagance when I splash out on something? It is not as if my latest purchases have been wildly frivolous. A new blade for my food processor; total cost one penny plus of course postage. The food processor I have is so old no-one else wanted to bid on the blade. Another item was a tablecloth with a print of game birds on that I thought John would like and which I will use for shoot lunches. Again no-one else wanted it, so it cost very little.

In fact I seriously question my own tastes. Seems the things I like no-one else does. My frugality (self-interpretation) is set against what I see as the small fortune John is prepared to spend on restoring a gun that has recently come into his possession through the family. Because of the gun's sentimental value – it had belonged to his grandfather – he wants to make sure it is safe to use again and so it is off to a gunsmith to be reproofed, tightened up, etc., etc. Originally I thought, after it had turned up, that we could disarm it and hang it over the fireplace on one of the inglenook beams. I had checked out with a blacksmith to have a couple of locking supports made so that the gun, even disarmed, could not be lifted down from its display. But disarming a gun costs a lot of money and a lot of bureaucracy as well, as it all has to be done legally through the police. So now, once back from the gunsmith, it will be securely kept in the gun cabinet.

What we have both agreed to spend on recently, however, has been some new fencing for the farm entrance. For Christmas, the children bought us a farm sign for the entrance. The previous one, roughly painted on an old piece of board, was only decipherable if you were an expert at word searches and could guess what the gaps in the lettering said. Delivery men, especially with my eBay purchases, could never find us. Now we have a farm sign in gold lettering, on a green background and with a beautifully painted pheasant to set the whole board off. There was no way we could display such a prestigious sign on the old sheep netting that formerly constituted our farm entrance. Even the sheep held the fence in contempt and regularly climbed over, under or through it. Now we are post-and-rail fenced from off the road right up to the gated entrance. There is even a concrete slab to walk on to hook the gate onto the fence, where previously you slurped through the mud to hitch or unhitch the gate hook. With the sign proudly displayed for all to see and no excuses from any delivery man that he couldn't find the farm as he couldn't read the farm sign, I can click back onto eBay in confidence. And secret.

6th

Decided to make soup for a shoot lunch from game bird carcasses and the remains of a haunch of venison. After a few hours I had some super stock to add to caramelised onions, plus all the leftover vegetables from New Year still lurking around in the veg basket. A quick whizz in the food processor and no-one knows what wrinkly specimens they had become. Unless they read this of course. After boiling and bubbling for thirty minutes the stock still needed a little body. Rummaging around in my pantry, and you need to rummage and utilise a satnav to find anything in there, I chanced on a packet of soup broth mixture. A faded date on the packet indicated a use-by instruction from the end of the last century, but who would care once the contents had been soaked and boiled up? Grain, lentils and split peas have survived in old Tutankhamen's tomb, so my pantry was nothing. Except perhaps a trifle more disorganised. I soaked the mixture for an hour or so, and once added to my stock pot, it made a satisfyingly thick soup. Now all I needed to do was leave it in a cool place overnight before freezing.

7th

A mysterious plop and gurgle disturbed my thoughts as I read the morning's paper and sipped a guilty cup of tea. The sound emanated from the dining room, and seemed to be coming from behind the still-drawn curtains, as I had not got round to opening them. A strange smell also assailed my nostrils as I walked towards the sound, and, most mysteriously, the curtains were trembling. Could there be an intruder lurking? No. It was my sinister, and now very lively, pan of soup. It had gone into a Quatermass fermentation and was apparently considering an attempt to take over the world, starting with the dining room. The mixture was literally escaping out of the pot. Bubbling and heaving, reproducing even as I watched. Quickly I slammed down the lid and flushed it down the loo. Well. Made several attempts to flush it down the loo before the last bits finally disappeared. The loo empties into the septic tank. I am getting a little worried as I write. The concrete lid on the tank is quivering, I am sure. What lies beneath?

8th

Granddaughter Jessica came into the kitchen looking very smug and superior. 'Pappa' (our grandchildren's name for John) 'and I have got a secret,' she said. 'And I'm not allowed to tell you but shall I give you a clue?' As she was being closely followed into the house by Pappa carrying a handful of plucked game birds, the downy feathers around her head creating an angel's halo effect around her head, it rather gave the game away. Apparently she has taken to the task of plucking pheasants and partridge with gusto, displaying a lot more enthusiasm for the job than me. I will pluck when necessary, but never make as good a job of it as John does, as I frequently tear the skin on the pheasants and leave the ducks looking almost as feathery as they were when on the wing. Perhaps I am not trying hard enough. The place where John chooses to pluck is just about the most godforsaken, cold and draughty spot on the farm. There is no heating and no door. Seating is represented by a couple of upended feed buckets and the atmosphere enhanced by the ghosts of hundreds, if not thousands of pheasants, ducks and geese that have been denuded of their feathers over the years. Spooky, but Jessica loves it. 'It's mine and Pappa's special place' she says. 'Pappa says Mamma won't find us here.' You are not kidding. Mamma steers very clear.

9th

After three days of mucking out the foldyards where the suckler herd are overwintering, there is an impressive heap of steaming muck maturing in readiness for spreading later in the year. If the frosty weather had continued, it could have gone straight onto the land, but currently the land is not hard enough through frost, or dry enough through drought. Just nice and claggy. We would either end up with deep sets of wheelings or a bogged-down tractor. Neither desirable. To bed the herd up again John has been rolling out the stack of big bales stored under cover in the biggest shed. They take up a huge amount of room, but at least when under cover the big round bales do not weather and deteriorate.

Over Christmas John was talking to a friend who has a straw business about storage of big bales. We did stack bales outside, but they became a haven for rats and foxes as well as losing condition and therefore nutrition. 'Which direction did you stack the bales outside?' the friend asked. John admitted he had never really given it much thought, but on reflection considered that they usually stacked them north to south. 'Ah,' said the straw expert, 'you want to be stacking them east to west. That is the way the wind is normally blowing and it keeps the bales drier and fresher. Leave some space in between for the air to travel through as well.'

'It was like someone had walked over my grave,' John said. 'I suddenly remembered a conversation my father had had when he was farm manager and telling a farmhand where to stack straw sheaves. My father told the man to stack them east to west for the very same reason, and I had forgotten all about it. The man asked how he could tell which way was east and my father told him to look up at the church on the hill. He said churches are always built east to west and that the nave is in the east. I should have remembered.'

It could be a little more difficult to judge east to west on our farm. No church is in sight, although we can visualise which way our local church is sited and maps do show there was once a chapel in the garden.

Not all of his father's words, however, were as instructive, John recalls. Bill, or Pop as he was always known to his family, could sometimes lack specificity when giving directions and instead relied on his men knowing exactly what he thought and planned to do next. For example, one year it was after harvest and the land was ploughed, harrowed and ready for drilling. Pointing in the general direction of a barn where several varieties of seed corn were stored ready for drilling and then waving his hand in the general direction of a section of the farm where at least three fields were ready for working, Bill issued his orders for the day. 'Go to thingamajig field and sow it with whatdoyoumacallit,' he said. They did. And got it right first time.

10th

A successful prosecution by the RSPCA against two brothers who overfed their Labrador caused me to cast an anxious eye over our own collection of dogs. All currently have honed physiques, but if the RSPCA had come calling when we owned our much-loved Labrador Jill, we might then have been suitable cases for persecution. Jill had the body shape of a well-fed seal. She would steal food from anywhere. Even raiding dustbin bags, in one case with disastrous consequences when she ate two pounds of frozen broad beans that were past their sell-by date. Anywhere remotely near her backside was best avoided for a week after. Then was the case of the chocolate treasure trove. Several boxes of Christmas chocolates in a box in an upstairs wardrobe were sniffed out and consumed. She only had a problem with the chocolate brazils. Well, the brazils anyway. Her backside had a health warning. A veritable scatter-gun effect. But her chief foraging trick was the calf buckets.

At that time we were milking a substantial number of cows. The calves were taken off their mother after twenty-four hours, once they had had the colostrum, and afterwards bucket fed. Pails of milk were always stood in the dairy ready to take to the calves, but only if Jill did not get there first. Even if thwarted at that stage, she provided a very hygienic washing-up service on all the buckets. That dog waddled, and no matter how hard you tried to think one step ahead, she out-thought you. Despite her size she was surprisingly agile and possessed the magic of Houdini when it came to slipping out of her lead, nosing open cupboards and squeezing into where she should not be, but where food was. Once when food shopping on holiday, I tied her lead to a rail outside of a supermarket. 'Would the owner of a very fat old Labrador please retrieve her from the delicatessen counter,' boomed a voice over the tannoy. I rushed to find Jill licking her lips from the consumption of some rather tasty sausages.

So it came as no surprise to John, when enquiring after the astonishing girth of a spaniel slavering affectionately over anyone who was unfortunate enough to sit next to her in the shoot trailer, that she came from a farm with a dairy herd. Not any old herd either. A Jersey herd. This dog had access, despite his owners' best intentions to keep her out of them, to bucket after bucket of the creamiest milk available. 'I can't keep my Lab out of the sugar beet heap,' said another shoot member. 'Our front lawn is covered in beet that he has selected from the heap, taken onto the lawn, half eaten and then abandoned for another beet. It just piles the weight on him, but he's taught the young pup I have now the same trick, so there will be even more beets on the lawn next year. And the young dog will be just as fat.' Even as I write this I can hear our Labrador Pip's teeth scraping clean the remains of the roast potatoes from their tin, before moving on to lick out the gravy boat. Labs are just born greedy. Fortunately, the dishwasher destroys any incriminating evidence.

11th

John has been a guest today on a shoot on the edge of the moors. Towards the end of the day, John and friend Dave were walking up the hill to the moorland for the next drive. Dave lifted his dogs, a spaniel and Labrador, over a stone wall onto the moor. He himself then climbed over, followed by his wife Rosie, who was picking up fallen birds with her dogs. John clambered over, lifting Pip. He was backstop on the drive, and concentrating on keeping Pip by him and having a look round to see when the first of the birds would start to fly over.

'Have you seen my spaniel?' Dave shouted. John hadn't, and until then had assumed that she had returned to Dave after the usual preliminary root around that all spaniels need in order to ascertain the territory. Once over that wall and onto the ground, the environment was very rough indeed. Bracken, heather and boulders made walking difficult. 'It was just a bit rough,' John said. Throughout the drive no birds came over him and there was no sight of the spaniel either. But in the lulls between shots from the other guns John thought he heard a whimper. Nothing more than that one whimper, nothing at all. The drive finished and a by now very worried Dave came over to John to decide what they were going to do to find the spaniel. John suggested he went further up the hill with Pip in the direction of the whimper to see if they could find anything, but wherever they looked there was just bracken and heather, nowhere at all where a spaniel could hide. No more stone walls, in fact no nothing. Just bracken, heather and boulders.

Pip, who had stayed close to John, suddenly stopped in her tracks a few yards away and looked directly down into the ground. John came closer and noticed a small hole a couple of feet wide. The hole itself was invisible from six foot away amongst the bracken. Looking down into the hole John could see the spaniel about four foot below the surface, stood on a ledge, but not uttering a sound. Beneath the ledge, John also glimpsed a flash of running water, and when he leaned down and looked in further, keeping away from the edge, he realised there was a large cavern underground. Relieved, delighted and concerned, John called Dave over. 'I think it's what they call a wash hole,' he said later. 'It is where an underground stream in wet weather flows downhill and washes the ground away under the moor, so that what looks like solid ground, is anything but.'

To try and rescue his spaniel, Dave lay prone on the ground with John holding onto him. 'The last thing last I wanted was Dave down the hole as well,' he said. Dave reached down into the cavern but all he could get hold of initially was the spaniel's ear. Luckily he could get a grip and managed to lift her a few inches. John could then reach past him and grab hold of her by the scruff of her neck. Together they pulled her free. 'It was a thousand to one chance we came across that hole,' John said. 'We could easily have walked by and never known it was there.' Unless they'd fallen in as well, I presume.

12th

Snow and ice are giving us a lot of problems. The sheep can't find any grazing so they need to be taken hay. The cattle require the most complicated shuttle system to allow all of them access to the one water trough that remains frost free. All the other drinkers and pipes in the yards are frozen. The cows have to be shut into the silage area so the bullocks can be brought through, then the bullocks have to be herded back (riotous) so that the heifers can come to the trough. Then that skittish lot have to be persuaded to return so that the suckler herd can drink next. The poultry are fine, they scrat around in the foldyard, and the dogs are either snuggled up in the house or under their heat lamps. John has been engaged in his regular requests for a pull-out of various hedgerows around the village when drivers have entered them at speed. Some of the cars return with a thankyou, but not many, and one or two drivers appear to expect farmers to offer a rural rescue service.

Not a road or lane has been gritted within three miles of the farm, so it is not us creating the hazardous conditions, and it's not even our hedges that they are driving into.

13th

A dozen newborn calves are snuggled into the deep straw bedding of the big foldyard. All gave no problems with their delivery or feeding – bar one. There is always one. John had noticed that this particular heifer had been ready to calve last night. New to the job, she had just not been making progress, lying down, straining, and looking uncomfortable with all the new sensations. In the early hours we walked her into the crush and John was able to feel inside the heifer to discover that the calf was breech. That is, coming backwards. John repelled the calf and managed to turn the young creature round and attach a calving rope to its hooves. Success. It is a skilled manoeuvre and a credit to John's stock skills that both calf and cow suffered no harm. All I had to do was to keep the pressure up on the calving aid whilst John readjusted the calf's legs and eased its passage into the world. Normally it is the shoulders of the calf that present the broadest part of the calf when it is being born.

Older cows do sometimes give us a problem when they calve. Their udders are often so big, and their bag, not the shopping variety, so pendulous, that the calf simply can't get hold of a teat to drink from without lowering its head right to the ground. A trick they can adapt to after a few days, but not in the immediate aftermath of calving. To deal with this anomaly, John is in the habit of milking these cows to take off that first surplus of milk, and then tube feed it straight into their calf's stomach. Saves a lot of messing around, and with the pressure literally off the cow's bag, the calf can get on to drink. That is the theory anyway.

Initially this particular calf was very slow to feed and the heifer rather disenchanted with her new baby. Not a winning combination. John had noticed over the course of the day that the calf was on its own for most of the time and that he had not seen it feeding. Mum was spending most of her time hanging round the silage face. Walking this reluctant, maternally deficient heifer back into the crush, John realised she did not have a lot of milk and that the calf was hungry rather than slow to feed. He took off what milk she had, containing the valuable antibodies for the calf's protection, and then milked one of the other cows in the yard with a calf at foot. Normally this is not a simple task with a suckler herd. They are not like dairy cows, which are amiable and stand for anyone to milk them. Our suckler cows are quite skittish, but they know and trust John. As long as he does not push his luck. Happily this latest calf only needed one supplementary tube feed of milk and then its mum's milk came in. They bonded at last. Tonight you can't get near the pair of them.

'She's blocked this way too!'

This new system requires a degree of IT literacy. Now I am perfectly well aware of how IT literate many farmers are. But many are not. I know a lot of them. One very intimately. He views with horror the thought that the missus might have to be more involved on the book-keeping side of the business than she is presently. He has seen my book-keeping style and is still taking pills for the headache it gives him. We avoided the system as long as we could, but eventually conformity beckoned. The United Kingdom and the Republic of Ireland produce more sheep than any other country currently in the European Union. But there are a lot of sheep and goat farmers in Eastern Europe and Mediterranean countries who will be subject to the same requirements as us. Why do I hear hollow laughter when I think of the rest of our EU partners being as compliant as we are required to be?

16th

'A thousand happy hens and three ecstatic cockerels' read the sign outside a farm advertising free-range eggs. I thought about my little flock. Twenty grumpy hens, bantams and pullets and two frantic cockerels who are outclassed, outrun and ignored. Like me, comments John.

Chat-up, or cluck-up, lines are not a high priority for these two. Any seducing they do has to be on the sly. They wait until the hens are head down scratting and pecking around and then rush them from the rear, try to get a grip, then lose it. Shrugged off with a derisory flick, the cockerels pretend they were really only meaning to have a game of leapfrog that went wrong, and the bantams get on with the main task of foraging for food. I bet those three cockerels at the free-range farm are neurotic, frazzled and worn out from trying. Certainly not ecstatic.

I was delighted to see eggs in the nest boxes again after several fairly barren weeks. Mine are obviously fair-weather hens: they sulk and cease production when it's cold and the days are short.

For most of this winter the poultry enjoyed fox-proof accommodation. Or so we thought. But the other night Mr Reynard dined on three of my bantams.

The majority of my hens roost in the hen house, which is situated in the orchard. The guinea fowl roost in the plum and apple trees and

Checking out the hen house security systems.

I had noticed that some bantams were copying their sleeptime habits. Although the hens' wings were clipped, they were still able to access the lower branches and from thence the higher ones by a sort of cross between a hop and scrabble up the tree. Some of the fruit tree branches hang outside the fence, however. And these three must have chosen a vulnerable roost. A pile of feathers foretold their end.

Fox numbers are definitely on the rise. A neighbour who farms free-range hens recently shot seventeen foxes in his fields. As his hen houses are near our farm, we benefit from his vigilance. The only ducks we have left are the five I hatched from eggs bought visiting the Castle of Mey during our holiday in Scotland. Since the demise of the Aylesburys (they are safe in the freezer), my royal ducks have had the run of the paddock and farmyard. We still do not know what breed they are as they resemble a cross between a silver appleyard and a penguin. Since they discovered the rolled barley in the meal shed, there is no stopping their raids. Could be a bad career move. From looking rather lean and fit, they are now all sleekly plump. I advise a diet if they want to see the spring.

17th

'I've left my boiler suit in front of the washing machine,' John said. 'It's covered in clarts from chasing that cow that's just calved.' It is of course a known physical and mental impossibility for men to make that link that opening the washing machine door, putting in the garment, adding the washing powder and turning a dial produces a clean garment with little effort. The cow in question had lost her ear tag just prior to calving. The new calf needed tagging, but the number on the mother's ear tag had to be recorded for a cattle passport to be issued for the new calf. The cow has two tags, but the one still in her lug was covered in the aforementioned clarts and printed in numbers so small as to be impossible to read unless in close proximity. John had earlier asked if I would help him walk the cow into the crush so he could confine her and read the number off the remaining tag with the pair of binoculars he refers to as his glasses. He was a late convert to wearing reading specs. Gradually I noticed whatever he was reading was being stretched further and further way from his face, until eventually his arms were outstretched with whatever he wanted to read as far away as possible. This is in contrast to me, who can read anything close up like books, papers, labels, etc., but had never appreciated there were leaves on the trees until I had glasses. For many years, however, I have worn contact lenses, and as I only wear one in one eye, I can both read without strain and drive without danger of hitting other cars on the road. For the most part.

To return to the cow. She had been leading John a merry dance around the foldyard, which, especially near the silage face, is a slippery, slidey place in which to chase an errant beast. John therefore sought to bring in his lassoing skills. Which are impressive, I may add. He slipped a halter around her neck, but then the chase turned from pursuit to drag, hence the muddy boiler suit. John finally managed to get her near to a gate and then wrapped the halter around the bars. Cunning, eh? We were then able to get the number read off and all of DEFRA's formalities completed. Traceability has a lot to answer for.

18th

Another day gone by without being able to sex my youngest guinea fowls. My grand scheme for breeding a bigger flock of them for the table is falling apart for a very basic reason. I have six guinea fowl hens and not one guinea fowl male in this little gang. I think. Apparently, when young, guinea fowls are difficult to sex. From two months old, and this clutch must be about four months old by now, the females call with a different note and frequency to the male. These have not yet developed a musical repertoire. They twitter away to themselves, but nothing that I can definitely say is a distinguishable phrase. And they all look the same. When they are older the males develop a bigger wattle, similar to the red coxcomb of a cockerel. None of ours has anything remotely like that yet. Roll on guinea fowl puberty and perhaps also a more welcoming attitude from the other guinea fowls on the farm.

Guinea fowl can be very parochial and on occasions we have had several distinct gangs of them roaming the farm and village, only coming back to the barns and orchard at night to roost. This particular clutch were hatched from eggs I bought from eBay. I thoroughly enjoy guinea fowl antics. They are not nearly as destructive as my pesky bantams and chickens. The latter will scrat out a flower trough without remorse. Pull up young vegetable plants and seedlings. The guinea fowl by comparison are interested only in insects. Not a hint of a chemical. They are the original organic pesticides and in the summer will forage virtually all of their own food. Another bonus is their built-in alarm system. When disturbed, they set up an unholy racket and alert us to visitors at night, both vulpine and human.

19th

Most of the cows are lounging about, in a matronly fashion, awaiting the birth of their offspring or cuddled up to their recently delivered offspring. Two, however, are exhibiting a very provocative and uninhibited desire to be mated. All this passion is not good news for them. If, after a summer with the bull, they are not in calf, then I am afraid it is a one-way ticket to the market. With the bull out of their yard, the whole provocative performance is going nowhere. It is, however, stirring up all the young lads in the neighbouring bull yard, but they are not allowed out to play, so there is no joy there either. To confirm the cows' barren condition, John had decided to call in our vets for a detailed examination, as he has known cows to be bulling even when they are in calf. Some of them are just too passionate for their own good.

As luck would have it, Simon, a visiting friend, is a vet. No sooner had he and his wife Marian rolled up for lunch, than Simon was in his shirt sleeves with his arm half way up the business end of a cow, checking to see whether she was in calf or not. She wasn't, and neither was the other one. At that point we took the ropes off and let him back in the kitchen. To be fair, Simon thoroughly enjoyed helping us out. Although originally a Ministry vet working with large animals, he now runs a small animal vet practice and employs a large staff to carry out most of the hands-on stuff. So this, he said, was a very welcome trip down Memory Lane. I think he needs to keep his hand (and arms) in regularly with this sort of trip. So they are booked in for lunch whenever they fancy and definitely at lambing time.

20th

With John off for the day shooting again, I have been on maternity duty. Calves are coming thick and fast. At least one new calf every day and twins at the weekend. John has taken the bull calf of the twins away as, despite the heifer twin looking more fragile, she is actually taking more of the cow's milk than the bull calf. He is now bawling his head off in a little pen in the big shed. All alone but getting a lot of attention. Even noticed a few of the teenage guinea fowl roosting on the bars of his pen last night, so he does not lack company.

Although it is a blessing to get twins, the heifer will not be able to come into the herd, as she will most probably be sterile. Apparently, in the womb, both of these twins, known as freemartins, share the placental membranes connected to their mum, and nearly all the female twins are completely infertile because of the transfer of hormones. Various other peculiar differences also occur which I will not mention, you will be relieved to hear, and moving on from this small diversion into bovine anatomy, the other calves are doing fine.

What does divert us, however, is our cows' propensity to lose their ear tags. John and I quite often have to track through the herd records to identify which cow is which either from a scrap of ear tag, a barely discernible number on an ear tag if the cow still has one, or a process of elimination from those cows that do have their tags and are easily identifiable. I tell you these bureaucrats have no idea what it is like to actually carry their regulations. A dimly lit foldyard with a herd of very curious beasts crowding round you bears no comparison to a well-lit office where the rules are made.

21st

A cold snap has provided an excellent opportunity to get on the land and spread a bit of compound (phosphate and potash) on the arable crops. The frost in the earth enables the tractor to travel along the tramlines and not compress the ground. John has usually had to finish by mid-morning, as the frost starts to ease then. It has meant some very early starts to the day, earlier than usual, but John has welcomed a hot bacon butty delivered to the tractor cab when he comes back into the yard to top up with compound. No tractor work this morning, however. Off to market with the two cows who are not in calf. They had come bulling yet again and all the rumpus and charging around in the yards was putting some of the newly born calves at risk of being trampled underfoot. Return to serenity.

22nd

The hens have hatched (yolk) a successful escape plan. Many of them spurn the hen hut at bed time and face chilly nights in the bare branches of the fruit trees, following the example of the guinea fowl. Usually in the morning the hens flutter down into the hen run whilst the guinea fowl fly off into the adjoining field. Now the hens branch-hop from tree to tree until they reach the perimeter of the hen run and then flop down into the field. They have watched and learned. Who says hens are dim?

23rd

John is waging an unremitting war on wood pigeons. This is the time of year when pigeons are voracious feeders on oilseed rape. But he cannot be in the field all the time, so to this end has invested in a Terror Kite to do the job when he is not there. This kite is remarkably effective in imitating the dip and recover action of a bird of prey and seems to be doing the job of keeping pigeons away. The 'hawk' hovers and swoops at the end of a string, attached to heavy-duty swivels which themselves are attached to a flexible 15ft launch pole. I think that is how it works. It all resembles a graduated fishing rod stuck straight into the ground. The main scary feature of the 'hawk' are a pair of sinister reflective eyes. Rather like a demented Angry Bird. Given even a slight breeze, the 'hawk' is constantly on the move. Very realistic. Well, the pigeons seem to think so. There has definitely been fewer of them.

24th

A trip out today to pick up some drench for the ewes to prevent liver fluke. A neighbour called yesterday to say that he had lost some of his flock to liver fluke disease and had realised too late that treatment was needed. Problems with the disease do manifest themselves at this time of year, especially after a wet summer. And didn't we have a wet summer. The intermediate host for the disease is a tiny snail, which, delicacies aside, permits the passage of the infected spores through its guts, if snails have guts, and leaves them stuck to meadow grass to be consumed by sheep and cattle as they graze. All this science, so clinically expressed. We'll be liver fluke experts when the quiz question arises.

So my job today is to pick up the medication. The disease is not a dramatic killer. The sheep quietly progress through the acute, sub-acute and chronic stages of the disease. They lose condition slowly at first, then rapidly, then roll over dead. Sneaky things. All that wool they have on them this time of year hides any weight loss, as does the fact that they are in lamb. But, obviously, having an anaemic mother with diarrhoea, another pleasant side effect, does not bode well for premium lamb production.

25th

Despite the guinea fowl early warning system and, we had hoped, fox-proof netting round the hen run, Mr or Mrs Fox has returned. Disastrous consequences ensued in the hen house. The fox did not even have the decency to eat his victims. Just chewed their heads off and left the carcasses littered round the run and in the hen house. Previously the fox had focused on those hens and bantams silly enough to consider themselves invulnerable and inaccessible on a low branch. Now the fox has found a way in because I forgot to close the shutter on the hen house entrance last night and was too lazy to get up and shut it after I had gone to bed. 'The fox won't get into the run,' I muttered to John. How wrong I was. The hen house is now more secure than any of Her Majesty's prisons, but it is too late for many of my girls.

26th

We had a drop-in call from the manager of a meat retailer today. He had seen our suckler herd in the yard from the road and instantly spotted what good-quality stock they were. We flatter ourselves. But apparently with the drop in the pound's value against the euro (and these things can change dramatically, so it may no longer hold true), exports of our meat are proving economically attractive once more to foreign buyers. We cannot make anything of it at the moment as we have no beef animals ready for market and it will be late spring before we start selling again. Also, we are now finishing lambs to a heavier weight than the export market demands. They like an animal that is about ten kilos lighter than we finish to, so no luck there either.

This buyer wants to deal with us directly. This company has its own abattoir, but it would involve quite a long journey for us to take stock there, and this in its turn piles up extra costs for us, as well as the welfare considerations. Currently we take all our stock to the local market for sale. A journey of about ten miles, half an hour at most. Any journey over forty miles, and this would encompass the meat buyer's abattoir, would mean John or me needing to pass a special test, and probably a new Land Rover as well. Our old girl can manage short trips on the flat quite happily. Dragging stock up hill and down dale over any distance would soon have her engine spluttering and complaining. Plus selling through a market opens up competition amongst buyers, and our local mart has always paid up straight way into our bank account. Selling to a private company might give us a guaranteed cost, but you are putting your eggs, or hooves, all in one basket. Unlike the banks, we are not keen risk takers, so we will stick as we are.

There is an enthusiastic new auctioneer at our local mart now who very helpfully rings us with the results of any stock we have sold and pushes for more. As he saw that the trade in cull cows is good at the moment, John sent in another cow this morning. She had not held in calf and was continuing to show signs of bulling; that is, she was restless, head-butting, bellowing and generally throwing herself about in a provocative manner. Goodness. Wonder if that is what is the matter with me?

27th

With everything Christmassy finally back up in the lofts until next December, several items and gifts from the festive season still hang around at this late date to be incorporated into daily life. One is a virtually life-size metal pheasant that a close friend bought for us, as it 'spoke' to her from a garden centre display as being exactly the sort of thing I would love. Big metal pheasants do not have a natural niche position in our house, but coming with such affectionate thoughts, I am determined to make one. It is this attitude that drives John mad and has determined that we are due a big clear-out of household knick-knacks, furniture, pictures and crockery. Of which there are at least three dinner services: two of them inherited and never brought out of the boxes they arrived in. Cupboards hold a plethora of such things as Victorian meat dishes and cut glass that never get used in case they are broken. And we do not have the grand life style they portray, preferring to eat in the kitchen with family and friends on a large table that can seat twelve at a pinch. Plus the table in the dining room is always stacked high with toys belonging to the grandchildren. So today I am off to our local saleroom for one of their entry forms. Be brave, I am telling myself.

The giver of the pheasant came over for the day with her husband and their Border Terrier Hattie. Both these friends are vegetarians and their dog too is fed on a vegetarian diet. At lunch I cooked a duck for John and me, but a vegetarian dish for them. Things went well. Hattie is a sociable little dog and quickly made herself at home with Millie our Jack Russell, who unfortunately has atrocious manners and begs imploringly at the end of any meal so that she is given scraps from the table. I know I have made her as bad as she is, as I feed her from my plate. Something I should heartily disapprove of if anyone else does it. Shows what a hypocrite I am. Hattie was intrigued by the smell of roast duck. Entranced by the taste of it. Fairly batted Millie out of the way to be given a few more scraps. Her owners did not at first realise what was happening, as they had stated emphatically that Hattie was not interested in eating meat. 'She loves cauliflower,' I was told. She loved meat too, I found out. So did they, when after about thirty minutes the impact of meat on a set of virgin carnivorous bowels was felt. Or, more appropriately, smelt. I swear the interior of their car was clouded by a greenish haze when they left. And they had pegs on their noses.

28th

I have been assisting our friendly electrician Keith today with connecting up our new diesel tank for red tractor fuel. The old tank had to go as it was starting to leak. A plastic bunded tank is not deemed secure enough, as a determined oil thief could pierce both the tanks with a sharp implement and drain off the oil. So we have gone for a steel bunded tank. And what, you ask, is a bunded tank? Well, that's what I asked anyway. A bunded tank is basically a tank within a tank. The larger outside tank can hold 110% of the capacity of the smaller tank, so that the surroundings of the smaller tank are protected from any oil spills or leakages. New regulations, you see. Plus with all its locks and sealed covers it is hopefully theft proof. Not that anything is ever totally proof against theft. But three determined dogs setting up a warning racket and CCTV are quite a convincing deterrent, as has been shown on more than one occasion.

29th

John has been out shooting with his friends, much to the joy of Pip our Labrador, who is never happier than when retrieving. Especially when she is not meant to. Pip has a wonderful nose. She can smell out food wherever it is. So far a goose carcass, garlic bread, panful of hot sausages, couple of bacon sandwiches put out for John's breakfast and a tin of roast potatoes have fallen prey to her appetite since Christmas. I think I have put everything out of her reach, but always forget one thing. Her acute sense of smell does, however, lead her to find game out on the field with consummate ease. Picking up and bringing game straight back to John. Even when it actually belongs to someone else's dog. We are going away for a night to shoot at a friend's and taking Pip with us. I have borrowed a cage for the back of the car as Pip has already chewed all the wiring in the Land Rover. Love Pip though I do, and respect the fact that she has a healthy appetite, it is not enough to let her make a meal of my car.

30th

Our friends with the shoot we are visiting today have a deer park on their farm. The park dates back to medieval times and its revival by Joy and Kevan to stock with fallow deer is proving commercially successful in producing venison from the culled deer. There have been ups and downs with escapees. The area where they live is very scenic, and although there are no rights of way through their farm, it is attractive to walkers. Not all who walk there secure gates behind them, so that deer have escaped. Over the last few years, fences, gates and security have increased, and trespassing is proving less of a problem on the farm, so that escapes have become rarer. The hunt proving to be the last transgressors.

Joy is now planning to open up the farm as a luxury camping venue, complete with honesty shop, a shower and toilet block, rent-a-chicken and stroke-a-sheep experiences, plus home-cooked meals and ready-made beds in the tents. All at extra cost, of course. They hope the deer park will be an added attraction, and the lakes in front of their farmhouse, which they keep stocked with trout. Separating the lakes from the house is a ha-ha – I think that is how you spell it – into which the lakes flow. As the lakes are situated in a field, Joy and Kevan thought it would be scenic and picturesque to have deer in there. Whilst the perimeter of the field had the usual mile-high deer fence – I exaggerate, but it is high – they assumed the ha-ha would prevent escape by the route directly in front of their house.

Thinking too that their existing deer might not settle in the new field, three fallow does and a buck were purchased and released into what they hoped was an escape-proof home. This was all in November. Plenty of time for the deer to settle in over winter and be ready to pose in model fashion when the trendy campers arrived. But then the weather grew colder and colder and the lakes started to freeze. Still Joy and Kevan were sure the new deer had plenty to eat and were totally settled. Then one night in mid-December it really really froze. Ha-ha, as well as the lake. 'Oh look,' the deer must have thought, 'we have a cunning plan, we can walk out of here if we want to.' And they did. So today whilst we were there we did get a glimpse of the escapees, but nothing more than a glimpse. And perhaps when the campers are there in the summer and sit out in the evenings admiring the deer over the fence, they might see four of them rather closer to home than they reckoned for.

Pip loved her day out. Behaved herself well and the back of the car is still in one piece.

31st

John came in to tell me that he had sighted from his tractor a falcon crouched over a kill on the edge of a field. He climbed out of his tractor and walked over to take a closer look. A peregrine falcon rose up from the pigeon it was feeding on and flew into the sky to be joined by another peregrine. 'I wondered if it is the same pair that nested in the pylon last year,' John said. 'They reared a couple of chicks and they must have returned to this area, but I think it is too early for them to start nest building.' Although this is not good news for any future game bird chicks in the area, we are very pleased to welcome the peregrines back if they are scaring the pigeons off the rape field. The gas gun and terror kite seem to have lost their effectiveness, but a pair of working peregrines will soon sort out any pigeons that are brave enough to fly in their territory. Last year, when they were nesting in the pylon, John saw the most incredible piece of aerial teamwork between these falcons. The male swooped down onto a luckless pigeon and caught it in mid-air. Mrs Peregrine left her nest, then flew upside down (it appeared) so they could pass the hapless lunch between them to take back to the nest for her chicks. A big welcome back to our aerial pest-control technicians.

February

1st

Sex on four wheels, two legs and a straw visited us at the farm this morning by way of the artificial insemination technician. John scanned a mini Facebook profile of bulls to decide who would best suit our heifers, and now hopes that a suitably dashing, but more importantly, easy-calving, suitor has been picked. The technician removed the straws from the flask where they were being kept in sub-zero temperatures, stuck them down the back of his neck to 'warm them up a bit' (the heifers already being considerably warmed up if all the mounting of each other was anything to go by) and set off to do his job. We have the Limousin bull for the suckler herd for beef calves, but to serve the heifers who are herd replacements, we are using Aberdeen Angus semen. That way John hopes to get some Aberdeen Angus back in the herd as potential breeding mums but have Limmy calves for beef. When we had a dairy herd, the AI man regularly called, as we had stopped keeping a dairy bull. Insemination took place in the milking parlour. Cows knew the routine and just walked into their stalls. Heads down, munching the considerately supplied dairy nuts, oblivious as to what was happening at the business end. Suckler cows are a completely different going on. They are not used to walking into crushes on a regular basis. Trying to spot when one is ready to serve in the field, and then isolate it and bring it into a crush, is a fool's game. So a bull does the job much better. However, this morning the job went well and two heifers were inseminated.

2nd

The answer to all our cows' prayers is becoming increasingly impatient to get on with his life's vocation. He is currently living with the boys in the beef bull yard. I noticed this morning that he has his eye glued to a peep hole in his gate where he can see the cows in the main foldyard next door. And interestingly the occasional cow on the other side peering back. Star-crossed lovers. With this introduction of fresh testosterone (or whatever) into the yard, several cows are bulling. But with so many young calves in the foldyard, if we put him in with the cows, all that lust and racing around when the action starts could put the youngest calves in danger of being literally trampled underfoot. So for now, Mr Limmy can just put up with the tranquil life and get used to the sights and sounds of our farm. I am sure when the fun does begin and he is being pursued and harangued by all those willing ladies, he will look back to this time and long for a bit of peace and quiet.

Today has been a busy day calving. Most of the herd (there are always late and early calves to ruin the pattern) have waited very reasonably until the end of the shooting season before they start to add their halfpennyworth in earnest to the farming calendar. Very frustrating. Just when I thought I had a fair chance at getting a few of those important little domestic tasks completed, like a new floor in the back corridor where the damp is coming through, something like that turns up. Another friend is completely stymied by lambing. 'He's done nothing but shoot for the last three months,' she said of her husband, 'and now all he's going to do is live in that lambing shed. What about all the decorating that needs doing?'

Some men. They'll do anything to avoid a domestic challenge. But when John came in with his boiler suit sleeves rolled up to his elbows and his arms and hands streaked with blood and gunk, you just know he's been having a rummage round the more intimate areas of a cow and have to forgive him the odd transgression on the home maintenance front. He'd come into the house for a bit of assistance and a cold drink. It might be below freezing, but nothing warms you up so much as calving: I've seen him stripped to the waist when the going gets really rough. Could be a new pin-up calendar man. Could be. Probably not, however.

In this case it was to help a rather reluctant calf make its entrance into a cold, frosty world. 'I'd seen the cow was bagging up,' John said, referring to the milk that swells the cow's udder prior to her giving birth, 'but she was not getting on with it at all and was starting to look uncomfortable with herself.' So it was roll-up-sleeve time. The calf, it turned out, was coming out backwards. Usually when they opt for this reverse-style delivery, the calves have the decency to have one of their hind legs sticking out as well, so that at least it is possible to get a purchase on its leg with a rope or a calving aid, and pull the calf out that way. This calf had its back legs neatly folded up under its tummy, pointing forward, and as John said, 'Pulling it out by its tail alone is not to be found in the calving text book.' For another half an hour he grovelled around in the depths of the cow to get hold of one of the calf's legs and pull it backwards enough to get a grip on it. Finally he succeeded, reached for the calving aid, and the little hoof shot back inside its nice warm mum. 'At least I know it's a live calf,' he said. 'That's some gratification.' Or at least that's what I know he wanted to say. *****!!!!!!! was what it sounded like. Next time he got the leg back, he got the rope round before it had chance to disappear back inside. One down, another to go. Finally the other leg was eased back under the calf and out of the cow. This is where a new calving aid comes into its own. So much easier on the cow, calf and cowman. A gentle winching pressure that inexorably drags the calf out inch by inch, then with a final slip and shudder, and a final heart-stopping tumble to the ground, the calf was delivered. Mum was instantly trying to get round to lick it clean, and after making sure that its nose was clear of any membrane, we just left them to it. Hot shower time for both of us. Except the shower door has just fallen off and John has been going to . . .

3rd

Time to start getting some money in. Big artics are rolling into the yard as John is selling corn again. Plays havoc with my windows, all this corn dust, when the wheat is tipped into the back of the lorries. Not that I am excessively house proud: I like the cluttered domestic look, or rather I cannot seem to achieve anything else. But I did spread the Windolene a bit last week and for why? It is almost as though John has decided to move corn out of sheer badness, rather than trying to get the overdraft down again.

Another significant piece of housekeeping on the farm has been cleaning out all the yards. The weather has been milder of late and the build-up of muck in the main yards, where the herd is, contributes to raising internal temperatures to a point where diseases such as pneumonia could be a problem. You do not want it warm and muggy inside when there is young stock about. Our cattle-handling system comes into its own, as John has found it much simpler to contain young stock, bullocks and the herd and followers in different areas of the yards. That way he can safely get in with the tractor and muck out without danger to himself, or stock, or the tractor. There was a bit of chasing around as the bull sensed there was an opportunity to get near to that tempting gang of ladies, but 5ft of cattle pen soon stopped that. So he is back again to peering through his peep hole at the cows, and at a considerably lower level than previously. A true voyeur.

4th

A heifer booked in for the AI man this morning was clearly not ready to play the game. She should have walked straight into the cattle crush for her big moment. Instead she jumped over the crush gate and bent it. Plunged into a water trough; splashed water everywhere; slipped and slid. Tried literally to climb a wall and demonstrated every intention of flattening John. Each time he got near the crush, the cow put her head down and went for him. It was very dangerous. The AI man and I stood well back and just hoped John would get out without a broken leg. In the end he let her go back to the yard. 'I doubt she would hold in calf, the state she is in,' John said. So she will encounter the real thing in a few weeks with the Limousin bull, not a long straw. Perhaps she's not such a daft cow after all.

We have a proper system of cattle pen sections in the collecting area that fit onto the cattle crush and can be repositioned to suit our needs. And at 5ft, our cattle would have to be related to the cow that jumped over the moon to clear them. Additionally, unlike the big bales, there is no chance of these sections being knocked over by a stroppy cow. But even the best-laid plans and best-organised systems are no match for a headstrong cow.

Good news, however, about a cow that was causing us some concern. Cows normally cleanse – that is, get rid of the placenta and afterbirth – fairly quickly after calving, but this one cow had not. John was concerned that with the afterbirth not 'unbuttoning' from the wall of the cow's womb, she would develop an infection and lose her milk, or indeed we might lose the cow. She is responding well to a course of antibiotics that the vet has left us. The calf has been fine and there is plenty of milk there.

5th

Millie, our Jack Russell, has decided to see off quite a few vermin this week. She has been doggedly (I know) burrowing under the hen hut, convinced there was something worth digging out. And she was right. A big fat rat, on a big fat nest of baby rats. Good girl, Millie. 'It's as good as a day's work when a rat's killed,' John says. So Millie has certainly earnt her day's pay in scrambled eggs this week.

Last week we moved the ewes to fresh grass as they had eaten up the field they were in. Apart from ensuring there are enough of us around to round up independent-minded ewes who fancy a walkabout to the next village, moving the ewes does not generally (I will regret saying this, I know) present many major problems. The ewes know the game. They are fed from a bag on a daily basis, whether they need it or not, to ensure that they always associate the bag with their shepherd. That way a brisk shake of a feed bag makes sure you have a devoted bunch of sheep ready to follow you to the ends of the earth. Or along the lane anyway. The field the ewes were moved to is a part of a hundred-acre block of land just next to the farm. Most of it is down to grass, encompassing three large fields separated by a corral where stock is gathered for such jobs as worming, dagging or injecting. The ewes went into a field immediately adjacent to the farm, as this way they are accessible for feeding and checking on their day-to-day health as lambing time approaches. The furthest field in this block is occupied by the hoggs, which are last year's lambs. Hopefully these will be sold at market this spring and maybe make more money than if they had been sold in the autumn or late summer.

6th

John returned to the house for breakfast looking very downhearted. For some reason a gate between the fields had been left open. By whom we don't know, but there was a party of ramblers in the area the day before. No-one should have been across the fields as there is no right of way, but that is not always appreciated. As a result, the hoggs had decided to go visiting and were all mixed up with the ewes. 'That means we'll have to bring all of them home and sort them out, half a day's work I could do without,' John said. 'We'll do it after lunch.'

Lunchtime came and went and I prepared to go out after doing the dishes to give John a hand. He came in looking exultant. 'You wouldn't believe it,' he said. 'I went in with the Land Rover to the first block and couldn't see any of the hoggs, only the ewes gathered round the feed troughs. Then I went round to the hoggs' field and found them all waiting round their feed trough. I hadn't bothered to shut the gate again and the hoggs had found their own way back.'

7th

The lambs left unsold from last year's crop are gradually filtering into the market system. I thought they had all gone, but John keeps miraculously appearing with another twenty or so that I think he hides in a field deep inland. He waits until he sees me comfortably ensconced with a cup of tea and then demands a 'quick turn' through the village to get them into the foldyard. My first job is to drive along our lane making sure that all gates into other people's properties and fields are shut. With a growing number of new folk moving into our village, all very proud of their neatly trimmed lawns and gardens, tolerance of the country life can be severely stretched by sheep trampling up the garden path. The actual lane through the village is becoming increasingly narrow, as new householders place rocks, stone pillars and chained posts almost directly on the verges of the highway. The rise in traffic as cars and lorries use the lane as an alternative to a busy main road, has meant that what roadside is available to vehicles to pull off onto is churned into deep muddy ruts. Car can pass car, just, but there are stand-offs when vans meet, or no contest when a lorry uses the lane. But a notice on the village board indicates that help is at hand, with lay-bys planned in the near future for the narrowest sections of road.

8th

Sometimes the best-laid plans go horribly wrong. Or could go horribly wrong if sense did not intervene and an action was stopped before it became truly dangerous. So, when you know you are going to move a flighty young heifer, you must risk assess the situation, however bureaucratic it sounds, and make sure that the whole operation is as safe as can be anticipated. The idea was to take the heifer to market. She is now nearly eighteen months old, not intended as a herd replacement, and by virtue of her unseasonably late birth, there are no other heifers or bulls of the same age ready for market. Therefore with no other stock fit, the plan was for her to travel alone in the trailer. She didn't fancy that idea one little bit.

John backed the trailer up into the collecting yard and brought her through a chicane of gates and big rectangular bales to get loaded. So far, so risk assessed. Do you think a heifer can clear six foot? Well, it can. This heifer had no intention of making that one-way trip to market alone. She wanted to be back with her friends. Probably had even taken notes when the heifer who was to be artificially inseminated had managed to avoid it by flailing her hooves about. Eventually we got the point and the heifer in question is now back in the yard and will not be travelling until a number of other cattle are ready to go. There comes a time when you just have to realise that to rethink is the safest course. It is just not worth tempting a nasty accident.

9th

Today's risk assessment is taking the old Land Rover for its MOT test. At twenty years old it is not exactly an historic vehicle, but getting on for vintage. Strangely, John gets a lot of offers for the old girl. The Land Rover, not me. I'm probably not worth as much. Mark, the garage owner, says old Land Rovers' popularity lies in the fact that most of the jobs can still be completed without the need for the plug-in laptop required for the majority of diagnostic tests on today's modern vehicles. John can do a lot of the repairs himself, as he did the other week when the universal joint went. I did entertain the fantasy that we were going to keep the Land Rover as an agricultural vehicle for limited use. This means we could travel for 1.5 kilometres, on the road, between land owned by us, using red diesel, whilst not requiring the vehicle to be taxed. And that we would buy a lovely new 4x4 for me to swan around in. Not yet, I think, from the affectionate way John is talking about the old girl (again the Land Rover and not me; it can be confusing). Must consider a way to bribe Mark. Passing must not be an option.

10th

I have Pip the Labrador at home craving my attention and seriously annoying Millie, our Jack Russell, and Fizz, the sheepdog. It is because the shooting season has ended. Their master is actually having to get on and get some serious farming back under his belt, plus all the odds-and-sods jobs I have been saving up for him. From one tile loose on the kitchen floor, there now seem to be about a dozen that creak and rock ominously when you walk over them. These tiles are probably laid on sand. The kitchen is a Victorian extension to the main Georgian part of the farmhouse. The floors in that part were wood over bare earth. No wonder we used to get a plague of slugs whenever it was wet. When we ripped up the old rotten floorboards, it was to find about six inches of water and several very startled amphibians. Now, although those floors are concreted and insulated, we still have a persistent little slug visitor or two. Somehow also, two holes by the skirting boards have appeared in the carpet at the edge. Mousetraps have gathered a fair harvest of the perpetrators, but it will not be until now that John has the time to take the carpets up and fill in the holes. I shall miss that sharp snap of a trap as another little shrew or mouse meets its end.

11th

Returning from a fortnight's holiday in Portugal, my friend Tine was looking forward to the simple pleasures of a slice of toast and decent cuppa of tea with real milk, not UHT; all to be relished in front of a roaring fire in her comfiest chair. Instead of which, after leaving her daughter and partner to house sit, she came back to find the cupboard, the freezer and the coal bunker were bare. "But we assumed house sitting came all inclusive," an unrepentant daughter told her. "Just think. You were able to enjoy your holiday knowing we were here to look after things." Ummmmmm.

12th

'Don't go in the yard today when I'm out,' John warned. 'That cow with horns has just calved and could be lethal if you go anywhere near her. Caught me on the shoulder and if I hadn't moved quickly she would have gored me.' This particular cow needs watching. She is the only one with horns in the herd, and she knows it. The other cows are quite wary of her. She bullies her way into the silage clamp and the barley trough, knowing that the other cows will scatter in her path. Calves are still arriving regularly in the foldyard. John is up and down like a yo-yo at night checking on the cows and so far the calves have either arrived on their own, with only a few needing assistance with the calving aid. As a couple of bantam hens have also proudly introduced us to their little broods of chicks, carefully and secretly raised in some hidden corner of the barns, it is beginning to look as though spring is starting to have sprung. The moles think so too. Suddenly, over all the grass fields, molehills are erupting. And not only in our fields. As I drove back from market with John, from my vantage point in the Land Rover I could see hundreds of molehills in fields, where a week ago there were very few. Something is stirring down below. If you listen carefully you can hear the patter of tiny male mole feet in hot pursuit of lady moles. Or so I fondly imagine.

13th

Each day John feeds one particular cow from a bucket with rolled barley and pellets. This cow is relatively undersized and gets pushed out by the other cows when any feed goodies are on offer. Now she knows to wait by the foldyard doors for John to come in with her treat. But so does Mrs Horned Cow too. She chooses her moment to push in for the bucket and it has got so that John closes the collecting yard gate behind him so that she cannot get through. But as soon as it is open, she whips in and scavenges for any remaining grains.

The big problem John has is getting an ear tag into her new calf. The numbers on Mrs Horned Cow's tags are quite faint, and John dare not get too close to her to read them. We have tried a few times to get her into the crush, but she is not having that game at any cost. Being deliberately separated from her calf for even a few minutes drives her into a frenzy. It really does come to something when to ensure we do not compromise our compliance with regulations, it is necessary to risk a goring. All the calves are generally doing well except for one, and it is not the calf's fault. She has a feckless mother, according to John. A chav mum, according to my son-in-law. Can't say that I have spotted her in a Juicy Couture tracksuit and Burberry cap, but there you are.

This particular heifer will have nothing to do with her calf. The night she calved, when it was obvious that the calf was hungry and that she would not let it near her to drink, John and I got her into the crush. John then stripped her udder of any milk and the calf got that all-important first drink of colostrum to boost her defences. Next morning the calf was hungry again, but the heifer was not in the mood to be walked back through the gates into the crush. Too busy at the silage face, chewing her cud (nonchalantly), or just fluttering her lashes at those fit-looking bullocks in the next yard. She jumped the gates leading into the crush, putting herself, and us, at risk. An hour later saw me at the agricultural merchants to buy a bag of milk replacement powder, a purchase that always mortifies John as it is so expensive and, as he sees it, totally unnecessary if the heifer conducted herself properly. Ah. Youth today. Sadly this particular heifer will not get the chance to redeem herself if, over the course of the next few days, she does not pull her act together and let the calf near her. She will just be fattened up for market. It's a one-way ticket, I'm afraid, if you don't conform round here. In a week or two, with many more of the cows and heifers giving birth, the calf will learn just to nip under any cow that will accept it and take its milk from there. Problem sorted.

14th

Got her. Mrs Horned Cow, that is. We waited till she had gone to feed at the silage face then moved the calf into a holding area where the crush was and restricted the entrance. She shot in and we were able to secure her and check the number. What a performance. I have done some travellers in the area a good turn tonight. Their horses and ponies are frequently a risk to vehicles, as they are often tethered with a sufficient length of chain for them to stray onto the road. One of them, Charlie, had actually broken loose when I drove past and cars were having to brake hard to avoid him. Lurchers and terriers appeared out from nowhere under the vans when I drove up to let the main man know about the pony. Mutely he climbed into the Land Rover and silently I drove him to find Charlie, who was calmly holding up any passing traffic. Without a word my passenger climbed out and took hold of the pony's broken chain. But I got a big thumbs-up and a grin as I drove off.

15th

John's grandfather's gun has now been returned, fully restored. It came to him because of the generosity of his Uncle Fred, who passed it onto him before he died. Uncle Fred had always said he knew John would appreciate its history and value the gun as a link to a previous generation of farmers and shooting men. It is an old hammer gun with Damascus barrels and still in proof. John has fond memories of forking sheaves onto a horse-drawn rully at harvest time with his uncle. The tractor ran on iron wheels. In its day a modern piece of tackle, but looking back a real bone shaker. He recalls his uncle taking him to look at a peewits' nest (called tirfits by Fred) on grassland and pointing out a chaffinch nest in a horse chestnut tree that he had grown from a conker. Thinking back to the old family farm and Uncle Fred, John reminisced about the privy down the garden and that they had to use candles at night when everyone went to bed early. May I add John still does go to bed early. The old privy at our farm, however, is now a locked chemical shed. Same warning about dangerous fumes, I presume.

16th

'Have you had my torch?' came the querulous demand. No. Why should I? I have my own torch, jealously guarded so that it does not walk, as it no doubt would if I did not have a metaphorical lead on it. John has a few of those mega-million-candle power torches, none of them ever in the right place or fully charged. It must be me, of course, who has hidden this one, although I think this particular torch is probably to be found in the depths of the combine.

The combine has been stored over winter in the big grain shed. John has been poring over his last remaining heaps of grain like a miser in a fairytale with his hoard of gold. Grain prices are so volatile. For twenty years they were rock bottom, soared just over three years ago, dropped again and may or may not be rising once more. With grain so precious, John is determined to keep it as pristine as possible, and that means war on vermin. Try as you might, even in a vermin-proof shed it is extremely difficult to keep mice and rats out. In the last week John has ordered and had fitted metal plates for the sides of the grain shed doors to prevent any vermin squeezing their way in. Previously there were strips of wood, but the rats had eaten through those. They will get blunt teeth if they try that trick again. Even though rats and mice can no longer get in, we were left with the problem that at least one rat was probably still in there. A resident in the bowels of the combine. John could hear it skittering about and even shone a torch into its beady little eyes before it scampered back into the combine's innards. So Plan A is to drive the combine out of the shed, shut the shed door tightly and then work out a Plan B to trap the rat.

17th

I was surprised to hear a chorus of baas when I got out of the car last night. As it is cold, I am parking under the big shed opposite the house. With the cows in the foldyard in close proximity, the windows on the car do not ice up, but I do have a bit of a slippy slidey walk over to the farmhouse if it is really frosty. The baas came from a pen of some of the last of last year's lambs. They have not been thriving outside. Despite daily feeds of hay, the cold weather has just pulled them back and John wants them fit and off the farm before we start with this year's lambing. Pip is fascinated by them. Too much so. She stands and barks and they huddle together and stamp their feet at her. Fizz the sheepdog could not care less. All she wants to do is curl up and snooze away in the warmth of her kennel under a pig lamp. Occasionally we see a black and white nose peep out, but it soon pops back in again.

The lambs are hunkered together for warmth. Just think how much colder they would be out in the field, I tell them. These particular lambs were wormed around Christmas. Well, half of them were. At that time, the weather was very wet and they were not doing too well on grass. John went through the flock and pulled out the poorest doers to worm first. They have done well, but as there is a fifty-six-day withdrawal period, and they are still within that time and not ready to go to market yet. The lambs John thought were doing well, and that did not need worming, have not thrived to the same extent. So he has wormed them as well, but using a wormer requiring a shorter withdrawal period, so hopefully all of last year's lambs will be away by the time we start lambing again in March.

18th

The biggest and oldest cow in our herd has calved today. John even called the vet in last week to look at her as he was so concerned that the birth appeared imminent but that she was not getting on with it. The vet took in her enormous girth, her distended bag, the drip of milk from her teats and said there was nothing he could do to hurry things on. John's worry has been that the calf was getting too big for the cow to calve unaided.

Brrrr. Even a woolly coat isn't always warm enough.

The moment he spotted she was starting to look uncomfortable and possibly in labour we walked her into the crush.

A brief investigation revealed one of the calf's hooves coming forward, just ahead of its nose. John threw a halter around her neck and walked her back into the foldyard and tied her to one of the gates to stop her dropping down when she started to calve. Such a big cow would be very difficult to manage then. With a quick rummage (that is the nicest way of putting it), he found the tip of the other hoof, brought it forward, made sure the nose was clear and then attached the rope of the calving aid to just above the calf's ankle. It works on a ratchet principle, perhaps a little too indelicate for human deliveries, but quite acceptable for a cow. In a couple of minutes the biggest calf you have ever seen was flopped down onto the straw. He is huge. Dwarfs some of his peers who are a couple of weeks old. Very alert. Quickly onto his feet and trying to get under his mum, who was now pouring milk.

19th

We have had to bring the ewes inside to the big shed for a few days. Although they are still a few weeks off lambing, with the recent foul weather they are doing no good at all outside. Plus, if one of them decided this was its time to lamb, its newborn would fare much better under cover than getting a freezing and/or sodden start to life in the field. I have done my bit for the lambs by starting to have a whisky and dry ginger at night before bed. This leaves some empty dry ginger bottles (not whisky) ready for those pet lambs that will inevitably figure large in our lives and need to be bottle fed. It's a sacrifice, I know.

Populations change rapidly on the farm. Five new calves have been born to the suckler herd in four days and several of the other cows are bagging up prior to giving birth. Four of the calves are heifers and only one a bull calf. We would prefer bulls. John is delighted with how swiftly calving is going. 'What I have been looking for is a tight calving pattern,' he told me, rather pedantically, I thought. I do need to stop giggling and look serious on these occasions. A tight calving pattern? Is that plain stitch or purl and on what size needles, chief? No, you dope. It means that the herd will all calve within a short period of time. Cows are 'bulling', i.e. keen to be served, for twenty-four hours in a three-week cycle. The aim is to get all the herd back in calf by three months after they have calved. With a gestation period of nine months, the Limousin bull must have worked his magic and turned all the herd on within that space of time, plus satisfying their carnal desires as well. It is no wonder he spent most of the summer grazing very quietly, breathing heavily and trying not to catch the eye of any passing cows or heifers in the field.

20th

A night out with friends, one of whom is clerk to various charities in his village. He had taken advice from John over the valuing of parish land willed to the village in the seventeenth century. The land, after all this time, was going to be registered with the Land Registry, and he needed an idea of what the land was actually worth. The issue is complicated because fields were not measured in the deeds in European Union hectares, but in the language of yore, oxgangs. Not only in oxgangs, but roods and perches. A rood being equivalent to 0.1 hectare and a perch much smaller, 0.002 hectares. To further muddy the waters, one field had been robbed of a corner by that newfangled invention, the railway. Our friend Richard delighted in regaling us with the seventeenth-century dialect that the deeds were written in. Each bequest was introduced by immensely wordy diatribes. Written, for example, by 'an elderly man, frail in body but not in mind'.

An oxgang was at best an uncertain quantity that differed by locality and soil quality, but was roughly the amount of land that was tillable by one ox in a ploughing season. The field in question was half an oxgang, equivalent to about seven acres, or just short of three acres in today's measurements. Today, DEFRA measures to a hundredth of a hectare in a field inspection. I wonder how they would cope with the looseness of yesteryear's dimensions. With global warming, who knows how long a season entails? Would DEFRA accept an excuse that the oxen had got bogged down in a muddy field or that land was so parched that their plough could not bite?

21st

For the past few months John has been bagging up any waste plastic material, prior to taking it to a certified waste-disposal site. A big burn-up used to deal with all of those bags and baggages very conveniently, including old paper sacks, surplus household waste (the bins were never big enough for all the packaging and wrappings) and garden rubbish. No longer. When DEFRA comes a calling, they will want to see that we are disposing of our waste responsibly. Unlike the fly tippers, who they can't catch, farmers are sitting targets and milch cows combined. They cannot fail to miss us. And what a mucky job it is too. John was filthy when he came in for lunch.

'I hope there is nothing toxic in any of those sacks,' I thought. Normally he does not need to handle the big fertiliser sacks, as they are all lifted into the tillage spinner by the forklift and then ripped open without any direct contact. But folding and packing these paper sacks meant John was breathing in all the dust and muck. Meanwhile the dogs have set up their own waste-disposal system. They have discovered how to access their biscuits in the meal shed and have been making gluttons of themselves on a daily basis. We had all commented on how fat they were getting again but had not put it down to extra rations. Originally we thought Pip's increase in girth was down to a lack of exercise after the end of the shooting season. She tends to loll around the yard, chasing the odd chicken or pigeon if the fancy takes her and soliciting snacks and leftovers whenever she can. Once a day all three get taken for a really long run around the farm or down to the wood, but it is not the same as a full day out on the shooting field for Pip, and no dog is allowed to harass the ewes when they are so close to lambing. At this very moment all of them are stretched out in the kitchen in front of the Aga, noses twitching if a morsel of food passes nearby. It is a miracle if any edible kitchen waste makes it to the bin.

22nd

How much time can you waste just looking for things that seem to have mysteriously disappeared into thin air, and then just as mysteriously reappear? And in the exact place you have looked at least three or four times? Hours, days even. Today I have successfully relocated a mobile phone, cheque book, accountant's bill, television remote control and car insurance document. All had vanished from the face of the earth yesterday. In searching through documents, old handbags and carrier bags, I have come across long-lost bank statements and bills which I shall be delighted to have discovered when I come to sort out my accounts for this tax year. Mind you, by then the safe place I have put them in will once more have vanished, Atlantis style, under a mound of assorted household ephemera and rubbish. John meanwhile runs a very tight ship for all his documentation. He has to. But it does mean that all the rubbish piles up in my office whilst his is pristine and uncluttered. He has to be organised though. So much paperwork. With all the new calves arriving, each one requires its very own passport, herd number and tags. Let just one day slip in recording the birth, and chaos would soon ensue. Not that the cows make it easy.

Once more we have had a set of twins. And once more one of them has died. It is so sad. And all to be recorded as well. These twins were born to another of the oldest cows. She had started bagging up and I helped John walk her into the crush, our equivalent of the delivery room on a maternity ward. Soon, with a little help from John, she delivered her calf and we walked her out of the crush. Despite the cow being mad keen on the calf, however, she was still not settled. Did she have another calf to deliver? John was worried about her trampling on her baby, or us, if he tried to get her back to the crush to have another look to see what was going on. Eventually the cow was persuaded and after a brief investigation, John realised that there was another calf inside but that it was facing the wrong way. A breech birth, and needing to come in a hurry before it drowned inside Mum during the delivery. With some deft and arm-crushing manipulation – a cow's contractions can be very powerful – the calf was safely delivered.

By now the other calf was up on its feet and staggering off round the yard. John penned up Mum and her babies and came in for lunch and to complete his records for the delivery. Everything looked good. A brief relaxation over *Bargain Hunt* well deserved. But tragedy awaited on his return to the yard. The second calf lay peacefully curled up. Dead. Life, tragically short, can be very cruel.

Last year this same cow had given birth to twins. Again one died, but the other, against all our normal practice, we named Freddy. He became our special needs calf and, eventually, bullock. Freddy now takes his place in with the heifers (he would be bullied by the bullocks), pushing and shoving to get to the rolled barley, but he still takes very slowly to any changes in his diet or care. He would not be weaned off his bucket of milk for months, and even then it took him weeks to learn how to drink out of his bucket. John had to tube feed him till then. When he eventually started to cautiously nibble at the calf mixture in his bucket, it took some persuading to get him to eat enough to justify withdrawing his milk. Then he had to be introduced to hay. Now the heifers are on barley straw as well as their rolled barley. Freddy is not keen and it will take him a few days to appreciate that it is edible, but, in time, he will get used to it.

23rd

How times change. Once huntsmen passing by at a fast trot relied on verbal tips from roadside followers of the hunt to give them a clue which way a fox had gone. Now it appears to be done by mobile phone. At least that's how it seemed yesterday when John passed two of the hunt leaders in their pink jackets, one hand on their reins, the other clasping a phone to their ear. Wonder if the same rules apply to phoning whilst riding as to driving. Could be just as dangerous. Maybe they were receiving a frantic phone call from the missus to ask when they would be home for tea, but maybe it's another incursion of communication technology into one of our oldest traditions. Not that we object to the hunt, even though we do not follow it. It does a good job of moving the foxes around and currently they are a real pest in our area. The foxes have killed quite a few of our hens and bantams. Our guinea fowl survive because they have the sense to perch either up in the barn or at the top of the highest trees in the apple orchard.

We would be lost without the hunt kennels to take our fallen stock. The government dispersal scheme for fallen stock is prohibitively expensive and burying fallen stock banned. So the hunt kennels are vital to livestock farmers in our area. Normally you would expect a real town and country divide on the issue of hunting. So I was surprised at how supportive friends of ours, Sue and Paul from Liverpool, were to the idea of giving the foxes a run for their money. At Christmas, their elderly and much-loved cat was torn to shreds by a fox in their back garden. 'We always thought it was an urban myth until we saw Spice being attacked and killed with our own eyes,' Sue said. They took to their farm weekend with gusto, although their Mercedes convertible is not the most practical vehicle for our muddy lanes. I'm afraid Sue's struggle to clamber out of the low-slung sports model was as nothing when compared to her efforts to climb up into the Land Rover. 'My knees. My knees,' came the agonised squeal. 'Get in,' and a shove was her husband's less than sympathetic response. And no inhibitions either at joining John at pigeon shooting. Nor any qualms at tucking into guinea fowl for dinner. They had admired them in the paddock that morning, and eaten two roasted that night. 'I must admit I felt rather reproachful about the guinea fowl,' Paul said. 'It's not often you get asked which bird you think is the best looking, and then end up with it on your plate.' Mind you, it's fair to say that admitting a guinea fowl is attractive could open you to some curious looks in town. Good job we didn't ask which ewe Paul thought was the most appealing. Now that really might be worrying.

24th

It was very quiet when we entered the foldyard. Unusually quiet. The heifer calf John was bucket feeding after its mother had abandoned it was not at the foldyard door. She has developed super-sensitive hearing, and nanoseconds after the scrape of the door's opening, she is up on her feet, head lowered and bawling. Straight after that she has run towards the door to butt your legs and let you know she is there and hungry. But she wasn't. John was concerned. A couple of days earlier he had found the calf in the silage yard under a fall of silage. Whether it is because it is warm, even in comparison to the yard with its cosy carpet of straw, this calf has taken to lying under the silage face. The cows' access to the silage is regulated by a bar that is moved forward every day to allow them to feed, but does not permit them to clamber onto/into

'Are you sure you all belong to me?'

the silage and spoil or waste it. Occasionally, if the cows pull the silage from the bottom, it creates an overhang of feed, which topples down when it is unbalanced. The calf had been lying at the face when such a fall occurred, but fortunately John was able to pull her clear before any harm could be done.

So, had she got trapped again? No. She'd found a surrogate mum. There she was under an obliging cow, suckling away. Just what John had hoped for. She was not interested in the substitute milk any more. Which left all the more for one of another set of twins. They were born at the end of the week and John has them partitioned away from the main herd so that they, or the cow, do not wander away from each other until the feeding and bonding is well established. They have bonded, but only one of the calves is suckling properly. The smaller calf is being pushed out by the bigger one and we are having to supplement the little one's feed.

25th

Our big worry for the flock this year is the Schmallenberg virus, which can affect sheep and cattle and of which there have been reported cases of deformed lambs being born on a farm only a few miles away from us. There is no vaccine available to farmers for their stock yet. The disease is carried by midges, and the affected lambs in our area were all from flocks that started lambing early, and that must have gone to the tups at the end of summer. Our tups went in early autumn, but there were still a few midges about. The disease is a mystery. It suddenly emerged in an area of Germany and the disease vector is a midge, more commonly associated with transmitting diseases such as Bluetongue in Africa, Asia and Australia. There were big concerns about a Bluetongue outbreak several years ago, but now the UK is considered free from the disease.

We genuinely thought, however, that we had had a case of the Schmallenberg virus on the farm this week. A neighbouring farm has had three cows deliver deformed calf foetuses, and another early-lambing farm multiple cases of deformed lambs. There is a very narrow window of opportunity for the midges to transmit the virus as it needs to infect the ewes or cows during the very early stages of pregnancy. Hit or miss indeed. For us, our relatively late tupping date will hopefully be an important preventative factor, as we will have passed the main midge season and the risk of infection will be reduced.

We went into major alert recently over Schmallenberg when a calf was born with a twisted leg that prevented it from being able to stand. When the calf made an effort to get up, it just toppled over and would not or could not stand to drink from its mum. We knew that SBV-affected foetuses can often present calving difficulties, because if the calf has rigid or stiff limbs, delivery is complicated. Was this why we had a wonky calf with a twisted leg? Fortunately not, the vet assured us. He diagnosed an extended hock ligament that he thought would have resulted possibly from the calf's awkward position in the cow's womb.

Or that is what he hoped. Which was not quite so reassuring, but he was probably placing his bets either way, like most vets do, as in 'Well, it might live, but don't be surprised if it dies.' The good news today is that after a week's coddling, tube feeding and isolation from the rest of the herd whilst the leg grew stronger, the calf is now part of the general melee in the yard and doing well. At first John made a pen for Mum and calf that allowed her to access the silage clamp and drinking troughs, but kept the calf safe. For three days he was stripping the cow out for milk for the calf, which the cow showed she really appreciated by a neat up-tail and splatter. Clean boiler suit required after each session. Then the calf suddenly twigged what he should be doing to drink, his leg strengthened and he was up on all four feet. Success.

I meanwhile had been working hard to send John off his feet. One of the many domestic, wifely, tender tasks I administrate is trimming John's toenails. At 6ft 4in, his toes are a long way off from his hands. He claims. Whilst shopping I noticed a fantastic gadget that would slice off nails in a sort of pincer, plier motion, not unlike the tool John uses to clip the sheep's hooves. And, it transpired, with a similar effect, as I neatly sliced off the end of his little toe. Was that a cheer I heard from the ewes' field?

26th

Can spring be just round the corner? An insistent blackbird is singing very loudly each morning and hinting that maybe it is. Even the occasional sunny, dry day is reminding us of seasonal changes and there is a definite ramp up of hormones in the guinea fowl, with a lot more hanky panky. More than a few feathers will be flying when the bull goes back into the herd next month. Nearly all the cows have calved now. Just a few persistently late calvers remain to surprise and confound John by dropping their calves mid-summer at some far corner of a field. Usually these are the older cows in the herd that have somehow gone out of sync, perhaps by not holding in calf when first served and then being successfully served at a later date.

Daddy Bull remains a voyeur, spending much of his day peering through a gap into the main foldyard where the herd is, and sussing out the talent. He is even refining his mating skills on some of the young bulls who share his yard. I tell you, same-sex relationships are quite the norm here. Even in the foldyard, cows that come into season and have no bull to satisfy those urges, mount other cows and cause havoc rampaging around.

Millie, our Jack Russell, has also spotted that there is an increase in squirrel love life around trees in the paddock that advertise luxury dray opportunities. She spends hours sitting at the bottom of a particularly fine des res, determined that no squirrel will sully her reputation as chief vermin terminator. When she is dozing peacefully it only takes a mere whisper of 'Cyril squirrel' or 'Rats' to send her into frenzy. Simple pleasures are all we ask for. But we have offered her another job this week, one she has completed with relish, and ease. Mouse hunting. Mice are polyestrous and can breed all year round, and certainly do in our house. I have traps set in all the rooms, usually hidden so as not to surprise and startle visitors. The mice that located the Christmas nuts in the front sitting room have now all been caught, we hope, but a sudden rush to my head that prompted a clear-out in the attic bedrooms, revealed evidence of even more little visitors.

And to add to this, John wanted revenge. The mice have feasted on his chest waders, rod covers and fishing bag. All of which if he had hung them up (nag, nag) would have been safe. But tossed onto the floor were fair game for Mrs Mouse and family. Millie and I went into the first room and shut the door. I pulled everything out, beds, boxes, bags. A scuttling alerted Millie. In she darted. Snap, snap. Game on. Not as much fun for a Jack Russell as a rat or squirrel, but it'll do, and for the moment, we are mouseless and she is zizzing.

27th

My new obsession is waiting for the guinea fowls to start laying eggs. It should be any time soon, and apart from their eggs being quite delicious to eat, I intend hatching some of their eggs in my latest purchase off eBay. An incubator. The minute I told friends of my purchase they all said, well, some of them, 'We've got an incubator you could borrow.' But apart from the fact that all the incubators mentioned hold up to a hundred or more eggs, I hate borrowing. 'Never a lender or a borrower be,' goes the old proverb. I don't mind lending friends anything, but I would rather not borrow. So my new toy can not only hold up to a dozen hen's eggs, but also about eighteen bantam or guinea fowl eggs. Perfect. That way if we find a clutch we can get them in the incubator and then ideally hope for a broody hen to usher them into the ways of the farmyard once they are hatched.

That currently is an impossibility. The fox, or several foxes, for all I know, has slaughtered many of our pullets from last year. There are a few hens and bantams, I am sure, hiding their nests up in the haystacks, but we appear to have seven cockerels left and one rather anxious hen. It's all right being desirable to the male of the species, but seven all at once? Too much. Miss Farmyard has now gone broody on a nest of her own and gets thoroughly fed up of being chased by all these cockerels every time she gets off the nest to stretch her legs and do what a girl has to do when you have been nest bound all day. So the cockerels are to go, or some of them anyway, to get the odds down a bit. Then I shall either buy, or get given, some fertile eggs for the incubator for now, and keep a sharp eye out for a guinea fowl nest. Last year some of our guinea fowl laid obligingly in the hen house. That is now deserted, but I have left the trap door tantalisingly open and fluffed up their old nesting area. There are still a lot of guinea fowl, although gradually diminishing in number as we have the occasional lunch from one of their numbers. They need to get laying now to save their necks.

28th

With lambing less than a month away, we brought all the sheep back home yesterday to vaccinate the pregnant ewes against clostridial diseases. These are organisms that actually occur naturally in the soil, but which can affect lambs during their first few weeks of life. Badly. They usually manifest themselves in infections of the intestine, but also as pulpy kidney. None of it nice. Normally we would bring the sheep for vaccination into a gated enclosure between fields, but the land is so wet it would just be a mud bath. Becoming even claggier by the time we chased the sheep round to try and catch hold of them for injections. So the easier course was to bring the whole flock back to the farm and do the job in a nice dry shed. Makes sense for us and the sheep. And they are now getting quite used to being brought home for a few days for a health check. As it happens, the job was a doddle. Our lane is closed again as road contractors are here to put in some much needed passing places. They resurfaced the lane last year, but did nothing to widen what is essentially a road built for 1920s-width cars. Now tractors, lorries and massive 4x4s attempt to get past by running each other off the road into muddy roadside verges. These currently resemble, from my recollection of history, the aftermath of the Battle of the Somme, or Flanders mud. John has been called out countless times to pull vehicles out of the mud since the original resurfacing work was done and the verges left in such a chaotic condition. Must be costing the council far more to come back and repeat the job. Even then the new passing places are very narrow and short, and your average lorry, which in theory is banned on our lane, would still run off them.

March

Ow. Ow. The throbbing of my little finger not only reminds me of how careless I was to cause the injury in the first place, but also makes me secretly envy the palliative support the calves get when they go through a similar encounter. The blackened nail and bruised finger was entirely my own doing. Chatting away, with an armful of groceries, I slammed the car door shut. Somehow, and I still can't remember exactly how, I used my little finger as a doorstop.

Many of our downstairs doors sport a little rubber horseshoe on the top of them to prevent complete closure so that grandchildren don't slam them shut on their fingers. No such luck on the car door. My son-in-law, a surgeon, kindly offered to drill through the nail to ease the pressure and let the blood out. Sounded horrible and I refused. Now I wish I had agreed, as the only way to reduce the pressure is to squeeze the nail bed and let the gunky blood ooze out. Hope no-one is eating while they read this.

I can now completely empathise with the rodeo show that has been happening in the foldyard and which, because of my poorly finger, I have been unable to help with. This is the regular dehorning of the calves before the horn buds get too large to deal with without veterinary assistance. Quite a few of our calves are polled. A reversion back to the Aberdeen Angus heritage of their mums. But their Limousin paternal genetics (Mr Bull) does throw a considerable number of calves with horns. He sports miniature crumpled horns, the result of some unsuccessful dehorning when he was a calf. But as he is the quietest, most docile bull we have ever had, but still requiring respect and careful handling, his horns are not an issue.

John likes to dehorn the calves just as soon as they start to bud. At this stage it is a relatively painless and swift job. A jab of anaesthetic into each bud area, wait for half an hour for the calf to be sensitised, and then the buds can be removed with the dehorning iron. In truth, referring back to the palliative effect of the anaesthetic, my kind husband has offered to come to my assistance. 'I can relieve the pain for you very quickly,' he suggested with a nasty gleam in his eye and, probably, for me alone, a blunt needle in his hand. Good job I know he's not serious.

The biggest problem with the whole dehorning saga is the calves' mums. The calves have to be separated from them and brought into the collecting area, so John can catch each one up and deal with it individually. The cows create mayhem, and the calves aren't too quiet either. You can hear the bawling all over the village. Not as loud as me, though, when that car door slammed. I don't do martyrdom.

2nd

John is away for a day or two fishing before lambing starts in earnest, so I am (nominally) in charge. Walking round a big yard of cows, calves and a bull, can be a little creepy on your own when all is quiet and dark. The cows are generally very quiet, but if you happened to get in between one of the sucklers and her calf, it can be a different story, as one or two of the Limousin crosses are very protective indeed. And big too. So, bearing that in mind, I do not so much stride through the herd brushing cows aside to check if any of them need a hand with calving (in which case ring Geoff), as edge surreptitiously round the perimeter of the yard, making sure I don't come between big Mum and little calf.

Then I slip and slide my way into the silage clamp to make sure none of the calves is trapped under any fallen silage. Imagine my surprise then when tonight I came on a newly calved calf, plus Mum. The calf was having a bit of a struggle finding a balance on the muck, rather like Bambi on ice. I thought the best thing was to leave Mum and baby for half an hour or so. When I went back they were both safe on the straw in the foldyard. Phew.

There are still cows left to calve. The yards are very full and this is the time when you hope that all the attention paid to vaccinating the calves and their mums against disease will pay off. That and yard maintenance to make sure the herd is always bedded up on clean straw.

3rd

Poultry are in spring overdrive. Ducks and bantams all laying furiously. There are eggs in baskets, pots, mixing bowls and Tupperware containers. I hard-boiled some of the duck eggs for my granddaughter Jessica to take to school for an egg-decorating competition. They are a gorgeous pale blue shade and a good size for titivating. She plans to do a blue penguin on a surfboard with yellow tufts and chest. Don't know whether such a bird exists, but there again, I don't think many penguins are actual surfers.

Big thrill. I am easily thrilled. I have found where the guinea fowl lay. I knew they must be up to something from their raucous cries, but just could not locate the nest. Then, when I was cleaning out the greenhouse, I spotted a clutch of their eggs tucked into a nettle patch and the roots of a bush. I would never have seen it without looking at it from inside the greenhouse as it was very artfully hidden. But not well enough for me to be denied guinea fowl scrambled eggs for breakfast.

Topping even the guinea fowl excitement was discovering that once more our nest box with a camera in has an occupant, I cleaned the box out last week but never thought that the nest box hunters would be on the move so early. Not so. One spuggy is in. She even slept in the nest box last night. We would have loved a blue tit, but hey, it's a little bird and sparrows are quite endangered now. So the only other exciting things to happen that will really assure us that spring is underway and firing on all cylinders will be the swallows nesting in the trailer and the barn owls in the tea-chest nest box. The trailer is getting quite a lot of use currently ferrying ewes and lambs back out to the inland fields, but John parks it up in the same place every night. The swallows will expect nothing less.

I am inwardly raging after having just replanted all the stone troughs in the yard with primulas. Only to find them denuded of leaves and flowers by ravaging poultry. I mean ravaging in its literal sense. Every other instance, the cockerels are chasing after the hens for a bit of

'Well, if a worm is more appealing than me, I'm off.'

rape and pillage. So tonight all of the poultry is being rounded up and imprisoned in the hen hut. That will serve them right for ruining my floral display. In the autumn they wrecked all the pansies. They just cannot resist the lure of a fresh bag of compost in the troughs and will scrat wildly to displace any new plants, and then peck the flowers into extinction.

4th

John noticed another newborn calf on his first walk back round the foldyard. As he approached, the calf struggled to stand, only bearing its weight on three legs. The calf managed to get under its mum for a drink but then collapsed. John was able to get up close to the calf and deduced that it had broken its leg just above its hoof. He wonders if the cow may have stood on it, but to make sure rang for the vet. The yard is getting crowded and the calf may not have been able to get out of the way if it happened straight after it was born. 'It's certainly a coincidence,' the vet said. 'I've just put two other calves' legs in plaster today. I'm sure it will be fine.' And it is. This evening the calf is already bearing weight on its pot leg and starting to stagger around the yard with a clop and a clump. The 'pot' is purple, so we will not be queuing up to sign our name on its leg, and goes from the hoof to above the calf's knee. All in all it needs to stay in place for the next three or four weeks, by which time we hope the herd may be able to go out. Better check up and see we are not transgressing any rules for cross compliance with a calf plus accessory.

5th

The biggest grain shed is transforming into a lambing corral with the strategic positioning of stack bars and big bales. Big bales make such useful building blocks. Rather like using a giant set of Lego bricks. What else could so quickly render a huge space warm and windproof? The bales have virtually closed off the entrance, with just a gap to drive the ewes in at night and out in the mornings, and a space for the dogs to see out of their kennels. Fizz and Pip love it. Lots to see and super warm. Millie could not care less, as she is in the house for most of the time.

6th

The main foldyard is now really overcrowded. At night, cows and calves settle down close together, but during the day the melee in the yard is potentially hazardous. The level of muck in the yard has built up over the past few weeks to a height that John is unhappy with. The stock are literally climbing up onto the straw to settle down. But he is hindered from mucking out the yards as there is nowhere to spread the muck. Under our wonderful new cross-compliance regulations, the land is too wet for him to run on with the muck spreader. The new system of single farm payment and cross compliance can be a nightmare to observe, and our day-to-day farming lives are heavily influenced by these measures.

7th

I hope my latest tidy up and sort out for a charity shop and the wheely bin does not have to be registered under any of the latest government wheezes that farming has to deal with. I refer to agricultural waste exemptions. Another hoop to jump through and quite an eye opener when you begin to realise the extent of accountability that the Environment Agency is looking for.

For years I have piled up in the meal shed everything that I think can be burned, so that it does not add to the domestic waste. Friends have even brought shredded office files for incineration. Now John tells me he can't take it down the fields to burn, which is infuriating as I see other villagers having regular bonfires in the gardens. Therefore I can indulge in my own personal legal inferno on the vegetable patch and incur no-one's wrath.

Most farmers I know are closet pyromaniacs. Banning straw burning after harvest was seen as a criminal act by many. The sight of those flames leaping along the rows delighted the match-happy and lighter addicts in the farming community. Wildlife sheltering in the swathes of straw may not have been that keen and visibility on nearby roads impeded, but it was a countryside tradition and contributed to managing weeds by destroying all the rubbish and providing a sterile seed bed prior to ploughing.

Farmers adjusted to the new regulations. They always do. A good moan and then finding out ways to circumnavigate, avoid or get round the problem. Our combine has a straw chopper, which is used for bean and rape waste, and all the barley and wheat straw is baled, as we need straw for bedding up the stock. But it was initially quite an issue, for example for arable farms without an arrangement with a stock farm on a muck-for-straw exchange. It is complicated. You just have to hope you have understood all the regulations and ticked all the correct boxes.

Can't see anything anywhere that directs what you are to do with the increasing amount of fly tipping that is taking place on our lanes and down the tracks to the fields. A rather large freezer is currently gracing a dike nearby, and I can only presume that its previous owner did not want to be bothered with any of the normal disposal methods, especially if costs were involved. I think we can confidently predict a lot more of the same if the government/Environment Agency goes ahead with charging for household waste disposal.

8th

Alone in the silage area a newborn bull calf was bawling for its mum. Two more calves had been born earlier. One claimed and with its mum. The bawling calf an apparent orphan, although as it had been licked clean, there must have been a responsible adult somewhere in the vicinity. All the cows are back in the foldyard and not one of them looks in the least bit distressed about losing a calf. John walked the calf round into the big yard and ushered it up onto the straw. Then he left. Half an hour later he went back in to find the calf snuggled up to its mum. Not only snuggled up, but snuggled in. 'The cow was laid down with the calf under her front leg. 'The calf was peeking out just like a chick does under a bantie hen,' John said. 'I've never seen a cow do that. It's a first.'

Another mystery solved today was why a previously healthy calf is struggling to survive and seems to have no energy. John is supplementing its milk with milk substitute. Mum, a heifer, seems to have plenty of milk, and we had seen the calf drinking. But it was just not getting a bellyful. Then we rumbled the reason. A cow, which we are not certain whether is in calf or not, is nipping underneath the heifer and drinking all the milk.

Cows will let other calves drink from them occasionally, especially if its own calf is drinking at the same time, but it is unusual, for us anyway, to have a cow up to the same trick. John bedded up a corner of the foldyard and gated it off to give the little calf a clear run at its mum. But Mum has jumped over the gate (luckily with no damage to either), so that option is a no-goer. So we are calling in the vet. If the thieving cow is not in calf, there is only one option for her. The market.

9th

John has forgotten to check the oil for the cooker and central heating and we have run out. I heard the cooker coughing and spluttering when I came down this morning to get the bacon on. John has a two-part breakfast. Grapefruit when he first goes out to check the cows, etc. and feed round, then a bacon buttie with a cup of tea at proper breakfast time. I love breakfast and thought I had passed this onto the children. True they wolf down bacon, eggs, sausages, beans, all the trimmings when they are here. Go to their house and only toast is on the menu.

John has recently completed a Grand Designs hen hut for the orchard and most of the banties now reside in splendour and sulk in their pallet construction. Those that were missing have now been located and are doing a useful job of sitting on Aylesbury duck eggs rather than the useless one of producing yet more bantie chicks. Jessica was puzzled over his plan to substitute the eggs and then delighted over the joke of chickens hatching ducklings. 'How will a chicken teach a duck how to swim?' seems her main concern. I showed her some old video footage we had taken of anxious banties clucking at the edge of the pond as previous ducklings launched themselves into the water. She can't wait to see it all.

10th

The cows are acting up. John had already come in swearing after they had climbed over the fence in the silage yard and pulled over a load of silage, trampling and fouling it. He re-erected the fence, tidied up the silage and left the herd to it whilst he took some feed troughs down to a field for the ewes.

Half an hour later I went back out to the foldyard as I could hear bellowing from the herd. They had done it again. Climbed over the fence at the silage face and were once more wrecking their feed. Then I spotted that the connection that links the fence bar to a power source had failed. No wonder the cows were so reckless. They were no longer getting that little warning tingle on the ends of their noses that kept them at a prescribed distance from the silage face. By then John had returned and he reconnected the power source to the fence. We noted with grim satisfaction an old cow pulling back smartly once her nose end made contact. Shocking stuff.

11th

The Limousin bull, formerly known as Sex on Four Legs, is hobbling about on three legs tonight and clearly in some pain. John is worried that an excess of passion might have led him to topple over and sprain one of his back legs. He cannot put any weight on his hoof and the area is very swollen. His lack of libido is proving very upsetting to the cows that have calved and come 'mad a bulling'. That is, they have come back into season and want serving. So what we have is a nightmare. Sex-starved cows, hurtling round the yard, scattering calves hither and thither, all trying to climb on the back of each other in a confined space. Bet the poor old bull wonders what else could go wrong. John tut tuts away at the cows like a Puritan witnessing an orgy. 'It's nature,' I tell him. 'Well, they can just pack it in. It's annoying me,' he says. Or words to that effect.

12th

Prior to the vet's visit this morning we have had to get the bull into the crush. Not easy as he is so big. We managed to back him into a corner and secure him there within a set of gates, but the next big idea had to come from the vet. After an initial sedative jab, the theory was then to release the bull and lead him into the centre of the foldyard. Even sedated he could drag the three of us anywhere he wanted to go. But the vet was able to get close enough to the bull's backside to jab him with a knock-out injection.

Of course the bull decided to drop onto the wrong side. The leg the vet wanted a closer look at was under him. It took three of us again to roll the bull over. Then it was all go before the bull came round. The problem was an abscess under his hoof. With me sitting on the bull's head, John holding the bull's hoof high enough for the vet to excise the abscess, we provided the cows with more excitement in the foldyard than they have had all winter. John and the vet left me alone sitting on the bull's head whilst they went to look for a medicated spray and jab of antibiotic to finish off the job. 'Don't worry,' the vet said. 'You should be able to stay on for about thirty seconds if he decides to come round. If he tosses you up in the air, just hang from the beams until we rescue you.'

13th

John has just come into the house in search of a warm pad for his back. He has pulled a muscle when feeding the ewes and blames the cold for his injury. Jo, our daughter, always has cold feet and so I keep a sheepskin-covered hottie for her that can be whizzed up to heat in the microwave. So those extra inches around John's waistline are not a sign of overeating, but down to the fact that he has a hot water bottle tucked into the back of his trousers. As Geoff is giving John a day to rest his back, we are going off to a ploughing match for a trip down Memory Lane. Thrills galore.

The land under the plough at the match is much lighter than ours and has been down to grass for many years. We stood in silent reverence beside tractors John had driven as a youth. He started work on the farm when barely into his teens. No cover, no Q cabs. One of his David Brown's Implematics had a Lambourn cab, a sort of tarpaulin with windows. 'I thought it was luxury to have one of those,' John reminisced. Good heavens, it's hissy fits now if the air conditioning or heater doesn't work. A Massey Ferguson 65 chugged past, then a Fergie T20 and a Fordson Dexter. John by now a drooling heap of nostalgia. Men in overalls and boiler suits stood judging at the end of rows. 'Now he hasn't set his rigs straight there,' John would tell me. And I would hear the same echoed by the other boiler suits. 'He's not covered up the trash either,' they would mutter 'That won't make a seed bed, all that grass will grow through in next to no time.'

The ploughs in use were nearly all conventional, not the sort that farmers use now, where they can turn them over and start back up the field when they have finished one furrow. These have to set a rig and then make the first furrow, tuck in coming back round, then plough round and round in a sort of rectangular circle until they get back to the central furrow. If that makes sense. Next time they would set the rig up further across the field so that the last furrow would end in a different place. I've glazed over already and so, no doubt, have you.

14th

It is a requirement to fit all newborn calves with two identifcation tags that indicate their herd and their individual number and country of birth, within twenty-seven days. We like to fit the tag as soon as possible, while you can still catch the calf. This is easier said than done and frequently requires a very devious approach to getting close enough to the calf to do the job, but keeping far enough away from its mum to stop her having a go at you.

The mum of one of the newest calves was not at all happy. 'She'll break my leg if I try to do anything to that calf,' John said. 'As soon as I get near, she puts herself between me and the calf and then gets her head down to have a go at me.'

How John eventually got the tag in was to wait until this cow had gone through to the silage clamp for a feed, leaving her calf bedded up in the straw of the foldyard. John quickly shut the gate out of the foldyard, thus isolating the cow in the silage clamp and catching up the calf. 'It would have been impossible otherwise,' he said.

It demonstrates how far our herd has moved from the days when they were all British Friesian milking cows, to now, when they are virtually all Angus cross Friesian. As British Friesian they were placid and easy going. Freed of all maternal duties at four days when the calves were taken away, their life centred on a plod to pasture or silage clamp, and two visits a day to the milking parlour for a feed of dairy cake and the rhythmic relief of the milking machine. Even though all the bulls that we have had since our conversion from milking herd to suckler herd have been very easy going, their offspring have been a mite frisky on occasions.

The main change is that the cows are not being handled on a daily basis. When John milked, he leaned into the cow, talking gently to her before he attached the milking cluster. He was in close proximity to them for the six or seven minutes it took to milk each cow in the parlour and even gave the AI (artificial insemination) man a hand when he came to do his job. In hindsight, he was even more involved in the calving. Now, the cows are much more independent. The majority of the herd will calve without any assistance. A good number are regularly calving in the foldyard on their own. But John will still check them last thing at night and first thing in the morning and go out in the middle of the night too if he is concerned about a calving. The cows may not be as approachable, but when they really need some intervention in the form of their herdsman, most are too far gone to fuss about who gives their calf a helpful tug into the world.

15th

An air of anticipation continues to permeate the big shed opposite the house. All the farm vehicles have been cleared out, along with assorted bikes, benches, hen coops, dog beds and kennels. The guinea fowl are completely disorientated because their normal perch on a coop has gone and they are teetering on the bars of the bull pen grumbling away to themselves. Don't know who looks more discomfited, the bulls or the guinea fowl. All this to make way for the ewes and lambing pens. The shed floor is strawed out and secured with a 'fence' of big square bales. The dogs think it is great to race round the top of the bales in a mad scurry. We are now bringing the ewes home every evening so they can all be under the big barn and easy to check up on overnight. The job has improved enormously from when we used to wander around a field at night, often in the rain, looking to see if any of the ewes had lambed and needed bringing back inside. Then you had to try and hold slippery little lambs with one hand, hold a torch with the other, entice the ewe to come with you, open gates with your foot or your teeth (I'm joking) and get the little family under cover. Now it's a floodlit job. Lamb pens all strawed up around the perimeter of the yard. Dry. Warm. Five star luxury. We are ready to go.

16th

Overnight a start to lambing with two ewes firing the official starter gun. During the day a steady stream of pairs, singles and triplets. As the weather has been so cold and wet, the ewes and lambs will stay under cover in the big shed. Last autumn a friend gave John a trailer load of old wooden pallets. John first used them for making the fishing hut down by the pond, but since then has been knocking out stack bars for lamb pens. As a result the ewes and their lambs are each housed in spacious, airy and secure pens. Enough room for the ewes to lie down and not squash their lambs, and even to produce another offspring if appropriate. During the day the ewes are out in the field but they will be brought home every night into the yard.

Experience has taught the sheep that the yard offers a trough full of sheep nuts. It only needs a wave and rattle of a feed bag at the gate to bring them home. The road is firstly checked to make sure that there are no cars hammering round the bend and then the gate opened for a flood/trample/melee of ewes to dash for the sheep nuts and a dry bed on the straw.

17th

John is now pretty much full on during the day checking on the ewes. He brings home ewes he thinks are ready to lamb, watches out for the shearlings with their first lambs to deliver and makes sure that all the lambs are getting enough to drink. I help out with the night-time rota by getting up at three, and John does the midnight check. Last night he had to stay out for nearly an hour as there were several ewes lambing at the same time and he needed to make sure which lambs went with which ewes so that none of them were rejected.

18th

After a hectic start to lambing, everything seems to have come to a full stop. We have had the vet in twice for shearlings. Both shearlings struggled with large lambs, but both have come out the other end alive and kicking, and proud parents. 'Worth the cost of the call out,' John says. I noticed some of the natty little accoutrements that the vet was using, lamb ropes and a sort of snare. John relies on his big hands or my smaller ones to furtle around inside the ewes to see what position the lamb is lying in when matters start to get complicated. But sometimes you need a bit of technical help. Out of loyalty I tried our local agricultural supplier for some new kit, but they did not stock the items I was after. So I have been on the Internet. All the bits and pieces I wanted arrived the next day. Free postage too.

We have also bought a bag of ewe replacement milk powder in from our ag suppliers, however. 'Let's hope we don't need it,' John said. 'There should be plenty of ewes lambing and we can get a drop of milk off one of them if we're short for any of the lambs.' But it turns out we did well to prepare. A ewe produced two sickly lambs and had no milk. Unhappily one of these lambs died as it had an intestinal blockage. But the other has struggled on, supplemented by the formula ewe milk. Today its mum has suddenly decided to get her act together and produce some milk, so it now stands a good chance of surviving.

19th

A trail of straw from back door to bedroom gives a clear indication of our night-time activities. The midnight and three o'clock wake-up call to check on the ewes, demanding tracksuits for John, and fleecy pyjamas for me. I like to keep comfy and warm in the lambing shed. The straw trail does actually stop short of the bed's interior, but it gets very close at times.

It seems like every time we go and look in the lambing shed at night, or out in the field during the day, one of the ewes is heaving away and popping out a couple of charmers. It's not been all plain sailing though. It never is with livestock and there has been the usual mix of tragedies and triumphs. The latest downer being not there in time to clear the birth sac from a lamb's nose. Tragic to lose a lamb just after it has been born. If only one of us had been there. In another instance, a ewe trampled her lamb to death in a frantic effort to guard her triplets from an inquisitive Pip, who had jumped over the stack bars and got into the lambing area. But small triumphs, when you can sort out which lamb belongs to which mum when two ewes lamb next to each other in the lambing shed, with both of them wanting to claim all of the lambs born.

20th

John enjoys a traditional approach to communication. He is not keen to take advantage of technological advances. I'm the one who likes her iPad, mobile phone, PC, laptop, satnav, scanner, etc. It does drive me mad when he wants to chase up something on the Internet and won't learn how to do it himself, but at the same time, knowledge is power. Plus he can't check on my eBay account.

Where I wish he would edge a little further into the modern world is in possessing a mobile phone. As it is, he can check up and ring me as I always carry mine, but I can't check up and ring him, as he won't have one.

And at times it would be very useful to get hold of him.

This morning he decided to take a break and go off with his mates for a round of golf. 'Just nine holes,' he said. 'I won't be long.' I knew he had checked up on the sheep before he left, but as we usually look in on them every hour or so during the day, I wandered over to the field opposite the house, where we turn them out first thing in the morning.

At the far side, under a hedge, I spotted a gimmer, one of last year's lambs, pawing the ground. From her rear end a water sac hung. Lambing was imminent but she was decidedly skittish when I approached and it seemed best to leave her get on with it for half an hour or so.

Back in the lambing shed, a ewe who had not wanted to go out with the rest of the flock at breakfast time, flopped onto the straw and started to strain. Leaving her to it, I went back to the field to check on the gimmer. She was getting nowhere, so I thought my best plan was to bring all the sheep home, so both of my maternity cases were in the lambing shed. Except the gimmer wouldn't come. Even though I was carrying a tempting back of sheep nuts and the rest of the sheep were nearly knocking me off my feet to get at them, my gimmer was not to be persuaded. Probably because by now I could see the lamb's head protruding from her rear. To cut a long story short, by the time John cruised back into the yard I was screaming blue murder about the fact he never carries his phone so I couldn't get hold of him. 'The gimmer's lamb's got its foot stuck and I think the ewe's got a breech lamb coming and the rest of the ewes have knocked me flying,' I screamed.

John stayed calm. 'Don't worry. We'll soon have them sorted.' And he did.

21st

One of our oldest ewes has lost both her lambs. She had not looked well and appeared very uncomfortable. When John investigated, she was carrying two dead lambs. He gave her a shot of antibiotic to halt any infection the lambs might have set up, but doubts the ewe will survive. 'She's lost some of her teeth anyway,' John said, 'so I would not have kept her much longer.'

Talking of teeth, I have been under attack from a killer tomato today. Whilst biting into a sliced tomato, a back tooth that was pegged into a root canal has broken off. I was lucky I did not swallow it. Just a surprise crunchy sensation and a funny hole where my tooth should have been. Good job I am not an old ewe. Once their teeth start to go, that's it. Off down the slippery path to market. A shearling, a lamb just over a year old, has two broad teeth. Every year after that it pushes two more broad teeth up, until it has a full mouth of eight teeth. A full-mouthed ewe. Once the ewe starts to lose her teeth – that is, becomes broken mouthed – John is looking to replace her. So I shall not suggest that he gives me a dental check. He might start looking for a younger model.

22nd

John and Millie have been invited to join a rat hunt tonight. A friend is overrun with the vermin around her ponds, hen hut, dike and ditch sides and needed Millie to join another terrier, Stig, to get rid of them. The terriers missed the first bolting rat and it made a clean escape. As did several more. At which point, perhaps bored by this lack of action, Stig spotted a hen out in the field. Game on. Alarmed, the hen spotted Stig at the same time and swiftly exited through a hedge. Undeterred, Stig tracked the hen by scent. Closely followed by Millie. Needless to say, by the end of the melee, despite best intentions, much invective and threatened chastisement, the body count stood at, rats nil; hen minus several tail feathers.

23rd

By two o'clock this morning, John had lambed three ewes during the night and they had eight lambs between them. When he got up at half five, to check up again on the ewes, no more had lambed, but there were only seven lambs in the pens. One lamb could not have disappeared, so where had it gone? Squashed between two bales of straw, that's where. Sharing a tiny space with a broody hen that had also squeezed into the minuscule gap. He brought the little thing into the kitchen and I fetched a dog blanket to wrap the lamb up in and mixed some ewe milk substitute. The bottom oven of the cooker is just the right temperature, so I tucked the lamb in there, and as she was too weak to feed, tubed her some milk. She lasted until lunchtime. The smallest of the triplets, she just did not have the reserves to fight back. Why do lambs do such daft things? They drown themselves. Hang themselves. Garrotte themselves and, this time, and it's not the first, squash themselves to death.

24th

Fizz our sheepdog is on a report card for behaviour. The ewes have been moved into a field, across the lane and opposite the farm entrance. But the lane is increasingly used as a rat run for vehicles wanting to avoid a slightly longer route on an A road. Despite signs at both ends of the lane clearly stating it is unsuitable for heavy vehicles (tractors excepted of course), lorries thunder through. Because it is too narrow for two large cars to pass, cars, vans, tractors, lorries, even the school bus, must dive for the verges to avoid losing at the very least their wing mirrors.

But back to Fizz and her misdemeanours. As a sheepdog she instinctively classes sheep as delinquents who require discipline and is increasingly determined to sort them out. From the yard she spotted a newly turned-out group of ewes in the field opposite the farm. Suddenly she raced out of the yard, past the old milking parlour and straight across the lane. Missed being run over by a passing car by a whisk of her tail. I was left to apologise to a shaken driver who thought he had hit her. Fizz meanwhile was organising the next field full of heavily pregnant ewes and not taking a blind bit of notice of her demented owner. Luckily no harm has been done. We hope. There have hardly been any lambs at all these past few days. And the weather is beautiful and warm. As soon as it starts raining the ewes will be popping out lambs at top speed.

25th

Before the start of lambing John had made half a dozen extra pens out of old pallets and was sure that he had solved any potential housing problems for the sheep. Not so. Everywhere you look under the big shed, ewes and lambs are mothered up in cosy domestic bliss. We are full. Fortunately we are able to get some families out into the home paddocks fairly quickly. A few have passed the independence test and gone down the road to the big fields, but most are still milling around in the paddocks.

To add to our new arrivals, we have several hatches of ducklings under bantams. A new hut for the ducks is fairly bursting at the seams with bantams and ducklings. We have had to keep the clutches housed separately for fear that the banties would have a go either at each other, or their neighbours' ducklings. There has only been one standard batch of bantie and chicks. She emerged from a secret nesting place in the straw stack and if she could cock a snoot at the other bantams she would. 'Yah boo sucks, I'm the only one with a genuine bunch of chicks. The rest of you have hatched interlopers.'

Geoff still has about a dozen duck eggs for us in his incubator, so when they hatch, our bantie foster mums will find themselves with a few extra ducklings to mind. With all the joy at new births, there is, unfortunately, sadness at the occasional tragedy. John brought another ewe home with her lamb's head so swollen that she could not deliver it. After half an hour's sweating and toiling to lamb her of the by now dead lamb, the next lamb she delivered was so weak that it could only breathe in fits and gasps. I fetched a child's straw so that we could blow directly into the lamb's mouth to inflate its lungs. But that only gained us a temporary respite. That lamb died alongside its twin.

Swiftly John raced to fetch the smallest lamb of a set of triplets that were in a pen across the yard. Before the ewe had had chance to struggle to her feet, John had smothered the triplet in the afterbirth and fluid surrounding the dead lambs and presented her with a tiny, but perfectly lively, foster lamb. The ewe immediately set about licking and nudging it. We waited to see if she would see through the ruse and change from nudge to butt. Not so: within half an hour the triplet was underneath suckling away and the ewe was stamping her feet if we went anywhere near the pen. 'She's mad keen,' John said with relief. Triumph snatched from the jaws of disaster.

Another one of the other ewes has had to be tied up to accept a lamb that was hers, but that she was convinced wasn't. 'I'm sure I got it right,' John said. But the ewe was not so sure. Her lamb, however, was. A day or two in bondage sorted the ewe out. I tell the ewes (talking to the sheep is a surer sign of madness than talking to myself), 'There is no way you will beat him, might as well give in and feed them from the start.'

26th

A brief visit for me to a friend who is a committed horsewoman and whose daughter enjoys following the local hunt. Fleur rides out whenever her job permits. As the hunt was meeting near to my friend's farm, Fleur had ridden her horse to the meet rather than relying on Mum taking her there. I was impressed. When our daughter Jo had a horse, we had to be at the back of her the whole time to muck it out and keep on top of the tack. Fleur was out at the crack of dawn plaiting her horse up, brushing down her jacket and all in all presenting a beautifully turned-out ensemble of horse and rider to the meet.

Because of problems with hunt saboteurs, the police were present. Discreet, but obvious. The whole affair was very civilised. A very high quality of refreshment on offer. Jugs of mulled wine, champagne, fruitcake, sausage rolls, scones, chocolate bars. What tickled me most, however, was the attitude of the hounds. Quietly and persistently they stalked the youngest members of the meet. A little girl on her Shetland pony and several toddlers were all being kept out of the way of jittery horses and well-shod hooves. With the gentlest of mouths the hounds would tenderly lift a piece of fruitcake from a child's hand, snaffle a sausage roll or patiently lick a Mars bar until a toddler was left just holding a brown sticky smudge. At the sound of the hunting horn, the hounds' appetites left them in a rush. They gathered to the huntsmen and set off in an excited group, still licking their lips for a last taste of stolen delights. Not a fox was seen, by the way, but Fleur had a good day.

27th

Agonised bleatings when we went out first light preceded the sight of a ewe trying to deliver a big single lamb. The lamb had stuck in the birth canal and its head had swollen so much that the ewe could not deliver it properly and the lamb died. So all today John has been hoping for a set of triplets so that he could set one of them onto the ewe. Our luck, and the ewe's, was in. Tonight she is tied up in a pen with a hungry triplet making on and not believing his luck to have all that milk to himself. The ewe is a little ambivalent about her adopted offspring, but in a day or two hopefully she will accept the lamb and all will be well. The triplets' real mum is more than happy with only two lambs to feed.

28th

Lunchtimes are slump times in this house. John rolls in at midday on the dot, and after cleaning up his meat, no veg and sack of potatoes lunchtime repast, retires to the snug with his pudding. Thence to doze quietly in front of *Bargain Hunt*, one of the many programmes devoted to buying, selling and valuing antiques and collectables. Apparently this programme and its like – *Flog It*, *Antiques Roadshow*, *Cash in the Attic* – are all great favourites for inmates spending time at Her Majesty's Pleasure. I always knew John had criminal tendencies. It is with scarcely disguised envy and a dose of healthy scepticism that we watch some apparently guileless participant producing a carelessly wrapped object from screwed-up newspaper to see if 'it's worth anything'. They of course claim to have no idea at all. Despite probably several hours trawling for valuations on the Internet.

But my heart began to beat a little faster when we were briefly (we are lambing) out this evening with friends for a bar meal. At the end, with a flourish and from out of a plastic carrier bag, one of them produced a roughly wrapped object in a parcel of old newspapers for our combined valuation.

The story went thus. These friends, Joan and Chris, live on a small farm previously owned by other friends who were out with us, Pete and Tine. Heavy snowfalls in December wreaked havoc on Joan and Chris's farm buildings. The roofs on the hay barn, hen hut, stabling and a Dutch barn caved in under the weight of snow. Fortunately none of their livestock was injured but it has necessitated a huge clear-up job and extensive rebuilding. In the course of this work, areas of the farmyard became exposed and dug up to allow for fresh foundations to be excavated.

'We had already gone over everything with a metal detector just in case there was anything buried there,' Joan said. 'Nothing of interest turned up but the hens had started scratting around and I noticed a gleam of brown shining under the earth. Something half concealed in the mud.'

By now we could all scarcely conceal our excitement. Brown glaze. Didn't we remember that funny little brown owl brought to an expert on the *Antiques Roadshow* that was worth a fortune? A piece of naïve pottery. What could it be?

'I was really careful exposing the pot,' Joan said. 'I didn't want to damage it so I just tickled it out like you see the archaeologists do on

Time Team.' Where would we all be without the TV? Obviously none of us has enough to do apart from watch the telly.

Breathlessly we watched her unwrap sheet after sheet. How fragile could it be? 'Just wait,' we were told as we bombarded Joan with questions. The last piece of tissue paper (really fragile object therefore) came away. To reveal a sturdy brown pencil pot carefully crafted and fired by the maker V. T., Pete and Tine's daughter Victoria, in junior school. Something you could never put a price on.

29th

A sad anniversary, as it is exactly a year since I lost my spaniel Holly. She was totally my dog. Never made a fuss at night about going into her kennel, unlike the others, who would all prefer to snuggle up to the cooker each night. Holly knew her biscuits plus treat were in her kennel waiting for her and was always straight there at night. On the day before her death I had taken all the dogs for a long walk and met up with Joan who was running her bitch across our fields prior to taking her to Crufts to compete in the field trial section. The dogs rough and tumbled and at one point Holly did go topsy turvy in the general melee and gave a brief squeal. But then, so did all the others at one time or another.

The next day I went to Holly's kennel to let her out for a breakfast snack. She was lying in the run of the kennel, unwilling to get onto her feet and follow me. I was instantly concerned, as that was not Holly. John helped me lift her into the back of the Land Rover and I obtained the first appointment at the vets and took her in. Holly's gums were white, she was cold and had a slight haemorrhage in her eyes. The vet's first thought was that she was poisoned. But then he palpitated her tummy and felt a mass in her abdomen. He proposed putting her on a drip, taking blood samples and if necessary operating to find out what the mass was in her tummy. I left her with a kiss and cuddle. She gave me one of her unfathomable, trusting looks.

That afternoon the vet rang to say she had died on the operating table. By night she was back home wrapped in a blanket to be buried with her friend Meg down by the pond where she loved to hunt amongst the reeds. My lovely Holly. I can remember bringing her home in a box from my friend's nine years ago and John saying as he watched the box waggle across the floor, 'That's not what I think it is in there, is it?'

Holly's favourite response to the command 'Sit', was to jump on your lap. We both loved the joke; she knew what she really should be doing. Every year at her annual check-up I was told she was too fat, but who could resist those big brown eyes that stared directly into your soul? I never heard her growl. She was always thrilled to see you. Losing a beloved dog is truly heartbreaking.

30th

Today has seen a distinct correlation between the state of my brains and that of the eggs my broodies are sitting on. Addled. These particular eggs are under two of my soundest bantams. They would sit on bricks if it were possible for a brick to hatch. Never budge. A clutch of Cuckoo Maran eggs under one and chocolate brown Orpingtons under the other. Both clutches bought against expert opinion (John's) and with my highest hopes off eBay. I am a sucker for a good advert. Show me a winning set of words and a cute picture of the goods and I am clicking away on that 'place bid' icon like a fiend. In the cases of these eggs, I just wanted something for my broodies to sit. Our poultry are a plain lot and I fancied something a little different.

Marauding foxes are a risk at any time of year. Over winter they are especially hungry, it seems, and constant vigilance is required. Sadly not always successful. Luckily most of our hens who do not choose to go into the hen house at night, prefer to sleep in the apple trees, well out of a fox's reach. Unless, as occasionally happens, they are nabbed on the ground as they descend at first light. When the snow fell, it was enlightening to see how a fox/foxes had been circling the hen run looking for a way in, so there is no doubt that they are out there watching and waiting. One night of forgetting to drop the hatch on the hen house and close the gate and that would be it. But returning to those special, and on reflection, expensive eggs, they appear to have been duds. We tested the eggs in warm water to see if they were rocking, but all the eggs just floated. And then exploded when I threw them away.

'Surprise!'

31st

There is hope of a hatch. Whilst moving some hay bales this morning, John has found a little brown bantie whom I had seen around occasionally in the day but who had not gone back into the hen house at night. Mystery solved. She has a clutch of eggs in a haystack. A bit precarious but she seems very settled. I do not know how long she has been sitting and she has a very sharp peck when I felt under her to check the eleven warm little eggs. So for once I am going to listen to John, not be seduced into buying anything different off eBay, and go with home-grown bantams. For the time being.

April

1st

Lambing had slowed down to a pair a day at most. And one of the recent triplets decided to stick its head under some pig netting and strangle itself. Lambing numbers clearly going the wrong way. But today the ewes have gone into overdrive. Five pairs. John is in seventh heaven even though all of his lambing pens are full and some of the lambs are getting watery mouth, as we have had to keep them inside the buildings for too long because of the rain. Being wet does not necessarily cause the disease. The lambs can appear strong and healthy when first born, but then they begin to show signs of abdominal pain and a watery fluid drips from their mouth. Without treatment, death would soon occur. John thinks we must have the disease in the buildings and that keeping them away from clean grass for an extended period of time after lambing is weakening their resistance. But there has been no alternative. It has tipped down day after day. As newborns, the little lambs would die of exposure if they were under such downpours. We breed Suffolk crosses, not your hardy hill types. Our lambs need a bit of comfort and cherishing when they are little.

2nd

Another day of mixed fortunes with the lambs. That's certainly farming. Yes the sun is shining and so we can feel confident in putting out the newborns, but the teeniest, weeniest, sweetest little lamb that we have been nurturing and feeding and hoping will survive, hasn't. It was born to one of the hoggs, so it had the equivalent of a teenage mum. No problem there. Most of the twenty or so hoggs that have lambed have done very well. But this one lamb was just perfection in miniature. Jessica our granddaughter was especially taken with it. We have about twenty or so photos of her holding the lamb, feeding the lamb, stroking the lamb, etc., etc. John and I took turns to get up in the night to check on the ewes, and at one o'clock and at four o'clock this morning it was still fine. At six, dead. Another of the smallest triplets has not been thriving. The two biggest lambs are getting in to Mum far more than he is, and there is not enough milk to go round. And yet another ewe rolled over and crushed her big single lamb to death in their pen. So at this very moment she is constrained in the same pen with the tiny triplet who is thinking all his lucky days have arrived at once. He knows what to do, he just has not had the opportunity to do it as often as he wanted to before.

3rd

A thunderstorm in the early hours was an unwelcome sound. Good for the grass, but we have had so much rain. The grass is now growing at the speed we like in order to keep pace with the demands of stock, and John is having to micro manage where the sheep graze to save grass for later access. The crash of thunder sounded uncomfortably close and we lay there hoping no-one who has their cattle out early would be struck. It has happened to two of our cows over the years. But the casualty of this storm was an oak tree. Split from top to bottom. Bark just sheared off. An amazing sight. Apparently in a direct lightning hit, the sap in the tree actually vaporises, as it is reaching such a high temperature. The gas takes up more space than liquid and the rapid expansion physically creates the dramatic damage.

4th

My eyes are dim this morning after a couple of turns on the night shift. A set of twins on one of my watches and triplets on John's. Bigger and better, of course. Must be the sunshine enticing the lambs out to play.

My eyes are not only blurry, but I am cross eyed as well, from searching for the guinea fowl's nest. I know it must be somewhere, but where? Over the last few days I have found the odd tantalising guinea fowl egg laid in the paddock or hen run, but guinea fowl are notoriously secretive about their nests. A friend who was given nine guineas necked them all for the freezer, as he declared that they were useless at laying. Only to discover a massive nest of nearly one hundred eggs which they had hidden in a forest of nettles. But too late . . .

To entice ours into laying in a communal nest, I have bought some dummy bantam eggs off the Internet and placed them in likely-looking clumps of nettles. Not the same as a guinea fowl egg, but near enough to my eyes. But not apparently to a guinea fowl's. The cackles of horror that come from the gang when they discover these interlopers is as if they have discovered a murder in their midst. Which I suppose they have. Guinea fowl eggs are very tasty and I immediately use any I find in my baking. So why not leave the eggs where they are and let them lay to them? is the intelligent query. Which I would do, but I suspect a black Labrador or naughty Jack Russell finds them first. They must attempt a mouthful, nearly crack their teeth and then drop the eggs. Guinea fowl eggs have shells like prefabricated concrete. Guineas are also a suspicious breed. Very Machiavellian in their ways. All scurry about as if up to no good with necks tucked down into their feathers, attempting to disguise themselves around the farmyard. I have taken to spying on them. If they can be sneaky, so can I.

Whilst searching for eggs, I rediscovered the greenhouse amongst the weeds of the veg patch. Time to clear out the corpses of last year's tomato plants, cucumbers, chilli peppers and courgettes. Needless to say, John, the last of the great carnivores, will eat none of them. But before I chanced upon the greenhouse again, so had one of the ewes. The sheep occasionally blunder through into the veg patch from an adjoining paddock. This old girl must have wandered in through the open door (I am a very lazy gardener and would have forgotten to shut it) and then wandered straight out through the other end. Glass panes notwithstanding. So now we have an extremely well-ventilated greenhouse with two entrances. One intentional, the other not.

5th

Millie, our Jack Russell, has learnt a new trick. How to climb through shrubs to get to the top of a wall and chase birds. Recently she also refined and extended her skills in rat catching. The problem being she wants to share the spoils. I am having to accustom myself to the gift of freshly caught rats and repeat the mantra to myself that that is what is to be expected of Jack Russells. But in the kitchen?

One of my guinea fowls has been lost. Despite trying to ensure their safety by encouraging them to roost in the orchard, a fox has had her. And near her corpse the missing nest. Most of the eggs eaten. I hope the fox cracked its teeth on the eggshells. The other guinea fowl are distraught. They have stayed around the nest all day cackling and chattering away at full volume. I hope they resume laying in the same nest otherwise I will have to start all over again looking for their nest in the midst of nettle clumps somewhere on, or near, the farm. The guinea fowl do not grace only us with their presence. We are only their owners, and guinea fowl are no respecters of boundaries. They visit every garden, farmyard and paddock in the village. Nobody seems to mind, because they are not destructive to plants, only to the bugs and insects they find. They are collectively called The Ladies and quite seen as the village pets. Everyone who has heard about the fox raid is very upset. I am anticipating bunches of flowers laid on Mother Guinea Fowl's nest and an In Memoriam message on the village noticeboard.

6th

Summer visitors have arrived, and almost immediately started nesting. When you are a swallow, speed not only on the wing, but also in the matter of assuring the next generation, is of the essence. An old cattle trailer is seen as the residence of choice for one pair of birds. That is what announced their presence back on the farm. John was just hitching up the trailer to take two bullocks into market when the irate birds exited swiftly, chattering their rage at the disturbance. As soon as the trailer returned from market and parked up, the pair were back on the job, building the nest in the corner of the trailer roof. They are really taking us on trust. Fortunately we do not have any long trips away and this trailer is rarely off the farm for more than an hour or two.

Another pair of swallows has taken over the meal shed. I did not realise until I went in tonight to get some scoops of milk replacement powder for the pet lambs' last feed. Two shapes swooped down from the beams and out of the door. I nearly jumped out of my skin. In fact at first I thought they were bats but then noticed they were a lot bigger. Still tiny but definitely not bats.

The pet lambs requiring a supplementary feed are very demanding. I am surprised that we have not had complaints about the racket they put up first thing in the morning. John and I are early risers and one or the other of us is usually putting Millie out for a wee at about five o'clock. The five pet lambs, who are lurking in the corner of the paddock by the back door, immediately start to clamour for their bottles. And don't stop for the next hour until we have drunk our first cup of tea and gone back outside again. You may have noticed I wrote that we also needed to put Pip out. Not only Millie but Pip too is sharing that early morning toilet call, having wheedled her way inside at night. But for how long I wonder? She had better behave …

7th

Tonight, Pip has come perilously close to eviction from the house. She frequently sleeps in the porch even though she and Fizz have kennels with runs under a grain shed. In the porch we have a large fluffy beanbag for her to sleep on. Miraculously, although she has chewed up many of her other toys and beds, the beanbag has remained intact. Until tonight. The porch looks like a snowstorm has hit with a vengeance. We shall be sweeping up polystyrene balls for ever. If she pulls off the impossible again and stays in tonight, she will not have a bed that moulds itself to her shape. It's a cold tiled floor instead.

8th

To take some of the pressure off the foldyard, John is turning some of the cows with older calves out. The rest of the herd were not impressed and bellowed to get out of this place and into those fields. With a family entourage to help, and stationed tactically on the lane to stop any passing cars being flattened by frenzied cattle, the chosen ones were ready to go. Road clear, and John now positioned to make sure there was no mix-up, the signal went up for me to fling back the gate. And move very smartly stage left to avoid being flattened myself.

It is a few seconds of madness. The older calves are up to chasing off with the cows although they are not sure where they are going. Others need to be chased and chivvied across the road. There are always a few who have to go in a trailer at the end, as they are not willing to go anywhere and just mill around looking baffled. So we shut the gate on them till they could be picked up later. Meanwhile one of the calves who had been left in the field to wait for his mum had taken matters into his own hooves. Pushed through the hedge and set off round the village. Now we not only had the cows racing round the field checking out all the exits, but a calf who had found one. One cross farmer and a few trampled flowerbeds later he was back with Mum. By now the feckless mothers who had dumped their offspring for a hedonistic life in the fields had remembered what they had done and wanted their children back. Ten minutes after the reunion, peace returned.

9th

My goslings have arrived and soon the Aylesbury ducklings I have on order from a specialist breeder/hatcher will also be here. The only problem is that the goslings will be out and about in the paddock before the Aylesbury ducklings are taking their first nibbles at, and exploration of, the grass. Geese are so bossy. Even when we have kept ducklings and goslings together in the same hut, the geese, as they grow, soon take advantage of their size and strength and routinely harass and bully the smaller ducklings. Just teaches the ducklings to waddle faster.

10th

The water level in the pond in the paddock is dropping. Usually the ducklings and goslings should be able, when they are older, to enjoy a

'Respect your elders at all times!'

good splash around until well into June. They will be lucky to learn to swim, the way the water is drying up. It has made us a bit concerned about the danger to calves from one of the ponds in the fields where the cattle we put out are grazing. Again because the pond is drying up, it is getting increasingly muddy and boggy around the edges. The cattle wade in to take a drink, as they seem to prefer the pond to their drinking troughs. The problem is that the calves are still relatively young, follow their mums' example and then struggle to negotiate the mud. Quite a number of the calves are sporting mud-encrusted legs. The worry is that one of the calves might damage a leg if it overbalances trying to pull itself out of the mud. 'I've never seen it happen,' says John, 'but, I'd rather not risk it,' so fencing the pond in is one of the jobs for today.

11th

By the end of the summer I might have a crop of wheat in the back garden to rival anything seen in our fields. To entertain Ollie, our grandson, who has a fixation with the big heaps of corn in the grain shed, I filled an old 'turtle' sandpit with a couple of buckets of wheat. According to John, an expensive toy resource. Ollie has loved it. As he is autistic, sensory experiences are very important to him. I enjoy watching him experience the trickle of the grain as he fills and refills his trucks, push his trains across a mountain of corn, bury the lot and then tip the whole works onto the lawn. It has absorbed his attention significantly more than any other of the toys, trampoline and climbing frame. And it has absorbed significant amounts of my time endlessly refilling the sandpit, scooping the grain back up off the lawn and sweeping it out of every little nook and cranny in the dining room and kitchen.

12th

Our fishing pond is still heaving with tadpoles. Several weeks ago, Jessica took a bucketful home so that she could see a few hatching in her 'frog habitat'. The rest she took for her school's mini aquarium. All went well at home until her brother Ollie decided to investigate by tipping the 'habitat' upside down. Luckily, the tadpoles survived. Psychologically scarred, no doubt, by the trauma of moving from pond to frog habitat to floor to mixing bowl to jar and back to the farm pond.

Ollie is on the autistic spectrum, so as the sibling of a child with learning and communication difficulties, it is important that Jessica is given time that is special to her, without the often destructive (unwittingly, I may add) force of her brother. Ollie loves being taken to big play barns. There children can run riot up and down slides and hide in their padded depths far away from their parents and grandparents (who seem to make up the majority of accompanying adults). I remember a challenging moment when Ollie decided to strip at the highest point of the climbing area and fling his clothes over the sides and into an area no-one could get to. Later he shot ahead of me to climb into the goat pen at a play barn with a Pets' Corner. 'Watch out, that Billy goat butts,' an attendant yelled at me. It butted me rather than Ollie. Good job I have a well-padded rear. And the hugs and kisses I get are total reward for the sleepless nights, backache and trashed farmhouse.

13th

We are now down to the last few ewes to lamb. The lambs this year are amongst the best we have had. What a relief not to have had a case of Schmallenberg. Coincidentally, the calves we have had over winter have also been the healthiest. John puts some of this down to the change in preventive feed measures he has taken, with the provision of more mineral licks for both sheep and cattle. For the cows and calves, the high-protein licks contained an ingredient for which we needed a vet's prescription, to prevent coccidiosis. This is a parasite that gets into the intestinal tract of cattle and causes severe dehydration and weight loss.

14th

Dangerous task completed today. Re-tagging two bulls that are due to go to market tomorrow. They had lost their ear tags somewhere in the muck and straw of the foldyard, either by rubbing their heads against a wall, snagging their ears in a gate, or maybe they just fell out. They do. At least two farmers have been killed or seriously injured recently putting ear tags back in again. The demand for traceability can demand a terrible price. To re-tag the bulls, John has to first order replacement tags and then coax the bulls into the crush, so as to punch a hole through their lugs with the new tags. Unsurprisingly, they are not keen to cooperate. The first bull went into the crush without any fuss. So did the tag into its ear. The second bull was having none of it, having watched his mate being assaulted. John had lifted the crush into their yard with a tractor and positioned the crush against a wall with a gate to swing round to push the bulls in. Twelve hundred cwt of bull decided not to play. As soon as the bull reached a critical point in the game, he just pushed past John and me and turned round to join his friends in the yard. 'It's getting too dangerous to continue,' John said. 'The bulls are getting more and more excited and we're not going to achieve anything other than a hospital admission for ourselves.' Eventually we managed, and collapsed inside with a reviving cuppa.

15th

Fun and games loading the two bulls intended for market. Our intention was initially to load the bulls straight from their yard into the trailer, but they would not play, or rather the whole yard of bulls wanted to. Not good. So Plan 47 was to take them through the main foldyard, into the old collecting area for the dairy herd, along a chicane of big straw bales, and, before the bulls realised what was happening, into the trailer. Worked a treat despite a slight mishap on my part of letting three other bulls through into the main foldyard, because, to be honest, if a bull wants to get past you, I choose the coward's option and let it. Once all the excitement in the yard had died down (the cows being rather excited about the presence of three virile young males in their midst), we led the trio back into their own yard without any fuss at all. Probably frightened to death by all those mature females.

16th

'Are you breeding racing banties?' a friend asked, spotting our resident white homing pigeon hoovering up scattered corn around the mobile dryer. The little bird arrived several weeks ago and has been virtually a permanent resident since then. I kept spotting this white bird but did not make the connection that it was the same one until I came to recognise his style of fluttering off when anyone came near, and then returning to the dryer to start eating again. Millie, our Jack Russell, gives desultory chase every now and then, as does Pip the Labrador, but by and large they have come to accept the pigeon as part of the poultry scene. Except this 'bantie' can fly rather well. 'Shall we catch him in a net and let his owner know?' I suggested to John. 'Not unless you want to see his neck wrung,' he answered. I had forgotten that the last pigeon owner we rang about a racing bird that had given up the racing urge and taken to farm life, had his flying days foreshortened by a quick neck twist. No-one wants a homing pigeon that doesn't want to go home.

17th

Delighted to note that it has been quite a long time since we spotted a rat in the yard. The numbers of feral cats we have around the farm are low. Few litters survive. As soon as they leave the safety of their hiding places in the haystacks, which is usually where they are born and reared, Millie finds and kills them. It is distressing but difficult to put a stop to. If the kittens survive long enough to get a bit of speed into their escape flight and enough knowledge of the barn layouts to know where they can climb to safety, they stand a chance. A very slim one. The same rule goes for rats. Millie is an excellent ratter but we seem to swing from times like now with few rats, to an increase in numbers following the impact of fewer cats to kill rats, as no litters have been able to live into maturity. Then the rats become remarkably bold. I remember last year when they would literally stroll around in broad daylight as if knowing there was nothing up to the job to tackle them. I even saw one by the back door and had to wake Millie up from a slumber to kill it.

18th

Rats are a hot topic currently. We visited a friend's house to pick up some Aylesbury eggs to sit under a broody bantie. Her ducks are in full lay at the moment and she has a surplus of eggs. As our banties are all going broody, it is a great opportunity for us not to waste their egg-sitting talents. Eggs safely in the Land Rover, we lingered to discuss the problem she was having catching one particular rat. As you do. 'It is leading a charmed life,' she said. 'I even know the way it moves now, I've seen it so many times.' As we spoke, my gaze was drawn to a huge rat waddling out of the pig sty, replete from pig meal and unusually slow in its movements. More of an amble than a scuttle. 'Is it that one?' I asked casually. Quick as a flash, John picked up a fallen branch (the sty is sited picturesquely under a tree for shade) and leapt into the sty after the rat. 'Careful,' Helen shouted. 'The sow is vicious, she's still got her piglets.' Just as fast, he leapt out of the sty, but not before having dealt the rat a couple of blows. By now Helen's terrier had sensed game on and was after the rat for the mortal crunch along the backbone that Jack Russells specialise in. And Mrs Pig had charged out ready for her own game on with anybody foolish enough to have strayed into her territory after her babies. In seconds the mood had changed from rural bucolic to battlefield carnage. That's country life for you.

19th

Walk into the foldyard and you are greeted by our pet calf, a rejected twin who is totally fixated on either John or me for its milk. It hovers around the foldyard door waiting for one of us to go in. The other calves race around together, mainly feeding from their mums, but quite often taking a quick swig from any udder in the vicinity. Not so this little calf. It stands hunched and solitary. Our special needs case. The race around the yard by the whole herd when the bulls came to join the party, highlighted its vulnerability. Whilst the other calves quickly got out of the way, our little one was in danger of being trampled. It lays down to sleep alone, amongst the trampled, soiled straw by the foldyard door whilst others settle to sleep cuddled up to their mums. So today it has gone into a lambing pen in the big shed with the remaining ewes and lambs. It will have its very own wrap-round care. Snug and warm in its own big bale house. Ahh.

20th

One of our oldest cows is ready to calve. A Friesian relic from the dairy herd, who has managed to hang on in there since we changed from dairy to suckler. John knows she is in calf from the way she is bagging up tonight, i.e. her udder is filling out prior to calving. Won't be long now. And not so many ewes left to lamb. Thank heavens we have chicks and ducklings to look forward to. As long as they leave my flower troughs alone when they are growing up.

John is focused today on land work to top dress the grassland and apply growth regulators and fungicide to the wheat. To do this he needs a plentiful supply of water to mix the spray. The problem this week has been that the tap he uses to fill the water bowser has ceased to function. So instead we have had a long hose fixed to my utility room tap. As the bowser takes an hour to fill up, I just hope that the tap gets mended soon, but I'm not holding my breath. Although the weather is warming up, the ground is still too wet to turn the rest of the cattle out. We want to preserve our pastures for the entire summer/ early autumn, and if they went out now, they would poach a good deal of the land and stop fresh grass growth. As a result we have some very sulky cows. Lurking around the foldyard gates. Wistfully gazing across to the fields.

21st

Another racing pigeon has decided to have a stop-off in our yard and not go home yet. This one has again taken up residence with several of the banties in the barn roof. They are the ones that seem to be able to escape from the hen hut. It's certainly on very friendly terms with our little flock and shows no inclination to leave. Pigeons, or more precisely fantail pigeons, have been exercising my mind more than usual lately. A neighbour has a dovecote, and when visiting her house you can usually rely on leaving with a well-splattered car from all the flypasts as the fantails flutter in and out of their home. I have recently flirted briefly with the idea of having a dovecote on the farm. Quickly stamped upon by John, who is not keen on the idea.

I can remember bringing three baby fantails home many years ago. I put the three baby birds in a box in the porch and left to finish a job outside. I returned, to find one of the farm cats had clawed her way into the box and eaten all three of them. I am sure John had sent the cat a map of where to find a tasty snack.

A friend Helen also has a dovecote full of fantails in her garden. Rather a lot of them in fact; so when she was asked for a few birds to set up a dovecote for an acquaintance, she waited until night and collected twenty fantails as they roosted. 'As far as I knew, I had virtually cleared out all of them,' she said. 'I thought I would have a fresh start and clean out the nests and muck and blather. I went back the next night to check and there were sixteen more fantails roosting. They must have all been roosting elsewhere and spotted that there was room for them once the others had gone.'

22nd

Jessica, who is staying with us over the holidays as her mum is working and cannot get cover (she is a GP), is telling everyone who visits, about my shortcomings as a shepherdess. 'You see Poppa told Mamma to look after the sheep and she was too busy washing up to go and look at them and one of the lambs was dead. It was all her fault.' If the death penalty was still in force I would have been for the gallows on her evidence alone with no chance of reprieve. True I did get distracted by domestic chores whilst John took a well-earned sleep after lunch, but on the other hand, I have saved at least two lambs this year from suffocation when they are born. Unless the mucous or caul around and in their nostrils and mouth is cleared, the lambs cannot breathe. It is a very dispiriting death to witness. To have got so far and then be unable to breathe life-giving oxygen just because no-one is immediately to hand. You feel absolutely drained, depressed and downhearted. What a waste. And then your granddaughter never stops going on about it and does not let you forget.

23rd

There may not be many ewes left to produce, but seven of them decided to lamb this afternoon. It would have been exhilarating if we had not lost a lamb. John is philosophical. 'You win some, you lose some.'

Jessica is having a wonderful time collecting eggs, including magical chocolate ones in the nests. She loves bottle-feeding lambs, playing with the dogs and taking them for walks in the wood. Plus picnicking in said wood whilst making sure that the wolf from little Red Riding Hood and the Three Little Pigs does not share our sandwiches (although three hungry dogs want to). Poppa has been elevated to magician status by his ability to produce lambs from 'sheep's bums' (we do not encourage too close a view) and hatching off ducklings from under chickens.

A most noteworthy activity this week has been choosing a new bull. After much deliberation we have gone for another Limousin. I say we. John has decided. I fancied an Aberdeen Angus, as I think this breed is always a popular seller on the butcher's counter. Sounds more patriotic, an Aberdeen Angus, than a Limmy. But I must admit he is a very handsome fellow. We have gone directly to the breeder, as buying one from the market previously very nearly ended disastrously. The bull we bought then was stunning. A real show bull. But after a few months working he ran off to nothing and needed solitary confinement, expensive veterinary treatment and feeding up to get him back on form. 'I guarantee you this one will not run off,' the breeder told us. We are sure he will not, as the breeder, Robert, is a good friend and shooting partner of John's, far better than an anonymous seller.

I was interested in the criteria they used to pick the bull out from the forty or so in the barn with him. He has an appealing face and impressive tackle, but they were not the features John held most important. I heard him talking to Robert as they moved the bulls round to get a closer look at them. 'I like my cattle with long backs and a good ar…e,' he said. Now I know why he married me.

It is a few days since our oldest cow calved. Later that day she cleansed – that is, passed all the afterbirth with no problems. The calf suckled and all looked well. Then overnight the cow went down. Nothing dramatic. She had not crushed her calf, as ewes are liable to do when they decide to lay on one of their lambs; she just lay down and has not been back up since. John called the vet immediately as he suspected the cow had milk fever, and his diagnosis was confirmed. The vet took blood samples, ringing back later in the day to say she was deficient in calcium and phosphate. This is despite the fact that licks are available to the cows for both of these minerals.

Off I trotted to the vet's, picked up the required mineral jabs, John administered them, all should have been well. As the calf could not get at his mum's udder, John stripped the cow for her milk and fed the calf. We waited then for the cow to get up and get on with the job. But she didn't. So the vet came back and took another blood test. She was still short of phosphate. I went to pick up another mineral jab. Luckily I checked before administering, as this time the vet's dispensary had put out a different medication that did not indicate it was for treating a mineral deficiency. At first the duty vet, as by now it was evening and the vet's was shut, tried to argue that was maybe what was needed, as the cow's muscles may have cramped after being down for so long. 'But the blood test said she was short of phosphate and that was what she required,' I explained. By the time we met up at the surgery, he had looked at the computer read-out and agreed. And apologised.

Meanwhile John had cunningly constructed a hoist out of split fertiliser sacks, spread them out and we rolled the cow onto them. By hooking the ends of the sacks through the tractor forklift, it pulled the cow onto her hoofs. She paddled away in the air but then gently sank back into the straw when released. So, what to do. She has moved a little by herself. Makes occasional attempts to get up. Eats and drinks with gusto. John has created a pen around her and the calf in the foldyard, and the rest of the herd mill around unconcerned. The calf is now totally fed on milk powder replacement as there is no way he can drink from his mum as her udder is inaccessible to him. She is bright, feeding well, quite content to lie there whilst her meals are brought to her. 'What's not to like?' seems to be her attitude. 'I'll get up all in good time.' And she probably will.

25th

It is amazing what good use a pair of poultry shears can be put to. Mine, and they are still intact, have been used for snipping through plastic pipe when a saw can't be found, baler band around hay when a knife is missing and dagging out the rear end of sheep when the sheep shears have gone walkabout. Today we've employed them to cut through plaster of Paris when nothing else was up to the job. The pot leg that needed removing was on the little calf (now considerably bigger and faster) that had its leg crushed.

It has become very nifty on three legs and a pot, no problem at all in navigating its way round the foldyard. Within the next few weeks we are hoping to be able to turn all the herd out, and once in the field, catching the calf will be very difficult to achieve. So armed with a bucket of warm water to soften the plaster (but no idea of how to get the calf to stand with one leg in said bucket of water), my trusty poultry shears and a rope halter, we entered into the fray of the foldyard. Cows are not daft. They knew something was up. The calf's pot had been covered originally with a purple-coloured cloth, but after several weeks in the foldyard, the cloth had absorbed the brown hues of cow muck, and the leg in question could hardly be distinguished from every other brown leg of every other brown calf.

We walked the calf into a closed-off section of the foldyard that had recently been occupied by our old bull and is securely gated to keep him away from the cows. Not securely gated enough, however. The crushed state of the steel gates revealed how strong his passion was and served as a warning not to come between a bull and his desires. Fortunately our little calf has not yet developed such tendencies. Give him time. His mum, however, was none too impressed with us leading him away from her. She bawled and bawled. The herd joined in. She bawled some more. The herd encouraged her. She tried to jump in. The herd ignored her and just continued bawling. All talk. Once we had the calf on its own, it was a relatively simple job to get a halter round its head and secure it to a gate post. Then my job was to keep it still whilst John tried to soften the plaster and cut the pot off.

Calves are not very cooperative in a tight corner. I virtually had to strangle the calf to get it to stand still. Gradually John snipped down the plaster, peeling the pot away whenever he could. A couple more squeezes of the shears and the pot came off. The calf's leg looked a little bent, but clearly healed. Once the gate was open it hopped/trotted/limped/gambolled back to Mum. But, importantly, put its weight on the leg, something it was not doing when the leg was broken. Mum shut up, the herd quietened down, the bull saw his way clear, we staggered off for a cup of tea, the poultry shears went in the dishwasher. All's right with the world.

26th

A frequent visitor to our big pond is a wily heron. I could also describe him as lanky, scrawny, predatory, scruffy. Not, I consider, a visually attractive bird, and an equal menace to fish in domestic as well as natural ponds. I was surprised to realise how little they weigh when we picked up a dead heron once that had flown into a power line. It was literally a featherweight. Hardly any substance to its body. Just a long beak, skinny legs and feathers.

They do, however, have their champions, and one of these is our friend Graham. He has been engaged for the past few weeks in ringing heron chicks at the heronry at Besthorpe Nature Reserve near to where he lives in Nottinghamshire. The heronry is situated on a large island, a safe haven from foxes and cats. It is also shared by a colony of cormorants. On a misty morning there is a prehistoric ambiance about the place. 'With a bit of vivid imagination' (such as Graham's) 'you could soon imagine yourself surrounded by baby pterodactyls,' he told me.

Our heron is thwarted by the muddy condition of the water in our pond. The demise of most of our rainbow trout and a takeover by Canadian duckweed led us to stock the pond with grass carp to clear the weed. This was all prior to visits by our local otter, who then developed a taste for grass carp sushi. At the time, the carp had been very successful in ridding us of all traces of the weed, although still leaving the water brown and muddy. The only sign of fish you could glimpse was their mouths hoovering up fish pellets. Increasingly bigger mouths, I noted.

When we had the rainbow trout, Mr Heron considered us one of his favourite takeaways. We are still on his regular drop-off route to back garden ponds, but now there is less evidence of speared fish on the pond bank. It used to drive John wild to discover a large trout, too big for the heron to take away, lying jabbed on the grass.

But plenty of evidence of the heron's main favourite takeaway dish are to be seen, according to Graham, on the land surrounding the herons' and cormorants' nests at the heronry. 'It's just littered with bits of goldfish. The ground is thick with them. They must rob all the back garden ponds in the area,' he said.

Graham's main job consisted of holding the ladder firm at the bottom of the trees, for the accredited/risk-assessed/professional climbers to reach the herons' nests to ring the chicks. It gave him plenty of time to survey the undergrowth beneath the trees. 'I was surprised to see a virtually intact goldfish lying there,' he said. 'Most unusual as it was a large specimen and not one I thought the herons would have discarded so close to their nests.' It was in fact a goldfish reject. A cruel trick. Poor baby heron on being presented with a fishy feast found the meal to be rubbery and inedible because that is exactly what it was. A rubber goldfish. Probably put him off fish for life.

27th

'That's the best field of winter wheat I'm looking after,' our spray rep said after his latest field walk over all the arable crops. It is not down to anything chemical either. Rather, John thinks, to an old-fashioned technique that he can use in this particular field. Grazing it off with sheep. The field in question was for many years down to grass. It was well fenced because of stock grazing it over the spring, summer and autumn months. Cattle and sheep both still graze in adjoining fields, so it was very easy to turn the pregnant ewes in at the start of the year. They benefited from a fresh bite, and the wheat benefited from being nibbled down to almost ground level. What the ewes did was remove any leaves that might have developed mildew over the winter. They were not in long enough to destroy the crop, but long enough to dismiss any disease and trigger the wheat into renewed growth. Result is a crop that has not even had to have any fizz (fertiliser) on it yet and which is virtually organic at this stage.

28th

The cattle are very alert to the fact that it is nearly turn-out time. The silage area, which is approached by the gates and yard that faces onto their fields, is crammed with morose-looking cows hanging over the gate and gazing wistfully at all that yummy grass. However, like children, they have to eat up all of their silage before they can go out to play, and there is still a lot of silage left to eat. We have spent some time shuffling the remaining pregnant ewes around so that the field we turn the cows out into initially can have some fizz and be ready for the onslaught of the herd. The ewes left to lamb are now in one of the farmhouse paddocks. Another house paddock has ewes and triplets in (they need to be kept an eye on) and all the rest of the flock and their lambs are inland, well mothered up with their progeny. So far we have relatively few pet lambs. Touch wood. Often we get left with quite a large number. The youngest will soon be joining the other pets in the paddock, as they are doing so well that they have all jumped out of their pens when they see their bottles of milk arriving.

29th

It is the first anniversary of the death of a member of our extended family in Cumbria. To attend his funeral last year meant leaving the farm for a whole day. At this time of year, that can take some planning. Geoff came in to keep an eye on the stock, especially the ewes left to lamb, and make sure the dogs had a run. As we turned off the M6 for the Lake District, the sun came out. It was magic. The day was even more poignant because the service was held in the same church where my husband John married his first wife and then said goodbye to her. They met in their teens at agricultural college, married, and then she succumbed to cancer tragically soon after.

I am John's second wife, and Bill, whose funeral we were attending, was her father. We remain very close to all of her family. John recollected that when he was courting Kath, he lived at her father's farm to help with the lambing. Lambing up on the fell is a very different experience to lambing in our warm shed. 'I spent all days walking the hills checking on the sheep,' John said. 'They usually only ever had a single lamb and were very hardy, but I still had to catch some of them that were struggling and give them a hand. At night the sheep stayed on the hill and I had to wait until morning until I could get outside again.'

With staying close to Kath's family, who have always welcomed me as one of their own, I knew many of the farmers who came to pay their respects, even though it is many many miles away from where we farm. Bill, Kath's dad, was the quintessential hill farmer. He had a hard life but a rich and fulfilled one. This was his favourite poem and very apt for the occasion:

> *The farmer stood at the gates of heaven,*
> *His face all weathered and old,*
> *And humbly asked St Peter for admission to the fold*
> *'What have you done, old man,' he said,*
> *'To seek admission here?'*
> *'I've been a farmer, sir,' he said,*
> *'For many and many a year.'*
> *The Pearly Gates swung open wide.*
> *St Peter pressed the bell.*
> *'Come in, come in, old man,*
> *You've had your share of hell.'*

30th

Back home, the hens are banished to the hen hut. Over winter and most of spring, they have had the run of the foldyard. Scrabbled amidst the rolled barley. Pinched corn out from under the noses of the bulls. Waited with the ewes for the sheep nuts to be dropped into the troughs in the yard. No longer.

Part one of the escape plan from the hen hut completed.

As far as I was concerned, the hens were nothing but a bunch of idle, loafing criminals. I have waited all winter for them to start laying again and earn their keep, but no sooner have they popped an egg or two out of their rear ends, than they have committed the worst offence known to poultry. Scratted out all the plants again that fill the old water troughs in the yard. Or so I thought.

The biggest trough in the yard holds a passion flower, which grows up against the back wall of the old dog kennels. A week ago, as the spot is sheltered, I planted around the edges of the trough with trailing plants and stuck plugs of petunias in every available space. Four days ago each plant was rooted out. And they had been doing so well, thriving.

Then the next day I found the area around three other troughs in devastation. In the morning they had been a picture, a riot of colour; but by that night, they were empty. Plants lay forlorn and rootless. Compost was everywhere. Plus a few feathers. Crime solved. Hens into hen hut. The only two hens left out were a couple of broodies sitting on clutches of Aylesbury eggs.

But once more my troughs were in disarray. All the compost that I had carefully swept up and refilled and replanted was again spread across the yard. It must be those two pesky broodies, I thought, so once more I swept up and replanted and made myself a coffee after all that work.

Kettle on, I looked out of window and spotted Pip in a trough, digging. I screamed. She froze. Have you ever seen a guilty Labrador? I have. Pip specialises in a range of looks. One minute jaunty and cocky. The next, when she is in trouble, abject and ingratiating. Ownership of her switches from John to me at these times, dependent on what crime she has committed. These vary from egg stealing, drinking the calves' milk, raiding the sack of dog biscuits in the meal shed, pegging a pheasant on a walk, chasing rabbits and eating all the other dogs' titbits. On this occasion she did not know whether to turn and flee, or sink into the trough and bury herself. By the time I got out into the yard, she was cowering in the back of the Land Rover, having decided to be less than valiant and beat a retreat.

May

1st

Six new baby goslings to care for. Huddled under a pig lamp, gently peeping away. Then when they are disturbed, making one mass dash straight into their water bowl, where they flail and flap in terror as I add to their poultry crumbs. Table manners leave a lot to be desired. The approved method seems to be to stand in the bowl and perform any necessary toilet requirements at the same time, and in the same place, as feeding. A sort of drive-through and poo arrangement.

Plus there are also six kittens under the barn. Millie is unfortunately on a mission to find and kill them. They were born on one of the haystacks. These are gradually reducing as we feed the herd. All the silage is eaten up and there is still not enough grass to put the herd outside. To stop Millie finding their home and destroying the litters, John has barricaded their domicile with big straw bales that Millie's little legs cannot climb or jump over. She can bark, though. Endless hours yapping. Drives you nuts. I just hope the mother cat is not as fed up of it as we are and feels driven to move the kittens to another place that is not so secure.

2nd

We have our nephew Thomas staying with us, who is soon off to work as a game ranger in Kenya. He has worked in different parts of Africa in similar jobs: setting up safari camps, conducting tours, and a few conservation jobs. His dream is to emerge as a sort of film/journalist/ reporter, but it is a hard area to break into. 'We had a problem with fencing and elephants at my last camp,' he said. According to Thomas, it was a drought period and the elephants could scent both water and food in the camp and surrounding field areas.

The camp and fields were ringed by electric fences, but these were not always successful in keeping the elephants out, as they had developed a special technique for ascertaining if the current was connected without actually getting a shock. The elephants apparently held the tip of their trunk close to the strand of electrified wire, without touching it, and somehow could sense/scent/divine whether the wire was live or not. If the fence posts were on the outside of the fence and the current was off, the fence was worse than useless, as the elephants just pushed the wooden posts over and walked in with a minimum fuss. They even managed to get in without a shock if the current was connected, as Thomas had seen them using the fence posts as a trapeze wire/walkway to cross the wire on, once they had pushed the fence over by using the posts as an earth. No wonder they were such good circus animals.

If the fence posts were on the inside, their problem was more complex and the fence more efficient. Then the elephants kept away, as they could not access the post to earth themselves against the shock unless they connected with the wire before pushing the post over. Fortunately we do not have those problems. A cow may have a good reach, but it's minuscule compared to an elephant.

3rd

A large number of day-old ducklings have arrived and are now housed in an equivalent of the Duck Hilton. They have heaters, fresh straw, water to splash in and drink, and big straw bales in front of the whole caboodle so that they are not subject to any rain, wind or draughts. Plus everything is netted over to prevent hawks swooping in for a tasty takeaway snack.

Sadly one or two have already perished, and to be truthful, we expect to lose several more over the next few days, as ducklings can get what is called starve-out. This is where the ducklings have failed to learn how to peck at their grub and eat, and just rely on the nourishment they have retained from the egg sac. If they are not eating by the third day, you lose them. Hopefully, not too many. As soon as we step out of our back door, our ears are filled with the sound of a quiet, persistent humming. Rather like the buzz you hear near an active hive. But magnified.

4th

Lost a lot of ducklings overnight. When the ducklings were delivered yesterday, the lorry had already dropped off several thousand ducklings to other farms in the area. We were the last drop. The driver assured me that the ducks had been kept warm at a constant 22 degrees centigrade and were fine, but John was immediately alarmed and called in the vet. He thought they might have a salmonella infection. An antibiotic to go in their drinking water as an interim measure has been prescribed, whilst he did an autopsy on some of the dead ducklings. This afternoon the vet rang to say he had been contacted by the other two farms who had taken delivery of the same batch of ducklings. Obviously the ducklings had carried an infection from the hatchery, but as yet he was not sure what it was. Not bird 'flu, he hastened to add.

5th

I walk the dogs as far inland as I can get on the farm in the Land Rover. I go there because it is away from any stock and the dogs can run freely. It is most amusing to see Millie, the Jack Russell, trying to keep an eye on the other dogs so she can keep track of them. The wheat is now getting on for two foot high and once she is in amongst it, she is invisible. And so are they. To her. To see, she stands on her back legs. She reminds me of a little meerkat balanced on her hind legs with her front legs crossed across her chest. Comparethemillie.com, in her case.

As a cross-compliance requirement of the Single Farm Payment we receive, all arable fields require a two-metre strip of either grass seed or natural regeneration (i.e weeds) adjacent to any hedge or dike bordering an arable field. This is to be an established border and not ploughed up on an annual basis. Grass seed was drilled into the clean seed bed of each strip and germinated well, and over time it is good to see that it has smothered and suppressed any weeds and rubbish.

6th

With family up from London for a few days, we had enough bodies on hand to make sure that the traffic could be stopped when we moved the cows and calves out of the yards, across the road and into their fields. John directed the whole exercise with military precision. The cows and their calves were gathered into the silage area. My sister and brother-in-law positioned themselves on the road ready to stop any traffic coming through the village. I was in the greatest situation of authority: to open the gate and get flattened in the rush as the cows stormed the opening.

The problem was that John told me to loosen the bolt on the gate so that it would swing open quickly. If I messed around opening up the gate and then just brought it back slowly, there was a real possibility I could get trampled in the rush as the cows forced it open. Literally, I had to lean against the gate to keep them in until John signalled to me that he was at the back of all the calves, and then I signalled to my sister on the road, who signalled back the all clear. Talk about complicated. Anyway, it worked and this year we were not left with any calves wandering around the yard wondering where on earth Mum went. Conversely, not one of the cows who had stormed into the field started wondering where her offspring went. Irresponsible or what?

7th

No smells (other than the normal ones) within the house, but a lot of cheeps instead. The clutch of bantam eggs that I set in an incubator has hatched off. These chicks are a few days ahead of a clutch of eggs sat under one of our few remaining bantams, numbers having been ravaged by another daylight fox raid. The hope is to slip these chicks under their foster mother when she has hatched her own brood. Normally works.

8th

We are both nursing sore toes, sore knees, sore elbows, in fact, sore bits all over. Today was spent in a rodeo session with the calves, and, I think, the calves may have won. Last year we lost some of the calves to coccidiosis, an infection of the gut. It was hard to spot that there was anything wrong with the calves at first, but then, when they failed to thrive and we brought in the vet, there was little we could do at that stage to treat the condition effectively. This year we are forewarned and forearmed and the calves have already been drenched once this year when they were in the foldyard – and much smaller and far easier to catch.

Now it is not a matter of simply moving the calves from one section of the yard to a smaller container area, as we could do when they were inside, but of coercing them out of a large field into a collecting area and then, and here is where the fun really starts, into a crush. Three at a time for good measure. John brought our mobile cattle crush from the farm on the forklift to the corral. Within the corral is a sectioned-off area in the form of a long passage, concreted over so we are not slurping around in the mud when conditions are wet. This is used for most jobs that need actual one-to-one handling of stock when they are out in the fields.

The plan is, and we always have a plan although it does not always work, to drive the calves down the passage and into the crush. Then, once John has them confined and they open their mouths obediently when he says 'say ah', they receive a good dose of no doubt nasty-tasting medicine to keep them well.

Of course, on the farm, nothing goes exactly to plan. For a start, the cows have to come into the corral as well and they are never calm and reticent when someone tries to manhandle their babies. Plus Daddy bull comes too now. And whilst he is the most stolid and solid of beasts, you just never know whether if his ladies get upset (assuming polygamy is legal in the cow world, of course), he won't too.

Luckily he didn't, and in fact I was shocked to note that he took advantage of the fact that one or two of the cows who might be in an interesting state to accommodate him were easily accessible and not able to gallop off across the field in order not to receive his attentions.

But the cows. Push, shove, moo, bellow. One of them in particular needs watching as she escaped dehorning and is quite conscious of the fact that she can use her horns to get her own way. Queen of the Silage Clamp when the cows were inside. But John and I are nothing if not nifty movers when threatened and John especially was quick and efficient when dealing with the calves' medication. I'd have the stuff squirted in their ears, eyes and up their noses. Ours too. We'd be immune to coccidiosis as well as the calves.

9th

Only one ewe left to lamb. The remaining old girls (all Mules, which is a Swaledale ewe crossed with a Blue-faced Leicester) that had not lambed at the same time as the rest of the flock, were left in a paddock next to the farmhouse. But they have over the last few weeks surprised us at breakfast time with some lovely pairs of lambs. This old ewe is biding her time. These latest lambs have all been by our Texel tup. Originally all our Mule ewes were in with the Suffolk tup and our Suffolk-cross ewes were with the Texel. But towards the end of the autumn John brought the flock together and Mr Texel must have fancied his chances where Mr Suffolk had not worked his charms.

10th

Twenty-five years ago, an elm tree in the small field next to the house fell victim to Dutch Elm disease and had to be felled. Then, a sucker from the dead tree grew once more into a handsome specimen, until, a couple of years ago, it once more was ravaged by Dutch Elm disease, and died. The thought that the weakened tree might crash into the lane if there was a strong wind was a concern. Plus the fact that a number of power lines ran very close to the tree and could easily be brought down by such an accident. Accordingly we contacted the electricity provider in our area to alert them to the hazard. They came out, did their risk assessment, and agreed that the tree needed felling and that they would do the job, as it was compromised by the proximity of the power lines. No other permission was required because of their consent and so we waited for action to be taken. Have they been to do it? Nope. Zilch. Not a sign.

Branches had been breaking off over the winter and there was still no sign of any contractors or tree surgeons. So when the electricity providers notified us of a power cut today, for them to carry out other necessary work in the area, John decided that it would be safe for him to cut down the tree himself.

Up bright and early to get the work done of feeding up the cattle and checking round the sheep, he was ready to swing into lumberjack mode as soon as the power went off. Fortunately he got the job done early, as the power came back on again three hours earlier than we had been notified. Could have been a tricky situation if he was only halfway through when the lines went live. As it was, everything has been sawn up and carted off and the brash collected into a bonfire for another day. In the next village to us, also affected by the power cut, one of our friends had made her own plans for the day. Faced with the prospect of a day at home with no electricity, she decided on a day out shopping. She too got herself up bright and early, prepared the evening meal, etc., washing in and out on the line, house tided up, husband Pete organised. They moved into the village several years ago after selling up their smallholding and calf-rearing unit to build a beautiful detached house, with a garage block to house their collection of vintage cars. Plus one modern vehicle for everyday use. The cars are housed in luxury, parked-on carpets, air conditioned and secure behind electric-up-and over doors. Therefore when the power went off in Tine's house and she had gathered up her shopping bag and purse ready for a good day's spend and self-cosseting, only one thing prevented the trip out. She'd forgotten one vital element in her forward planning. With the power off, and her car tucked up in its garage, the doors couldn't be opened.

11th

Clearing out the big shed always turns up a few surprises. This year it was an old bike with a butcher's boy basket on the front. I had used it to take John his drinkings down the field in the summer time. 'Get rid of it,' John said. I demurred. I might use it again one day, I thought, even though it was a real boneshaker.

But the subject of the bike came up again today. We were at a friend's house for supper. She was bewailing the cost of running her Range Rover. Not exactly a Chelsea tractor, as they do live on a farm, but a 4x4 is not totally essential to her lifestyle. 'Last week I filled it up, £100 plus, went to the local shop, round to my daughter's and one or two other visits in the area, and when I looked at the fuel gauge it was empty and needed filling up again. So I'm going to buy a bike.'

It turned out she was halfway through a bid on eBay for an old bike with a basket on the front. 'It will be ideal, I can go to the shops, get a bit of exercise and save myself a fortune.' Her husband looked suitably sceptical. 'It'll be as much use as that fruit press you bought for a pound, to process the apples in the orchard we've only just planted,' he said. 'And it's going to cost us a fortune in fuel to drive and pick the press up from Wales.' All the men nodded sagely around the table, apart from John, whose eyes had lit up at the mention of someone wanting an old bike. 'I've been pleading with Bobbi for years to get rid of that old boneshaker,' he said. 'It's clogging up the yard and she' (me) 'won't hear of it even though it's years since she' (me) 'has ridden it. Surely you'll' (me) 'let go of it now?'

And I think it is time. So tomorrow the bike will be hosed down, pumped up and oiled. Much cheaper than eBay. No cost at all to my friend. She's thrilled and John's thrilled. I'm just relieved.

12th

John is disappointed with some of the lambs from the hoggs. The hoggs themselves are fit, well able to cope with lambing at a year old, but some of their lambs have been tiny, and a few have not survived at all. On the other hand, we have had a number of giant lambs that the hoggs have struggled to deliver. No rhyme or reason to it. 'Can we blame the new tup?' I asked. 'Don't think so,' said John. 'He comes from a reliable source,' (a friend's flock) 'but it's strange that it is only his lambs that we are having problems with.'

It reminded me of when a few years ago we bought a magnificent Texel tup. They originally came from the Netherlands where Texel sheep were kept for their wool and the cheese made from their milk. Mr Texel went in alongside our Suffolk tups and made virtually no impression at all on our ewes for the first couple of years. Indeed some ewes gave birth simultaneously to a Suffolk lamb and a Texel lamb, showing a degree of uncertainty amongst the ewes as to which tup they fancied the most. They were just dreadful flirts. Then we got rid of the old Suffolk tups, brought in a young Suffolk lad, but kept the Texel. That year we had a magnificent crop of Texel lambs. With the competition out of the way and a youngster to show off in front of, our mature Texel must have really felt top tup. Unfortunately for him, and us, John sent him off to market before lambing, and before we realised how good he was. Too late. By then he was cat food, shepherd's pie or a biriyani. 'Another stunning example of good farm management,' John admitted ruefully.

13th

Today John has cut four acres of grass for some bagged silage. We normally have contractors in to make the silage, but there is not time to prepare the big clamp or cut the large acreage of grass we shall need for winter feed for the herd.

Winter feed. It is not summer yet but we are already having to make plans for what the herd will be chomping their way through come November. The four acres is one of the furthest fields on the farm and difficult to access with the big machinery owned by the contractors, whereas John, and his friend who will bag it up for him, can easily bounce their way along the rutted track. This particular field is alongside a small wood. It belongs to the hunt and is approachable down a green lane which only John, a neighbour and the hunt can access. There has always been a gentleman's agreement that John can shoot the wood if the hunt can ride over land immediately adjacent to the wood. Since the hunt ban, of course, things have changed and we rarely see any riders. But there are plenty of foxes and John showed me the flattened areas of grass just out from the wood where the cubs come out to play. They will be rather surprised tonight to find their playground has been shorn. So will the badgers too, of which we are sure there are several.

14th

The clutch cable on our tractor with a loading spike on the front for handling big bales has broken down and now we're stuffed because we can't find the spike for the other tractor. We know it is somewhere on the farm, but where? I can picture it clearly. It's blue and you would think that a blue bit of kit would stand out from all the green bits of kit. But it must have either camouflaged itself very effectively amongst all the tackle, or walked. Or, even, been borrowed and not returned. The last being the most likely.

Dealers no longer carry spare parts, as they do not like to have lots of expensive bits and pieces hanging around their sheds. Instead you now have to order the part you want, once it has been identified on the microfiche. Then you must wait for courier after courier to bring it to one depot after another until it reaches the dealer.

This has proved very frustrating and time consuming when feeding and bedding up in the yards. The big straw bales are in a field and have to be fetched home. Big hay bales for the ring feeders are only round at the back of the farm, but still need a loader to get them into the yards. When John bought Geoff out of the farm, he knew that he had to look to easier ways of handling areas of work. At one time all the hay and straw was in small bales. Took days, literally, to stack in the fields, load onto trailers, pitchfork off trailers into stacks at home and then pitchfork off the stack for use in the foldyard or stables. A lot of manual handling and aching backs.

That was until we switched to big bales. Purposely created for single-handed farmers. Or, to put it better, farmers working single-handedly. But you do need the proper equipment to handle it, so for example when the clutch cable goes on your tractor with the loader, you're stuffed. John's father used to say, 'It only breaks down when you're using it,' which is a wise truism, if an irritating one.

Fortunately a neighbour became aware of John's plight and is giving him a hand with his loader. No thanks to the dopey dealer who rang eventually halfway through the afternoon to say, 'We've got the part now. It came yesterday afternoon but we forgot to ring you and we've been so busy it just slipped my mind. Sorry about that.' By then there was no time to fetch and then fit the cable before the whole job of feeding stock started again for the night.

15th

I spent the day helping John reposition the pens of the ducklings. We need to prevent a build-up of waste water on the shed floor. Ducklings do not just drink their water from the automatic drinkers, they splash and spread it all over the shed floor. Now it drains away into the waste water system that serves the foldyard for the cows. The ducklings are totally absorbing to watch. Frantic in their rush from one end of the pen to the other in a hectic dash from water, to feed, to warmth under the gas lamp. It is like watching a swirl of fish, or those dips and swoops that starlings make before coming into land. In the end we decided the only word to describe it was a vortex of ducklings. I do not know if it is accurate but it seems most appropriate in its description. They are gradually taking over all the spare space and we have already had to move the corn dryer to provide more room to extend their pens.

16th

When work permits, John and a select group of his mates toddle off to play a round of 'Millionaire's Golf'. It is called that as the course they play on is owned by one of the mates, so, no matter how busy the course is, although they do start this game at an unholy hour, they can usually find an empty hole to tee off from. I think those are the correct terms, not being a golfer myself. As all the mates are self-employed, they can dictate this spot of leisure time. Holidays and the need to earn some money routinely interfere with this knock round; however, just occasionally the mixture of smart (theirs) and battered (ours) vehicles gathers in the club car park for this hallowed occasion. So any stock, if they are about to lamb or calve, have to clench all orifices and hang on. They need to picture a leisurely amble around the greens punctuated by wild and inaccurate shots, a running commentary on the wildlife (currently a swan is again nesting on one of the ponds), and then shut out the vision of them feasting on bacon sandwiches (poor piggies) that have been ordered from the greens by a phone call directly to the chef in the restaurant.

Mobile phone calls are a useful excuse for some of the less than spectacular swings. To be interrupted by a call from a dodgy trader wanting to buy or sell a vehicle at auction is one of the player's excuse, another regularly hears from his wife about corn prices, tractor breakdowns and spray calibrations, whilst the golf course's owner is constantly berating his groundsmen with jobs that need to be done around the course. For him the round is in the nature of a daily risk assessment, grounds maintenance sweep, and no blade of grass goes unnoticed. Noticeably silent is John. He refuses to have a mobile phone, knowing that if he did, it would never stop ringing, with me on the other end of it.

17th

The last of the ewes managed to keep such a close grip on herself that she failed to lamb at all within the prescribed time limits as written down by John in his orders for the day to all farm stock. Throughout April she failed to produce, but now she is showing a glimmer of bagging up and the merest hint that she might be persuaded to part with some progeny. The rest of the flock are contentedly grazing, lambs afoot, lots of gambolling, king-of-the-castling on grassy mounds, furious butting at their mums' bags for a slurp of milk.

Not this ewe. She stays close to home with the tups and a hogg in a paddock at the end of the big sheds. The hogg, a lamb from last year, has resolutely failed to fatten up, and seems to have discovered the secret of perpetual life on a farm. Not fat, not fit. It must have passed this mantra of unconventional behaviour and the idea of keeping the farmer guessing onto the ewe. 'What can I do with her?' John said. 'After every wet, cold night I get up expecting that ewe to have lambed in the middle of it. I'm convinced she's in lamb, so I kept her, but she looks like she's here to stay.'

18th

Mr Fox, or in this case Mrs Fox, has visited us one last time for a takeaway meal. She had even snaffled up two of the guinea fowl. Nothing gets the guinea fowl. The only one killed last year was by a car speeding through the village. Took out his headlight. Jolly good. Should not have been driving so fast.

This marauding vixen had become increasingly bold. She had even taken three piglets from a neighbour's Kunekune litter. These pigs are not an aggressive breed, otherwise I doubt whether the vixen would have been able to commit the evil deed. In our case we suspect Mrs Fox had been hiding in the undergrowth commonly referred to as the garden and vegetable patch, and taken the guinea fowl as they came down from the orchard trees in the morning. However, one morning there was someone waiting for her, and I have to report that she has gone to the happy hunting grounds in the sky. I feel no elation at her death but I am pleased that my poultry are safe. It will not last long without vigilance. John thinks she must have virtually adult cubs. She had clearly been feeding for some time and was thin and manky looking. So out there will be more poultry predators. It never ends.

19th

If it is not my hens who are a desirable item on the menu, it is their eggs. Top culprits here are the rats and Pip. Millie does a sterling job around the farm checking on all the rat traps and flushing out their possible hiding places. I actually found a rat that she had killed in the hen house, but largely ignored all her excited digging around and under the hut as terrier enthusiasm.

That is until I found some of the dummy eggs that I had placed in the hen boxes to encourage the bantams to lay had gone missing. I rooted around under one set of nest boxes and came up with three very well-chewed rubber eggs. So there really were rats in the hen house. With severe indigestion, I hoped.

So the plan today was to give the hen house a really good muck out and steam clean, and then catch up all the chicks and rehouse them. Step one was to pull out the nest boxes. I did, and then screamed with horror and fell backwards out of the hut at the sight of an enormous rat's nest, plus rat and baby rats, smack under the nest boxes. Millie was thrilled. I averted my eyes from the blood bath. A Jack Russell has to do what a Jack Russell is born to do. Good girl, Millie.

20th

A blood-curdling squawk echoed round the big shed. What was John up to? Surely he wasn't necking any of the banties? Those that are left have an important job at this time of year, sitting clutches of Aylesbury duck eggs.

John came into the house, hessian sack in his hand. The contents of the sack were clearly peeved and hell bent on escape. 'Fran needs a bantie cockerel,' he said, 'so as we've got a couple, I'm taking one up to her.' Friend Fran has an eclectic flock of chickens. Many of them come from another friend who keeps a commercial poultry unit. Fran could not provide a home for all of those past their best lay-by date, but a happy two dozen hens have had the chance of life in an orchard with the only cloud on the horizon a possible visit from Mr Reynard when they are out foraging for food. Better that than the possible alternative. A definite date with a chicken-processing plant.

Fran also has some of our old bantie hens, which they find useful for sitting eggs. Banties are wonderful mums. Fiercely protective and much better sitters than ordinary hens. For this reason she wants to expand her flock, but needs a cockerel to provide the necessary 'input'. Our own plans for expanding the bantie flock have been disrupted not only by foxes, but also by Fizz, who frequently finds any nests before I do, and ignoring the barrage of pecks on her nose, eats all the eggs before they have chance to hatch.

21st

For the past month or so Geoff has been collecting pheasant eggs for his incubator. He rears pheasants for his shoot and also to boost numbers in the wild. He has been keeping the hen pheasants in runs in our paddock where they can shelter under branches and foliage during the day and probably try to hide from the incessant attention of visiting cock pheasants. These besiege the runs day and night, totally flummoxed by the wire netting that keeps them from the objects of their desire.

In a week or two the pheasant hens will be released back into the wood. Plenty of time for them to rear a brood of their own. Meanwhile

'Can I interest you in a fine wine, dining and seduction experience?'

some of them are getting a little bored of being kept in captivity and have started to peck at and break the eggs they have just laid. Geoff has his own way of dealing with this. He blows a pheasant egg and fills it with curry or chilli paste.

This morning he came into the house for a coffee and asked if any of the dogs had been particularly thirsty and drinking a lot of water. 'Don't think so,' I replied, 'but I haven't seen Pip for an hour or so.'

'I left a tray of eggs filled with curry paste on the table in the porch to take out to the pheasants later on,' Geoff said. 'When I went to get them, two had gone missing. I wondered if any of the dogs might have had them.'

On cue, panting, tongue lolling out to cool it down, drooling streams of water, Pip turned up in the kitchen. Along her back, what remained of the eggs and curry paste was smeared where she must have rolled in the mixture, having decided it was not to her taste. 'I think we have found the culprit,' I said, 'and I don't think either of us will have any more thefts.'

22nd

An afternoon counselling session for Bill, a friend's husband who had recently been traumatised by a large vet's account.

The story goes thus. One of his wife's cats was killed in a road traffic accident. She decided another cat was needed to keep her remaining moggie company, and after a sizable donation to a cat rescue society, brought another cat home.

Like John, Bill does not entirely approve of cats. John will tolerate them around the farm buildings as they keep rats and vermin down, but that's as far as it goes. So whilst Sue, Bill's wife, was delighted to give another cat a home, Bill grumbled. Being a good husband, however, he did as all husbands must: he shut up, paid up and forgot about it.

Until, that is, the remaining cat in their household, the one who had stayed at home and been a good, faithful companion by the fireside, took umbrage at the newcomer. He went off his food, started wandering because he did not like being at home and lost weight. Sue was worried and went to a vet. One she had not been to before.

This vet was something of a cat therapist/counsellor/aromatherapist/reflexologist/reiki healer. I jest. But he did suggest that along with pick-me-up treatments, Sue should purchase an ioniser that could be plugged in close to where the cat slept so that pheromones (or something like that) would permeate the air around the cat, and relieve any stress the cat was suffering. All very holistic.

Then the bill arrived: £270. 'Stress? Stress?' Bill said when he saw the cost of the device. 'Never mind the cat. Plug it in by my bed: I need it now.'

23rd

Our ducklings and goslings have matured enough to be let out of their runs and have free access to the house paddock. The bantam that hatched some of them off, though, is having an upsetting time. She is thrown into confusion, throws motherly tantrums and goes berserk when they all decide to go for a swim in the pond. Not the kind of behaviour she would expect a chick to indulge in, and as far as she is concerned, they are hens, not ducks and geese.

Jessica, our eldest granddaughter, sees all this as a supreme example of her grandfather's male incompetence. 'I told you, Pappa,' she says with worldly authority, 'I told you,' (she has already learnt the need for repetition when nagging) 'that they would all end up muddled when you let a hen hatch a duck. That Mummy hen thinks they are going to drown.'

More ordering around comes when we go for walks. Jessica certainly knows her way round the farm. 'Keep the windows closed, Pappa,' she shouts as we drive past the beehives at the end of the wood. 'I don't want to get stung.' We were off on a walk with the dogs, bouncing along the rutted lane in the Land Rover. The dogs love this walk. So much to explore, chase, and opportunities to snuffle around in the undergrowth. There are currently about fifteen hives on the edge of the woodland. Strategically placed so that the bees can fly to the fields with rape and beans.

The scent of the bean flowers is heavy in the air and very pleasant. But rape flowers seem to stimulate every hay fever sufferer in the country for weeks on end. The air around each hive was surrounded by a buzzing horde of worker bees and the entrances clogged with others, vying to get in and unload (I presume) their cargo of nectar. Over the winter and early spring we have been accustomed to strolling past the hives with no fear of being stung, but with the bees in such a frenzy of activity, discretion appears to be the better part of valour. For this reason we were in the Land Rover, windows tightly shut as instructed by Jess.

'There looks like there will be a good honey harvest,' I said to John, but apparently, according to him, that is not going to be the case. Not yet anyway. The hives are still building up their working force after winter has taken its toll of worker bees, depletion of honey stocks, etc. Therefore there are not yet the number of bees in each hive to cope with the profusion of flowers in bloom. No wonder the bees looked so frenzied. So few of them and so much to do.

24th

The bees will be delighted when a field John has finished drilling today with wild grass and wild flower mixtures for a neighbour, comes to maturity. The land is going into a higher-entry-level environmental scheme and the varieties will encourage insects and beetles. John is amazed at the cost of the seed. Two tiny one-kilo packets at over a hundred pounds each. The wild flower mixture will grow buttercups, daisies, cornflowers, poppies and a host of flowers that John has been tempted to eradicate from our grass fields for the past twenty-five years. But there is an ulterior motive. The grasses and flowers will attract insects and beetles, which will attract and encourage all sorts of birds. Some of them game. Conservation and field sports living alongside each other.

One of our fields has had a game cover over winter. It provided a good feeding resource for birds and an ideal nesting site for lapwings. Throughout land work nearby, John took great care not to disturb the birds and is thrilled that they were all sat tight, surrounded by little banks of earth, built up to protect them from the wind. Lapwings, or green plovers, peewits, pewits, pie-wipes, pee-wees, chewits, lappys, tuefits, toppyups, peasiewhips, teeacks, teeicks, ticks nickets, tieve's nackets, thievnigs, thievnicks, peasiewhips or teewhuppos as they are also called, sit very close on their nests. A neighbour remarked that even when he lifted the eggs out of the way of the tractor, prior to replacement after his implements passed over the nesting site, the birds remained close by. One became so tame, he said, that she rarely strayed more than a few yards from her nest, whilst others watched from a distance as the eggs were carried from a nest in the path of the plough to a safe spot in a newly turned furrow, before being carried back again to the original nest site.

25th

Major excitement in the farmhouse. Our blue tit has apparently left his nest box. John's birthday present from Jo this year was a nest box with a camera inside. For two nights Mr Blue Tit has been absent. Where has he gone?

I understand that blue tits build several nests for their mates (or prospective mate when one chooses him) and that he takes her round them like a pushy estate agent. This nest box was originally investigated by a sparrow, but he abandoned any attempt to live there when the blue tit took over. The camera is fantastic. It is compulsive viewing, especially the nights that the blue tit sleeps over. He is certainly not a peaceful sleeper. Every few minutes he has a whizz round in the nest, reorganises the feathers, pulls a bit of straw over himself, tucks his head under his wing, preens a few feathers. We await developments.

26th

My friend Sue cherishes and spoils her two rescue cats. The ones with the expensive vet's bills. But Bill, Sue's husband, remains as unenamoured of the cats as ever. He accepts they have a place and purpose, but considers that place and purpose is definitely not in the bedroom. But, in order to keep Sue in there with him, a compromise was needed. As the new cat was still a little unsettled, it was to be allowed to come in with them for one night. 'As long as she sleeps in her basket,' Bill said. 'She is not coming on the bed under any circumstances.'

Unfortunately cats don't understand rules. After fending off the cat nibbling their ears and purring her gratitude for being allowed to share her slumbers with them, then dragging her out for the umpteenth time from underneath the covers, they all eventually drifted off to sleep.

To be woken in the early hours by World War III starting up in their bedroom and the cat spitting and hissing as she pounced around and under their bed.

'That's it. Out she goes,' demanded Bill. 'I've had enough. The cat's useless. I need my sleep.' Several hours later they stumbled out of bed to step onto the remains of not just one mouse, but two. Now that definitely is a Top Cat.

27th

It's not often John will acknowledge a management mismanagement, but occasionally, just occasionally, it goes so public he has to.

In this case John was cleaning out the heifers' yard. So that he could muck their yard out safely, the heifers were let out into the big foldyard for a gallop round. The main road gate into the farmyard was open, so that John could go back and forth with the tractor, but he was sure that the gates out of the foldyard were shut. Certain.

Then through a gap in the weather boards at the end of the yard, he glimpsed the heifers gallivanting off down the road. They had escaped. The gate was not shut. Reversing at full tilt out of the yard, he nearly wiped out a passer-by who had come to tell him about the escapees. John went one way in the Land Rover to try and head the ladies off, and the passer-by agreed to block off the other. Fortunately the heifers did not go far. Fresh wayside grass was too tempting and other motorists very sensibly decided to stop and watch the goings-on rather than try to drive past the heifers and upset them. Thank you, the public.

28th

'I'm off to check some fencing out,' John said this morning. 'The cows are putting pressure on that fence bordering the cottage field. They'll soon have it down if I don't get something done.' The problem is that a short dry spell has restricted grass growth and although it seems no time since the cows were turned out, it is getting perilously close to being eaten up in some of their fields. We can move them into a field with the sheep, but John is keen for the ewes to have a good bite as they are all feeding lambs. As are the cows for that matter, with their calves.

It is easy enough to take the cows supplementary feed, but the cows have spotted a good growth of corn in a bordering field. And they are not averse to reaching and stretching over the fence to snack on nice juicy wheat or barley. Round one field John has even resorted to spraying off a border of the field so there is nothing to tempt them. But despite that precaution, the combined weight of all those hefty ladies is proving too much for some of the fencing. So John will be hammering some new posts in today.

29th

It was a clever move to leave the sunroof on the car open whilst we had lunch. We watched the rain bucket down and I never gave it a thought until I got in the car to go and do some shopping. Soggy botty syndrome. But the rain is much appreciated. What a lovely fresh smell permeates the air and everything looks so green. It will do the pastures no end of good.

30th

The cows continue to surprise us with a late calf or two down the fields. It is the perfect situation for them to calve in. So much more stress free, calving out in a field rather than in the crowded foldyard. It's not so bad when the cows first go in in the autumn, but by the time the cows and their calves are due to leave the foldyard in the spring, it seems claustrophobic in there. The cows probably consider it cosy.

We have finished lambing as well. A triumph of twins at the end. All doing well. The pet lambs, though, are pests. Three of them, twins whose mum had died, and a triplet pushed out by its more aggressive siblings, bowl you over if you have to venture out into their paddock. Unfortunately I have to go through it to get to the hen house. Added to this, they have managed to ruin the gate into the hen run by pushing to get in when I go to pick up eggs. John has put a lamb creep in the

'Bottled not draught for me!'

paddock so they can feed ad lib from protein pellets, but the lambs would still rather have a bottle. Now that we have cut them down to just one bottle a day, they are very peeved pet pests.

31st

I've just been mugged by two very angry swallows. I had shut the door of the old milking parlour whilst I sorted out some of the junk we store in there. Completely forgetting that a pair of swallows have claimed one of the beams as the site of their nest. As I reopened the door they practically flew straight into my face. Chattering with rage, they circled the parlour and drove me out. I have been warned.

Other swallows are nesting in the meal shed and a pair that may fancy an itinerant lifestyle in the cattle trailer are flying in and out of the gap above the back trailer door. The swallows have struggled with the dry weather. There just isn't the mud about for nest building. We were down at our pond last night fly fishing with friends and commented on the number of swallows swooping over the water and at the edge where there is some wet clay.

But hurray. The guinea fowl have started nesting again. After the slaughter of alpha female guinea fowl on her nest by probably the same fox that killed the bantams, the rest of the girls refused to lay in the same place. I have been going cross-eyed trying to find out their new preferred nest. Success. In the midst of a nettle patch on the roadside. Very vulnerable to all the dogs being walked round the village. They'll have to be told to find somewhere better to lay – and soon. I need those eggs. They make the best Yorkshire puddings ever.

June

1st

We have been following weather forecasts more diligently than usual. As no rain is forecast for five days, John cut three grass fields ready for the silage contractors. Then it poured down tonight.

You just have to be phlegmatic, cut your losses and go with the flow when all your plans are dashed by the weather. So everything is now ready for silaging, except the weather. And one other important factor. Yesterday the mower broke. It appears the universal joint on the power take-off shaft (PTO) of the mower has had a funny turn and we are faced with the decision whether once more to repair the mower, buy a replacement or bring in a contractor to cut the rest of the grass. There is a sale later this week and several mowers are listed, but as John says, 'When you want to get rid of a piece of broken machinery, where do you send it but the sale?' so he is not convinced that he will find a good replacement there. 'If there is a good piece of tackle, everyone is after mowers at this time of year and the price will go sky high,' so the odds are in favour of a repair, at the moment. He has washed the silage yard and sealed it with Visqueen, a huge roll of black plastic. It is important not to have any seepage from the silage liquor other than into our dirty water system. From there it can be pumped out into the fields and spread far away from any watercourses. There are heavy fines for pollution. Having once had a milking herd, we are actually well set up for getting rid of any dirty water. A huge tank lies underground where all the washings from the milking parlour used to go. It was set up on the insistence of a visiting official, at vast expense, and as we went out of milk shortly after installing it, for most of the year is rarely full. But not at silage time. The liquor from the grass resembles a foaming beer and is viewed as very palatable by the cows. Their annual booze-up. Another factor in the equation is actually getting hold of the contractor. He has not yet rung us to say when they are coming, so the farm is both wet and unnaturally calm. The sheep and cattle are quietly grazing the fields. Spooky. There must be some natural disaster in the form of a strangled lamb or drowned calf somewhere.

2nd

At a standstill today until things dry out, so John is messing about with his pheasants. Geoff, my brother-in-law, is considering bringing his peahen to the farm to tempt a single peacock that is visiting our pheasants on a regular basis. The peacock has settled in the village and scavenges from our hens for its meals and has also been made a pet of by other families. It could be a risky business. We have never been successful in rearing peacocks. I was going to say pea chicks, but none of them ever got to that stage even. This peahen is definitely going broody, but she is only young and not an experienced egg sitter. Over coffee Geoff told the story of a very determined bantie, who had been sitting her own nest of eggs when for some reason they failed to hatch or the nest was disturbed and she was left with no chicks and an ardent desire to keep sitting. Meanwhile Geoff's peahen had also gone broody and laid a nest of eggs. Unfortunately with no peacocks at his farm, the eggs were infertile, so not willing to waste a perfectly good incubator, Geoff set a clutch of goose eggs under the peahen. She took to them without a fuss, but the bantie had noticed that the peahen was not yet the tightest of sitters, had a plum nesting site and wandered off a little too much for safety. She laid her plans. But no more eggs. The bantie snuggled under the peahen and presented herself as the sitter closest to the eggs. An extra layer of insulation, so to speak. The peahen tried to oust the interloper but was gradually twittered, pecked, nudged and wiggled off the nest by the indomitable bantie. She hatched off the goose eggs successfully and is now the proud mother of a clutch of goslings whilst the peahen has nothing.

3rd

'I've just seen something I've never seen before,' John said this morning. My mind boggled. My latest shopping trip rumbled. That 'I've had it for simply ages' exposed for the tawdry fib it is. But no. John is fortunately not tuned into shopping so is easily hoodwinked by the simple ruse of letting new clothes lie around in a heap for a day or two before I wear them. Then when the time comes to actually to put the stuff on, he – so the theory goes – has subliminally accepted their presence in my wardrobe. That's what I think, anyway. He probably knows all the time and just goes along with the game. But what he had really not seen before was a red kite flying over the tractor. Not a kite kite. Not a terror kite to scare off pigeons. But a bird kite. With forked tail, the lot. John is very excited. Not too thrilled about what it might mean to the game bird population, but willing to admire the bird in its own right and applaud the fact that it is being reintroduced back in the countryside. The bird may have been attracted by the exposed field, rapidly clearing of grass for the silage contractors. As, three cheers, the gang arrived today, it's just go, go, go. Three fields to clear and a huge mound to fill the silage pit. Miraculously the rain held off for most of the day and there was only one brief stoppage whilst a storm blew over. The grass is covered up tonight and tomorrow will be spent compacting the mound and sealing it. John was fascinated by the kite's flight. It circled the tractor for a long time. 'It must have been over a field that was being cleared before,' he said. 'Often when you are cutting you might catch a leveret in the mower and the kites feed mainly on carrion.' Although kites have been persecuted, they do not offer a threat as such to game birds, but they do unsettle and frighten them, as they are very similar, from a partridge or pheasant's point of view – so a game bird told me – to a buzzard. But bigger. When game birds are just hatched, they are tiny, and if the chicks scatter because of a supposed predator, they are facing one more risk to their survival.

4th

Silage has been completed in the nick of time. Today it poured but we did not care. The silage was in. Feed for the herd next winter. What a relief, as once under cover, the silage was safe. There is more grass to cut, but that will be for small bales of hay. Although we do not have Rupert any more, our old horse and hay connoisseur, it is still useful to have some small bales for calves and sheep. This evening we could admire a full silage pit. Very satisfying to see next winter's provender for the herd all gathered up and in place. When added to the ninety big bales of hay that John made at the end of last week, things are starting to stack up very nicely. John has opted for big bales as he wants less work handling fewer small bales this winter. His knee has been giving him pain again and a visit to a specialist has confirmed that it is arthritis in his knee and not another torn cartilage. When he was a lad he was always on his knees setting traps and ferreting for rabbits and his dad used to say that he'd get arthritis in his knees as his trousers were always soaked at the knee . . . and he was right. 'But you never listen at that age.' His father had a lot of country sayings in his repertoire. 'You should take a coat when it's fine and do as you like when it's raining,' being his favourite and most repeated. Would have been a good day to heed him. Sunshine and rain in equal measures. Whilst we have come through relatively unscathed, a neighbour has just phoned who lives eight miles away and had an inch of rain. Not surprisingly, their silage is rained off.

5th

John has started the sheep clip this year with the tups. He will do the rest of the flock later. After being shorn, the tups had to spend the night in the close confinement of the livestock trailer. If John had turned them out into a field straight after clipping, they were very likely to have killed each other. This is because they fail to recognise each other as bosom buddies, but only see a love rival. We know this from painful experience when two tups ran headlong into each other many years ago after clipping, and one was killed outright. More brawn than brain. Despite living together for over two years, grazing cheek to cheek and rubbing noses, once the tups were released into the paddock after being shorn, they were immediately head to head in combat. Fortunately, bruised egos as well as bloody heads soon sorts the business out, although they kept on taking a tilt at each other into late evening. With markedly less enthusiasm as the hours wore on.

6th

Our television viewing is now restricted to only one channel. Mind you, that is only when I have set channel viewing for John. He has not yet mastered the art of remote control technology. Or claims not to have. Funny that. A man who can recalibrate drills, drive complicated farm machinery, etc., does not know which button to press to get the channel he wants. 'Could you put me that DVD on about fishing?' a plaintive voice calls out just as I am settled to a read of the paper or a book. Or 'Can you find me that programme on birdwatching?' Both of which tasks he is just as capable as me of carrying out. But won't. The system should currently, however, be fool proof. This is because for John's birthday, Jo, our daughter, bought him another, improved bird box, this time with a colour camera inside. By dint of a hole being drilled through the wall behind the TV, and a lead going from the box to said TV, we are wired to watch the intimate goings on of family life, bird style. John only has to switch on with the remote control and he has an intimate window into avian home construction. A slight hiccup occurred when my son-in-law changed from AV to TV for a football match, but we are now back on track for voyeurism on a small scale. It has been exciting. The day after we put the new box up I switched on the TV expecting to see only the bare floor of the bird box. Nothing could have discovered it that quickly, I thought. I was wrong. Within twenty-four hours the nest box was already filling with straw and feathers. Something had been very hard at work. Then everything stopped. No action for a day. Disaster. Had our nest been abandoned? No. A sighting of a sparrow investigating the nest and bringing a beak full of straw cheered us up. She tweaked a piece of straw here, moved another piece there, and then cleared off. Not seen again. Now, however, there is a cloud of feathers lining the nest and we can't see a thing.

7th

Went back into the house to flop onto the settee and have a restorative cup of tea. John followed me in. He had sorted out some cattle for market and carried with him the fragrant aroma of the foldyard. Cuddling up close, he whispered into my ear, 'Do you fancy coming to look at my mole traps?' Irresistible or what?

The mole traps have been set in one of the fields that have recently been cut for hay. This particular piece of land is not drained and in winter it's virtually waterlogged. As a result, the moles all take off to a neighbour's field, which is set on higher land and drier over the winter months. Our neighbour is not such an enthusiastic mole trapper as John, but there again he does not use his land for silage or hay and only grazes it. The loose earth in a mole hill can make a mess of a hay bale and John spends quite a bit of time trying to discourage the moles from using the field. Because of the damp soil, it is beloved by worms, and thus a huge draw for mole gourmands who like nothing better than a large, juicy nematode.

8th

Added to the silage, the hay is now also all in. Can't believe it. Cut, dried and baled in just a few days. John has a saying that 'Good hay takes no time to make, it's bad hay that takes for ever.' It's very true. If you are constantly trying to dry out hay that has been rained on, and then perhaps over a fortnight watch it gradually blacken out in the fields, that is two very bad weeks, with nothing to show at the end of it. We did have a little help in the form of a big baler. That saved a lot of aggravation, as if there is anything on the farm guaranteed to upset John, it's the baler. Anything and everything goes wrong. So we brought in the latest piece of tackle, and the contractor brought along his wife and toddler son to keep him company. Whilst the contractor was having a drink and five minutes' break, he let his little boy sit and play in the cab. No chance of turning on the ignition, he had the key, but the little lad soon had lights flashing, horn blaring, indicators winking. Five minutes later the contractor set off again to bale. The baler is normally preset to stop baling and then wrap and cut at about 4ft. This particular bale did not seem ready to come out at all. Eventually a 7ft bale was produced and need to be pushed out of the baler by John and the contractor together. It's massive. Won't fit in the ring feeder and is the result of some very nifty finger work on the control panel by an eighteen-month-old farm worker.

9th

Despite an adamant approach to the subject of clipping the flock a couple of months ago – 'Never again. That's it. I'm going to get someone in to do them who is younger and fitter' – once more the clippers have been dusted off. I've raked out the ibuprofen gel to massage into sore knees and back once the job has been done and the woolsacks are filling up. John has decided he will clip the sheep for one more year. But now he is taking a steadier pace to the job than in previous years. Once upon a time he and Geoff would have a mad couple of days and get all the flock done at the same time. Now John takes a few sheep out here, a few more the next day, and this morning he is doing another twenty-four. Because of this staggered approach, the sheep are getting warier and warier about being driven into the collecting area. John has made this inland in order not to drive them through the fields that the cows are in to reach the usual collecting corral. He has fitted up a wide corridor between two fields with extra-high gates and used this area instead. It works well. Or rather worked well. The sheep now know that being driven out of the field into this race means either being dosed, dagged out, clipped or jabbed. None of which they appreciate. The first case this year, however, of a lamb with maggots means that this is an exercise they are going to have to learn to put up with, as an itchy rear end is something they won't appreciate. Fortunately the maggots had not started to eat into the lamb and John could just cut off the muck around the lamb's tail.

10th

John is soaking his aches and pains away in a hot bath. He has finished clipping the sheep again for another year, and, as usual, he is considering

There's only going to be one winner in all this . . . and it's not the sheep.

whether it is a task he wants to ever do again. According to *Farming Today*, our wake-up call each morning at a quarter to six, sheep shearers are in short supply. 'No wonder,' said John. 'It is backbreaking work. Unless you are regularly clipping like the travelling gangs from the Antipodes, the money is just not in the job.' When John was a younger man, he was in a clipping gang. They travelled all over, four of them, and had a regular round of sheep farms. If things were set up right with the sheep all in under cover and dry, with a team to feed the sheep to the shearer and then take the fleece and sheep away after the clip, he could get through up to thirty sheep an hour. Now he is down to ten or twelve. And unless I am involved, he is catching the sheep himself and rolling up the fleece and stuffing it into the woolsack on his tod as well. Mind you, his hands are lovely and soft after clipping. All that lanolin. 'I'm going to have to send my combs and cutters away to be reground before I do any more clipping,' John said. This is not for a new haircut for himself, or me, but to have them ready for those friends who will want their sheep clipping. Set up in the meal shed is a grinder with papers to keep the combs and cutters honed ready for clipping. But because of the wet weather we have had again, the lambs have got into the habit of climbing up onto the backs of the ewes to keep dry and warm. As a result, the ewes' wool has become clogged with clay, and it is the grit and dirt in the clay that has been blunting the cutters. 'Won't the people who collect the wool reject it if it's dirty?' I asked. I read all the dire directives we receive from them, warning about rejection if straw or permanent spray markings are on or in the fleeces. 'No, the clay will wash out,' John said 'They are not bothered about that, it is when matter is entwined into the wool and it won't wash out that they do not want the fleeces.' This has put paid to the charming habit of some sheep farmers of twisting coloured strands of wool into the fleeces of sheep up for sale at market. I used to think they looked very decorative with a plait of wool just behind their ear. The sheep, not the farmers. The wool collection company send us large hessian sacks to stuff the fleeces into. Literally. When Geoff worked alongside John, he used to fold and tuck the fleeces up into tight little bundles that dropped neatly and individually into the sacks. It was quite wonderful to see him toss the fleece up into the air before it settled onto the ground like a huge airy duvet, prior to his wool origami trick. Changes in wool preparation, and the huge drop in the price of wool, have meant that unwrapping the fleeces in the collection sheds has become too labour intensive. Now they just have to be ready to tip out ready for washing.

The most traditional moment in the job, however, is sewing the sacks together. For that John uses a huge silver needle that belonged to his father. How I manage not to lose it year after year is my most wonderful achievement. It has a secret place in my mum's writing desk. Not so secret that if I was not around John could not find it, but secret enough for it not to be used for anything else other than sewing sacks up.

11th

It looks as though the blue tit that had taken up residence in our nest box with a camera, has been killed by a predator. After laying several perfect little eggs, she failed to return one day and we can only presume she has been taken by a sparrowhawk which we have seen in the vicinity. Nature is cruel. John has taken the eggs out of the nest and we hope another bird will take up residence. I am not sure whether we should clean our nest box out to persuade another bird to nest, or leave it with the old nesting materials in. We are going to try leaving it 'fully furnished' at first, and see how we go from there. In the big shed a bantam has hatched out sixteen of her own eggs. A cunning little bird, she had hidden her nest in the haystack, but was revealed when a neighbour wanted to buy all our remaining small bales from last year to feed her horses. Mrs Bantie is there with her wings outstretched to cover all sixteen chicks, clucking away and very pleased with herself.

12th

Major excitement with a calving for a cow we thought was barren and off to market. She had wandered off away from the rest of the herd, was bagged up (udder full of milk) and shuffling around in a fidgety sort of way. All technical stuff, you note. Eventually we had to get the vet in, as after we had persuaded the cow into the cattle crush to find out what was happening, John found that the calf had presented with one leg, and the head, twisted behind. The outcome was good, although the calf had to be twisted round ninety degrees in the womb to pull the bent leg forward so that it presented correctly for delivery. Now we can't get near the pair of them to tag the calf.

13th

Nearly wrecked my marriage by heavy-handed tactics to create a fitting sauce to accompany a Christmas pudding left from last year's seasonal festivities, but still within its use-by date (just). I had rum, brandy and whisky to go at. So I did. Gave it a splash of everything. Tasted very good, I may add. But just to add that final oomph, I felt it needed one more splash of something special. And there before my eyes was a drop or two of malt whisky, Old Pulteney I think it was called, in the bottom of a bottle. Obviously finished as a drink. Not enough to warrant much of a mouthful. Or so I thought. 'This sauce is good,' John said as the final drops coated the last morsels of pudding. 'What did you put in it?' 'Oh, this and that,' I replied, 'Finishing bottles off, you know.' John's face turned grey. 'My nectar,' he cried, 'my last drop of nectar.' Not a recipe I can ever repeat, it seems.

14th

John is back tonight after participating in a living history project. Well, that's a posh way of saying it. What he has been doing is consulting (again hyperbole) with a friend as to the best way to drill maize, for game cover, using a disc coulter Fergie drill on a T20 grey Fergie tractor, circa 1940s/50s.

First. Plough with a two-furrow, conventional Fergie plough. The tractor was a twenty-first-birthday present for Adam, our friend's son. It was originally in the nature of a restoration project, but as the tractor is in good mechanical order and the restoration largely cosmetic, the Fergie is good to go. John was delighted to hear that Mick, Adam's dad, was pleased with his son's ploughing. Rare praise indeed.

Second. Power harrow your land for a good seed bed. Unfortunately not with the Fergie, as power harrows were not around circa 1940s/50s.

Third. Ring your mate John to ask if he ever remembered using a Fergie drill. Although certainly not on a tractor in the '40s and '50s, John can recall using one on the farm after he left school. So a trip out for the day was arranged and John set off, brain in gear, to help set up the drill.

Fourth. Calibrate to drill the maize in approximately twenty-inch rows. Not centimetres, you note. Inches. This was pre-metric drilling. Maize seed is much bigger than wheat, barley and especially rape, so the slides on the drill had to be opened up to take the size of seed.

Fifth. Tip the seed out of the bag, and trundle off to drill. The function of the crop is to be game cover. Mick is improving his shoot with the hope of holding more birds. Pheasants love to pick the seed out of the corn cobs, and most game birds feel safe in a field of maize as it offers them cover from overhead predators. The first strip to be drilled was on a hillside. So they started at the top of the hill and drilled down. 'Adam was making a super job of it,' John said. 'The seed bed was damp, so there was plenty of moisture for the corn and he was burying the seed well. When he got down to the bottom of the hill and turned round to go back up, the Fergie struggled. The tyres were spinning and it was hard for the tractor to pull the corn drill back up the seed bed.'

Sixth. Take a decision to drill downhill only and get back up the hill, running on the grass either side of the strip, without drilling. That worked.

Seventh. Roll the crop in; but by then John needed to be home to feed round the cattle and check the sheep. He spoke to Mick that night and he and Adam were celebrating a job well done. Perhaps all this new space-age tackle, with satellite technology and computer precision, isn't so necessary after all.

15th

Our ducklings have suddenly found their bearings in relation to grass paddock, big shed and the rolled barley heap. Since we let them out of their run about a week ago, they have stayed close to their shed and water trough during the day. Then they found the little pond in the paddock. Now, however, they want to explore wider horizons. Ones with unlimited access to rolled barley. If I've shooed them back into their field once today, I've shooed them back twenty times. They are still small enough to squeeze through the sheep netting of the fence. All that rolled barley will soon put a stop to that. Only a few fields on the farm remain undrained, and this is being addressed piece by piece as we can afford it. At one time there were government grants for drainage, but no longer, and this year we have just drained another few acres. And our bank balance. Currently the field is pasture for stock and John will not put it under the plough for at least another year as we still need the grass. But as soon as the rotation for planting crops allows him to do so, he will drill for winter wheat. Last year forty acres that had been planted with arable crops for at least ten years went back to grass for silage and hay, and in time the same field will go back to arable in much more fertile condition. A grass field that was ploughed up from pasture for wheat last year is producing a storming crop because the soil is in such good heart. Crop rotation works for us and is supported by Geoff's bees. He has taken a couple more hives of bees down to our bean field. 'Just be careful round them for a few days until they settle,' he advised. 'They might be a bit agitated for a day or two.' I am warned.

16th

I am being entertained on a daily basis by a tiny flycatcher who is using a fence post as a base for foraging for food for his mate who is nesting in a wasp trap I have hung near our back door. The traps are a cunning construction. You slice off the top third of a pop bottle, which has the spout. Then invert this into the remaining two thirds of the bottle after pouring an inch of two of syrupy liquid from jam or a sugar solution into the bottom of the bottle. Next pierce a couple of holes through the two sections of the bottle both to keep them together and to allow a length of string through, with which to hang from a tree/hook/branch. The wasps and flies (equally good for flies) climb down through the spout and cannot escape. But Mrs Flycatcher has thought of an alternative use. The cup formed by the inverted top provides the ideal shape for a nest base. She is sat on her eggs in a perfectly formed cupcake of a nest. If only she had left a little entry into the trap, she could have had flies lining themselves up as ready meals.

17th

'Millie. Millie. Where are you, Millie?' This is by now the routine call from the farmhouse to ascertain where our little Jack Russell has disappeared off to. Last night, after a frantic half hour, I finally located her where I least expected to find her. In her bed.

Plus one dead chick. We have encouraged Millie to kill rats as part of her job on the farm, and she possesses a collection of toy rats to hone her skills on. These stuffed rodents litter the house in various stages of disembowelment. But now Millie is targeting my little bantie chicks, who after being hatched out in the incubator, lovingly reared under heat lamps and cosseted in their own run in the big shed, have now been let out to explore the big wide world. And promptly been snaffled up by a wayward Jack Russell. Millie appreciates she may have done wrong, but when I waved the stiffened chick corpse at her and told her off in the grimmest tones, she merely wagged her tail at me.

Millie, unlike many Jack Russells, has a magnificent tail. Her breeder, a friend, would not dock her, and now it would be unthinkable to imagine her without her curly, constantly waving appendage. If I find it hard to tell her off, John finds it even harder. Millie is his regular companion in the Land Rover and races over to the driver's door whenever she hears the engine turn over. I fear for her safety. The other dogs leap into the back of the vehicle, but Millie is having none of that. It's the front seat or nothing. She leaps up and down at the door like a demented jack-in-the-box until John opens the door and she clambers/climbs/jumps into the Land Rover. Once in, she settles herself down until they are off road, when she is straight onto his lap with her face and front paws balanced out of the window. 'If we see a young leveret or baby rabbit in the field, she just launches herself out of the window,' John said. 'But she hasn't managed to catch one yet. The chickens must be too easy a prey.'

18th

Whilst their own house is being extensively renovated, friends have taken on the lease of another dwelling in the next village. Several planters in front of the house drooped with the remains of spring daffodils. Time to freshen up the flowers, my friend Angie thought, so after a visit to a local garden centre, she filled the planters with summer annuals. Eight pairs of crafty avian eyes watched with interest from the roof of an adjoining property, and spotted that lurking amidst the foliage of the flowers were potentially tasty, nutritious and highly edible and desirable plants. 'I heard Stig going mad,' Angie said. Stig (a Jack Russell) was throwing himself against the conservatory window, trying to get out. The watchers were eight peacocks, now in the process of pulling all the plants to bits. 'It was a nightmare!' Angie cried.

Peacocks can be dreadfully destructive. I once had dreams of a muster of stately peacocks to strut around the farmyard, but regular raids by a neighbour's peacock and peahen dimmed my enthusiasm. They are voracious. Any young, tender plants in the veg patch were demolished (that was when I had time to have veg in the veg plot, now it is just weeds), and all my flower troughs were seen as handy takeaway sites for hungry peacocks. Peacocks are the jump jets of the bird world. They can be aloft in seconds. Amazing for such big birds. This pair would head straight for the barn roof and then trumpet (they sound just like elephants) their defiance. Once I chased them onto a haystack and threw a heavy feeding bowl to frighten the pair out of the barn. All I succeeded in doing was missing the peacock by miles. The bowl disappeared over the edge of the haystack, immediately followed by a dull clang and surprised quack. A terminal quack. The bowl had dropped onto a duck and killed it. I hated the peacocks even more.

19th

Tomorrow morning two of our oldest cows are off to market. One is the cow who gave birth to the dead calf a fortnight ago. She has not accepted any of the suckler calves in the field, so John says it is not viable to keep her any longer as she may throw another dead calf next year. The other cow is the mother of the twin calves who were born in the spring. One of them died – the healthy, strongest calf – but we still have our special needs calf, the other twin called Freddy in the yard, in his own little pen. In the last three or four months he has steadfastly refused to be weaned off his milk and onto a calf mixture. John has persisted with him almost out of curiosity to see just how long Freddy would be prepared to hold off solids and stick with his milk diet. Then last week he started to nibble and graze in his bucket of calf mix. Not exactly keen, but definitely progress. And I think he has started to put on weight and grow. Without the other calves in the yard it is difficult to make an accurate judgment of his relative size to other calves born at the same time, but he certainly looked a scrawny little chap. Now he even seems a little chunky. Not a lot. But a bit. Added to this is the fact that he is starting to take more notice of his surroundings. He will even give a mini bellow when you walk past his pen, just to gently remind you he is there. When he starts to rattle his bucket, we will know he has made it.

20th

'Look, a cuckoo,' John said, pointing skywards as we drove to market. We were going at a fairly steady pace as we had the two cows in the trailer behind and no intention of throwing them around, but I still only caught a glimpse of the surprisingly large bird flying ahead. There has been a lot on the news about the decrease in cuckoo numbers this year, allied to decreases in the number of small birds whose nests they take over. It was the first cuckoo we had seen. Much much later than normal. Swallows too are always eagerly anticipated. Our swallow visitors have adapted to changes in the farm buildings by taking over one or two of the nest boxes that we have put up for other birds. They still love the old barns, however, and also what was the milking parlour. As a result we have doors and windows left open all around the farmyard and sheds, otherwise the swallows would not be able to access their nests. There is even a blackbird in the meal shed. She is nesting virtually at eye level and keeps absolutely immobile as you walk through, daring passers-by to acknowledge her presence. If a visitor does happen to look at her on the nest, she fixes them with an unblinking stare, still retaining the myth of invisibility and invincibility.

'Hope it's up to the wife's expectations!'

21st

To a machinery sale today. We farm heavy land and need to use a mole plough to create a continuous channel at fifteen inches' depth that enables the land to drain more efficiently. Our fields are criss crossed by drainage systems, but to get the water away and into the drains, it does need a little help. So to support the drainage systems John pulls a single-leg mole plough behind his four-wheel-drive tractor, but over the years, this mole plough has had a lot of hard work. And shows it. Three mole ploughs were up for sale at market and John bought the one fit for the heaviest duty. A Ransom single leg. He had flirted with the sale of the first two, but knew that he had to go all out for this one if he was to bring a new plough home. He was top bidder. John had gone to the sale yesterday in his Land Rover, so this morning he trundled off to market with the tractor to bring his latest purchase home. Probably brought a few lanes of morning rush-hour traffic to a halt in the process.

No sooner were we back on the farm than he was off down the fields to try his new toy out. The field he went to has been the subject of much kitchen table discussion. John has seen a pair of oystercatchers in the vicinity, suspected they had a nest, but had not been able to spot where it was until recently. Over winter the little birds have been able to pick over any spilt grain in the stubbles. Pheasants and partridges have hidden in it during the shooting season, and the foxes used it for cover when the hunt came for their chase round and gallop. The plan is to mole plough the field now, spread muck on it and prepare it for drilling this autumn for winter wheat. The stubble field has also encouraged ground-nesting birds. But until Mrs Oystercatcher has finished nesting, he intends to ignore that section of the field. She can remain safe and sitting snug on her beautifully camouflaged nest until her chicks hatch out.

22nd

Torrential rain. The yards where the bulls are kept have flooded, as the gutters were unable to cope with the sheer volume of water coming down. What is really distressing John, though, is the fact that a lot of the corn has all been knocked down by the rain. 'We had one of the best look-ons for years,' he said. 'I was expecting a really good harvest, but I don't know how it is going to turn out now.' Once the corn goes down, and stays down, it will not ripen properly. It may even drop out of the ears and, as the ground is so wet, germinate and start to grow through the fallen crop. Then when the time comes to harvest what corn there is, the combines will struggle to get under the crop. Plus, with the ground so wet, even though it is still some time off, any weight of machinery is going to find it difficult to travel without risk of getting bogged down.

With such wet conditions, the sheep, especially, can soon develop all kinds of manky (technical term) hooves, so John is expecting to have to keep an even more vigilant eye on the sheep and cows' feet than he does normally.

23rd

A wild goose has taken up residency in the paddock. It appears to be pining for the company of our goslings, although they must be at least a year younger than he is. The goslings and the Aylesbury ducklings are free to roam the paddock, some of the ducklings under the eye of the anxious banties that hatched them out, and perhaps it is the lack of any parental chaperone that attracts the wild gander. Planning a wild night out with a young gosling. Tut tut.

The ducklings have proved themselves to be amazing pond engineers. They have redesigned and excavated any puddles and wet spots in their paddock. Even though they have a pond available to them, any accessible wet spot inspires them into creating even bigger, deeper and thus wetter environments.

24th

Given how expensive a vet's call-out is, John's advice is frequently requested by friends and neighbours who have problems with their stock. Usually it is people who are hobby farming and have a few sheep to keep the orchard down (doesn't that sound grand). These friends have little interest in actually rearing animals for meat, and I think they are frightened that a vet might take drastic action, as well as costing them a fortune. Also, given the welter of legislation that we have to cope with in keeping stock, I expect, in fact know, that many of them pay scant regard to medication records, etc. And if the awful possibility of the animal dying actually transpires, whereas we have to follow prescribed disposal procedures now, I think most of them just dig a big hole for the dearly departed. John will always advise that a vet be called in if he considers it necessary to prevent suffering or if he even vaguely thought that anything was notifiable. What people normally want him to do is to sort out foot rot on their sheep, problems with maggots if a sheep is flyblown, help with delivery if a lamb needs an extra pull, but most often it is problems with feeding. A case in point. 'I've got a lazy calf and I can't get it to drink. It's a great big thing; it won't stand, but it is determined not to and if I hold it up under the cow, it still won't latch on. What can I do?' That was the latest answer phone message to our 'desperately seeking solutions' service. 'Have you tried milking the cow into a bucket and then getting the calf to suck on your fingers before plunging your hand into the bucket?' John asked. The theory being that the calf, rather than drown in the milk, will start to drink on its own. 'Sure have,' came the answer. 'It won't suck at all.' It had been twelve hours since the calf's birth and it should have been up for a drink by now. John took with him a tube feeder. This would get milk directly into the calf's stomach and so the calf would not miss out on the colostrum and have all the benefit of his mum's immunity. When we had a milking herd and were coming up to lambing, John often had a few pints of beastlings, the first milk after a cow has given birth, in the freezer. It used to be a wonderful pick-me-up for weak lambs. 'Keep the tube feeder,' John said. 'Keep stripping some milk off the heifer and put it into the tube feeder every three hours to sustain the calf.' Twenty-four hours later John was again rung for advice. The calf was thriving, but horizontally. Our neighbour was fed up milking the cow and then tubing it down the calf's throat. 'Stop feeding it for twenty-four hours,' John said. 'Make it hungry. You've no immediate worries, so it won't harm to starve it a little.'

That calf must have been listening in on its own line extension. It knew when enough was enough. With a lurch it stood up on its own. Another few lurches and it was under Mum. A bossy bang of its head on its mum's udder proclaimed the start of feeding time. Slurp, slurp, end of story.

25th

'What was that?' yelped my friend as she sat herself down in the front of my car and the sharp snap of a mouse trap twitched shut by her foot, narrowly missing her big toe. I had to explain. When giving my car one of its rare clean-outs, I had come across a neatly nibbled biscuit. Since I did not know whether it had been dined on before it got in the car, or inside it, and since I did not want the most obvious culprit, a mouse, to turn its attention to any of the car's wiring, brake cables or ignition system, I had placed two strategic traps in the car. One inadvertently close to her toe. My theory is that a mouse may have got in via Millie. She likes to jump in when I leave the back tail gate of the car up and survey the yard from a position of authority. Pip does the same from the back of the Land Rover. Millie also enjoys toying with the occasional mouse, I think she may have been closely related to a cat, and sometimes lets them go just for the thrill of catching them again. One must have got away. And still has. I have not caught my stowaway yet but regularly hear the traps snapping as I go over bumps or round corners. My friend Linda, having recovered from her near-amputation experience, settled, nervously, for the rest of the journey. She lives on the outskirts of a large market town and for the last few months has played hostess with the mostest to a family of fox cubs. Not only Linda, but several of her neighbours as well have been charmed by the comings and goings of a vixen and her litter. I am the first to admit that a fox cub is one of the most appealing of creatures. We have videos on the lives of foxes, and books and prints galore. We watch television programmes with interest and always feel sorry when we pass a fox road victim that has been flattened by a speeding car. 'How are your visitors?' I asked Linda, waiting for a lyrical recall of the joys of twitching noses, waft of bushy tails, pitter patter of tiny footpads and gleam of burnished coats. 'Not welcome any more,' she said. I was astounded. What had happened to turn Charlie (as Mr Fox is commonly referred to in our house) from champion to his sworn enemy? 'We love our garden,' my friend said. 'We have spent a lot of time and money in there to make it a special place. A real sensory garden. A few weeks ago my sister and her husband came to stay. The day had been beautiful and after our meal, we suggested we went out into the garden to enjoy the splendour of the evening and drink in the glorious scents of flowers.' They all sat down, relaxing with their coffee, prepared to share the floral aromas redolent of the height of summer. But instead her sister's nose took on a distinct twitch of disgust. 'What's that awful smell?' she asked. 'What have you planted? I've never smelt anything like it. It's disgusting.' It was too. Turned out to be not a voluptuous perfume but a vulpine one. The rank stink of foxes. Beautiful they may be. But a bed of roses they are not.

26th

Stacks of big bales only yards from the back door are not yet hermetically sealed and have a tendency to continuously shed straw, much of which blows into the house via the back porch, back door, back kitchen. It is never ending. Add to that muddy boots kicked off just inside the house, plus dogs paddling in and out, and you can see I need a road cleaner, or one of those trundling sweeper jobs you see in airports to keep the place clean. Away from the farmhouse, the continuing rain means a fresh approach to completing jobs such as worming the ewes and lambs and treating them against blowflies. When the weather is so variable, rain then sunshine, the warm, humid conditions are ideal for fly strike. The lush grass can inevitably result in very loose scouring around the ewes' and lambs' back ends; irresistible to a fly looking for somewhere to lay its eggs. The eggs initially develop into larvae with no mouth parts, but then metamorphose into voracious feeders creating open wounds on the sides of ewes and lambs that in themselves are vulnerable to strike. But we hope it never gets that far on this farm. John has a very systematic approach to animal welfare. All the lambs have now been treated with a pour-on that provides a long-lasting blowfly protection. Prevention is surely better than cure.

27th

'It's a lovely evening. It's been a long day. Come and have a drink outside,' was the request. How romantic. A glass of wine, a packet of crisps and an air rifle awaited me. We were after rats. There has been quite a plague of furry four-footed vermin. One of them, after an encounter with one of my mousetraps, is probably wandering around somewhere with fewer toes on his foot than he should have. I had heard a scuttly, draggy sound in the pantry and found a mouse caught by its back foot. 'You should have just knocked it on the head,' I was told later. But I am afraid I am a softy at heart. I swear the mouse looked straight into my eyes and pleaded for its life. The upshot being that I took the trap, plus mouse, down the lane, releasing the mouse to hobble away and enjoy another day. Less a couple of toes. Next day the trap caught a large slug. The moral being, if I invite you for a meal, think twice. You don't know what's been in that pantry.

But back to the rats. Whilst we had the ducks in the yard, John left several traps set to catch any rats tempted to feed on the duck pellets. With some success. However, as we then had Ollie, our grandson, to stay for a few days, and he loves the chance to poke around where he should not be, the rat traps were taken away. It does not take long for the rats to return. Several of our farm cats have been killed on the lane recently as drivers ignore the speed limit and whizz through. So the rats' natural predators have been reduced. At the same time, with the best will in the world, ad lib feed for bulls and heifers and ducks in the foldyard and sheds must provide a veritable feast for vermin. Hence my romantic invite. Some of the rats have made a home under a small shed where gardening equipment is kept. It is at the side of the big shed in the yard and handily placed smack outside our back door, where a table and bench are placed for cups of tea, farmyard chat, etc. During the course of the evening the rats have been seen to race from the old farm buildings, across the front of the big shed and pop under the gardening shed. It is whilst they are crossing such a large open space that they are vulnerable. Rather like one of those fairground games. Only it's not a duck you are aiming at. The venue is not without its merits. The big bales of hay are stacked just inside the big shed. It smells gorgeous, the balmy scent of summer. All is tranquil and I can marvel at the swoop of the bats who roost in the barn, chasing moths. The companionship of the dogs (who strangely are not interested in rats) adds to the aura of peace, as does the quiet clucking of my bantams as they usher their broods (which have appeared out of nowhere) back home to bed. And then comes the crack of the air rifle. Three rats down. Heaven knows how many to go.

28th

When off to take a walk down the fields with the dogs, I never go near the cows and calves. Cows might appear placid, and generally are, but take a dog in, especially if any of the herd has recently calved, and they are instantly in protection mode and will chase the intruder or intruders off. So if visitors want to take a look around the farm and express a special interest in the livestock, off we go on our very own farm safari in the Land Rover. I am often struck by how calm animals are when approached by a vehicle in film footage shot around genuinely wild animals. In wildlife programmes, the camera will pan back and reveal about five off-road vehicles, all full of tourists, gawping at a dozy pride of lions who seem blindly oblivious to their presence. Bet, however, if the tourists took one step out of the safety of the truck, it might present a different scenario. Game on. Lunch has arrived. It is similar to our cows and sheep. You can drive right up to them, slowly, not a mad charge, and more often than not they will stay where they are until you are virtually on top of them. In fact, when we took a drive round last night with a friend, on a glorious sunny evening, we imagined ourselves on the plains of Africa with our cows and sheep lazing in the last of the sun before dark fell. Even the bounce of the Land Rover as I hit yet another grip in the fields, added an authentic jolt to the drive. Our friend was very complimentary about the stock. 'Look at the gleam on the cows,' he exclaimed. It's true. They are in great condition. A diet of rich grass does wonders for their coats. And their bowels. Nearly all the herd lay quietly chewing their cud, calves nuzzled up close. Very peaceful. Apart from the bull. He had other ideas. As did a gang of adolescent bull calves. All of whom had their thoughts fixed on a cow who must just be coming into season. Talk about harassment. This poor cow was plodding about, trying to get rid not only of the attentions of a very determined Mr Limousin, but also of a gaggle of young bull calves, all stirred up by they knew not what, but whatever it was keeping them on the go.

29th

Geoff came in yesterday to take the cattle into market, as John was off on a day's jolly, invited to participate in a charity clay pigeon shoot. The shoot was on behalf of a services charity and very well attended. In days of yore John was a champion clay pigeon shot, and recognised names in the professional team, guns who he used to regularly compete against. Although doing fairly respectably in the shooting competition, John's team scored particularly well in an archery contest. One of the friends revealing hidden talents with bow and arrows. Life is full of surprises.

30th

Our biggest group of guinea fowl are parents. I am just so pleased. After weeks of wondering if they had any clue as to whether they knew what a sex life consisted of, or even if they knew what sex they were, we have keets. Not sat by the guinea fowl, of course. So far, despite laying loads of eggs, they have shown no inclination to sit any of them, and they have been 'surrogated' by an incubator and a broody bantam. And not a moment too soon. Mr Fox has nabbed two of the guinea fowl over the last couple of nights, and of those left, we still do not know which sex is which. They all do the same calls, where different calls are supposed to differentiate between hen and cock, and they all seem to have wattles. Ditto.

A month or two ago we clipped their wings so that they would be forced to go into the hen house at night, but, over the course of weeks, their flight feathers have grown again. Now many of the guinea fowl perch on the top of the hen run, but somehow they were either caught during the day by Mr Fox, or charmed off their perches by the same wily creature. The fox has done nothing to conceal his tracks, littering the paddock with feathers after his guinea fowl dinner. We have a problem now to catch any of the guinea fowl, as they are so wary of us after having been caught once before. They appear to have an inbuilt distance sensor. Get anywhere within what they consider is a dangerous area and they are off. Straight up into the air and heading for the grain store roof, house roof, shed roof, cottage roof, foldyard roof. We have a lot of roofs. There they sit, cackling down at us in a series of unearthly shrieks.

July

1st

Accompanied my friend Rosie to the vet's for a routine review of the medication for her two border terriers. Daisy and Meg are nearly fifteen and frail little dogs. My friend has invested in a baby buggy to take Daisy, the most doddery terrier, for a walk. Whilst we chatted and fussed the dogs in the waiting room, a Land Rover drove at speed into the vet's car park. A distraught farmer rushed into the surgery. His sheepdog lay stretched out in distress in the back of the Land Rover. After a hurried conversation, a vet, armed with a large syringe, accompanied the farmer back out to the vehicle. Things looked bad. But not to Daisy and Meg. Suddenly, from their prone positions on the floor, the pair of them perked up and trotted outside into the car park. They angled themselves for a ringside view of what were obviously the last moments of the sheepdog. Give them a set of knitting needles each and a ball or two of wool and they would have been dead ringers for the old ladies sat observing the guillotine and today's big show of executions. Job done, they trotted back in. My friend was too embarrassed to follow. Doggy review over, we went back to my friend's house. She and her husband are away soon on holiday and her mother is coming to look after the dogs, as they do not take kindly to the change of scenery and drop-in care standards which a visit to a kennels might entail. 'Mum is very worried about what she should do if one of them dies,' my friend said. 'But I've been very clear about what she should not do.' She then proceeded to tell me of the experience of a neighbour who had been left in charge of a very poorly terrier whilst the dog's owner went away. Apparently the poor state of the dog's health was known to the carer, but exactly how ill it was, was not. It died the day after its owner left the country. 'Whatever you do,

1 *Wedding day, 1986.*

2 *Matthew, Jo, Bryony and Chris at Christmas.*

3 Millie enjoying a spot of comfort.

4 Fizz and Millie in the wheat field after harvest.

5 *Me, John and the dogs out in the field.* © *Jim Varney*

6 *Daring bantam raiding Fizz's biscuit bowl and bone.*

7 Hens in a safe place.

8 The peacock terrorists!

9 Out in the field. © Jim Varney

10 The two of us together with a lamb. © Jim Varney

11 *Pheasant shooting at Braco, Scotland, 2000.*

12 *A shoot meeting in the yard.*

13 *Nostalgic trip back to shoot at John's childhood home at Blaco Farm.*

14 *Off fishing on Loch Dionard.*

15 Me fishing on Loch Dionard.

16 John on our fishing holiday at Loch Dionard in 2010.

17 *A rainbow trout from the pond on the farm caught by friend Tine!*

18 *Pet lamb being bottle fed, 2010.*

19 Bryony and Jess aged five months.

20 Sophie in hot pursuit of the guinea fowl.

21 John with Millie and Fizz in the big shed, 2012.

22 John on a shoot in the Highlands, 2013.

23 Harvest 2013.

24 Happy Birthday moment when fishing at Gualin, Sutherland.

25 *Pet lambs being fed, 2014.*

26 *The prime enemy of a terrier – cats!*

27 Jess (aged twelve) and Ollie (aged ten) waving hello, 2015.

28 Harvest 2015.

29 Tidying away, Lowther Farm style.

30 Pile 'em high! The grain shed. Harvest 2015.

31 On the tractor steps. © Jim Varney

32 Winter in the back paddock.

don't get rid of Binky until I get home. I want to arrange a proper send-off for him,' were the instructions. What to do with a deceased dog in a heatwave were not explained. At first Binky's corpse was laid out on a sheet, a fan wafting cool air over him, curtains closed to keep out the sun. A portable air conditioner was brought in to chill the room but the sun beat down outside and in desperation the carer decided to empty the freezer. It was casseroles for the next week as the dog took the place of frozen stewing steak, mince and chicken. The next hurdle was the return of the owners. How long to defrost a dog? Microwave instructions are not very forthcoming and microwaves rarely big enough anyway for this particular job. It was a slow, overnight, leaky job. Binky was arranged tastefully, front paws crossed on a towel-covered cushion, flower between the paws, soft music playing, candlelight to hide the ravages of being iced up and then de-iced. 'He looks lovely,' his owner exclaimed and proceeded to bring out her digital camera for close-ups. 'I'll let you have a copy of the pictures.' There are explicit instructions for my friend's mum: 'No freezer for Daisy, should she drop dead. It's off to the vet's and they can sort out what to do.' Rosie is, after all, a vegetarian and never knowingly had meat in her freezer, and I don't think she's starting with Daisy.

2nd

Rows of big hay bales, stacked end to end like packets of giant Rolos, fill the big shed. As rain threatened after this hay was baled, John brought it all home and created the rows to ensure it was properly dry before stacking under cover. I remember one year when he brought home a trailer full of fresh bales and left them stacked there for a couple of days. One morning we woke to find virtually the whole load tossed onto the ground, off the trailer, as if by a giant's hand. Fortunately they had not caught fire. Always the danger. Bales can heat up and in extremis spontaneously combust. Some years John has struggled for a fortnight turning and turning the cut to try and dry it out. Now, at the first sign that drying the grass for hay is not going to plan with the weather, John rings a contractor and we get the lot sealed up in big green bales. We now always make a four-acre field behind the wood into haylage bales, but that is a field that hardly gets any sun and is notoriously difficult to dry out. Plus, a few bales of haylage always comes in useful over winter for the sheep.

3rd

John called me into the foldyard. 'See that heifer?' he said. 'I was fattening her for market as I didn't need her for the herd. She has had a different idea. One of the young bulls must have served her.' Clever thing, I thought. Instead of market, she is going to get out in the fields for the rest of the summer. Much better alternative. The dogs and I go round the herd and the sheep twice a day in the Land Rover as John is busy with other jobs. I have been agitating for a quad bike for some time, but after doing the check on a rainy day, I can definitely see the advantage of being inside a vehicle, rather than out in the open on top of one. 'Just make sure everything gets up,' John told me. 'That way you know they are all right.' The calves can be very disconcerting. They lie with their heads stretched out almost backwards. To all the world they look dead. Then you see a tail whisk or they scramble to their feet if you pass close to them. The cows and Mr Bull scarcely move at all. In the morning the entire herd is laid up chewing their cud. They look so contented. There they are, three big fields to wander between. Plenty of grass. Water troughs handy. A mineral lick centrally placed in each field for a taste diversion, as John was the victim of a fast-talking salesman with one of the licks. 'It will keep the flies off the cows,' he was told. I don't think so. There's still plenty of head shaking and tail whisking going on. Unlike the cows, which always stick together, the sheep are scattered everywhere. If it was only the cows that needed observing, the job would be done in a flash, but the sheep . . . I have to trawl up and down trying to see if any are upside down in ditches, or upside down anywhere, and have banged my head on the roof of the Land Rover more times than I care to mention through failing to notice a grip in the field. In the back, the dogs do a wonderful levitation act. Then come back down again with a wallop.

'Mum, what have you been up to?'

4th

Another heifer which was planned to be in calf started to bag up yesterday and politely waited until after lunch to give birth to her calf. As it turned out, she needed a pull, so it was fortuitous that John was around and well fed. The calf is a beautiful soft grey colour, quite unusual, and must be a throwback somewhere as the bull is a brown Limousin and the heifer a black Aberdeen Angus. She is a most solicitous mum. From the start she licked her calf vigorously and then let it feed with no problem at all. She is extremely gentle. In a day or to she will go out with the rest of the herd. That job done, John turned his attention to test running the combine where it is stored in the grain shed. Imagine my surprise when half a rat was spat out at my feet as John ran the engine at full speed. The rat must have been somewhere in the combine's gizzards when John started up. Unfortunately for Mr Rat, he could not run as fast as the belts and pulleys when they started to turn. Wonder where the other half of the rat is?

5th

The farm trailer has stood empty for a week or two. With no cattle to take into market or sheep to move, it stays parked up outside the big corn shed. A lifeless aluminum hunk. When John came to use it today to take a heifer and calf from the foldyard to join the herd in the fields, he noticed a small pile of bird muck in the corner of the trailer. 'I thought I can't have cleaned it out properly,' he chastised himself, as the trailer has to be hosed down and cleaned out after every animal movement, 'But I thought no more of it as we were not moving off the farm.' The trailer was kept on the move that day, transporting ewes with triplets to different fields. They have proved very useful as a clean-up gang, and John puts them in to graze off several small plots that would be time consuming to get into with tackle. Instead this keeps the ewes happy, and the place looks tidy. All in all, the trailer was out of place for most of the day. When he parked it back in its allocated space late afternoon, he stepped out of the tractor and was nearly decapitated by a pair of enraged swallows divebombing the trailer air vents. 'I thought I'd just go back into the house for a cup of tea and then take the trailer back to hose it down,' he said. 'But when I saw the swallows I put two and two together and realised that the pile of bird muck must be beneath a nest.' It was. It is. And there are eggs in it too. The daft things have chosen a mobile home for their domestic residence, rejecting their usual nest-building sites in the old barns. Usually from May onwards we can never shut the doors on the meal shed or old milking parlour as they nest in the beams. They also make use of the big foldyard. There are so many gaps for ventilation in those buildings and in the silage clamp, that they are never in danger of being locked out. This is the first time that any bird has ever considered the trailer as a home. Perhaps with it staying immobile for over a week and because it is dry, warm and rain proof, everything was just too tempting. Maybe they are a very trendy pair of swallows, going for that minimalist, brushed aluminum look in preference to old-fashioned wooden beams and the traditional clutter and profusion of spiders' webs that every farm shed sports. But their new home presents a few problems. John pressure washed the trailer out but took care not to disturb the nest. Just washed the muck away. But next week it will be needed to take some fat stock into market and he is trying to work out a way of keeping the cattle away from that corner of the trailer so that their heads do not knock the nest down. Mrs Swallow is now sat tight on the nest, apart from when it had to be moved to get the combine out of the big shed. Then she flew out and sat on the telephone wire and waited rather impatiently until the trailer returned. 'Just not good enough,' her attitude reflected.

6th

Arrived at the vet's in a tangle of dog leads as it was an opportune time to update all the dogs' vaccinations. The vet took one look at Pip our Labrador and suggested we lift her onto the weighing table. 'She needs to lose at least three kilograms,' he said, 'otherwise as a working dog she will get increasingly arthritic as she gets older.' We know, but try telling Pip. She can find food anywhere. Ewe or calf milk replacement is a particular favourite, but she is also partial to rolled barley, sheep nuts and protein pellets for the bulls. Pip is quite fearless about actually stealing the food from under the bulls' noses. As John tips the feed into the bulls' troughs, Pip follows, a fat dog in amongst the big bulls. They have been used to her all their lives and do not bother. Of particular joy to Pip are the visits of our occasional resident guest Labrador, George. He is from Meg's, our old Labrador, one and only litter, and a frequent visitor when his jetsetting owners are off abroad. George brings exotic and delicious fare. Tinned dog food. Unknown to ours, who live off a complete dried dog biscuit and all the household scraps they can get their mouths round. George is not a big eater, however, never having had the competition of a pack of greedy dogs to challenge for every last scrap. As soon as he is out of his kennel, Pip, Millie and Fizz are in. When George returns for another snack, he finds zilch.

7th

We are currently enjoying a surfeit of field mushrooms. They are delicious. Many years ago we took some racehorses in for respite care. They grazed over several fields as they rested at the end of the racing season. Nasty bad-tempered things they were too. Any attempts to stroke or get close to them was met with a nasty nip and a pair of flailing back hooves. They were beautiful creatures but we were both glad to see the back of them, as they made walking across the fields a nightmare. But their legacy has been some super crops of mushrooms, kick-started aptly by their manure. The memory of the racehorses has reminded me of a seaside donkey that we homed for the winter. This was before we had Jo's horse Rupert, and we thought a donkey might just stave off the evil day that we would have to provide a pony for her. The donkey arrived in the back of a small lorry. Part of a consignment of seaside donkeys being literally farmed out for the winter. The donkey trotted docilely behind her owner, saddle still on, ready to go. For approximately two days she let Jo ride her round the paddock at the back of the house. Submissive and gentle, she seemed everything we needed to satisfy a seven-year-old's ambition to ride. Then the tranquillisers wore off. Or that's what it seemed like. The donkey suddenly appeared to appreciate that she had the upper hand here and that the day-to-day routine of trawling up and down a beach had disappeared. Her main aim in life was then to unseat

Jo. She was uncontrollable and her favourite trick was to canter under the low branches of the trees in the paddock and sweep Jo off her back. Several months later we waited for her owner to collect her for the start of the donkey-riding season. He did not reply to phone calls and the donkey responded to her new life of ease by getting fatter and fatter and producing the most adorable foal. Feelings were very mixed when they were collected.

8th

The barley would go now, but there is not a hope with the weather. The combine is ready. The grain store is clean. There is even more hay ready to be made. But not in this weather. It is going to have to wait until the barley and rape are out of the way. Combining will be a very difficult and sensitive job, however it is tackled this year. The story is going around about how a brand-new Class combine, fitted with rubber tracks, got stuck trying to cut winter barley last week. The farmer hired a winch to pull the combine out backwards. Unfortunately it caused extensive damage to the underside of the combine when it was scraping along the ground during the recovery operation. It bent the grain pan and the fan housing, effectively putting an end to that day's harvesting. Year's harvesting, probably, for that particular machine.

9th

My fifteen Aylesbury ducklings are down to thirteen. Unlucky for the two who landed up in Fizz the sheepdog's kennel. She thinks she is a retriever and not a border collie, but the tender touch was not tender enough. In her enthusiasm she has killed them. John was furious with her but then decided to blame himself for letting her wander round the yard with so many temptations in the form of fluffy ducks in her sights. And mouth. The ducklings have been under the charge of a very aggressive bantam. Under normal circumstances she would not have let Fizz anywhere near her charges, as they were in close confinement in a purpose-built pen on grass. Whilst the ducklings were tiny and could flee under the safety of her wings, they were safe from most (barring foxes) threats. Millie our Jack Russell and Pip both have a healthy respect for those sharp beaks. But as the grass in the pen has been eaten up, and the ducks are now of a size where they are almost as big as their foster mum, we decided to give them the full run of the paddock. They loved it. Darting hither and thither searching out insects and grubs, attracting the passing interest of an excitable Border collie. We had left the dogs alone for the day whilst at a clay pigeon shoot. Clays used to be John's passion. Every Sunday, work permitting, he was chasing prizes. But family duties eventually wore him down and over the past years game shooting has taken ascendancy. The shoot we went to was run by a friend. The pot paid for the hire of a cherry picker to hoist the clay trap up above the shooters, beefburgers and sausages for a barbecue, and anything left over for a local charity. A good idea. John really enjoyed it. He could still 'smoke' and 'powder' them and was able to give guidance to those who could not.

10th

Our bantams frequently choose to nest on the hay and straw stacks. Given the chance, they purloin each other's nesting sites, and this nest napping has been demonstrated on large scale at a friend's business. John and Rob have diversified from farm to golf club, and the clubhouse and restaurant are sited close to a lake on the tenth hole. The lake has attracted a number of nesting birds, mainly ducks and coots. A pair of swans has shown a passing interest in the lake, but never to the point of wanting to rear a family there. However, a coot's nest suddenly appeared to trigger their fancy, and the coot, having finished her own job of nesting/ hatching/dispatching, abandoned the nest to the next tenants. This nest was only a starting point. Over a few days, the swans cleared a site in the bullrushes around the original nest, and built a towering edifice of bullrushes and reeds to over a metre height. Mrs Swan took up residence and eventually brought off three cygnets. The whole business has been of intense interest to passing golfers and diners in the restaurant. The swans for their part have been undisturbed by swipes and wide balls. Once hatched, the cygnets needed feeding and here the friendly diners contributed to their lunch, tea and dinner. What could be nicer than to wander down to the lake after a meal and toss a few crumbs into the water for the swans? Except the swans soon realised the source of the food and took to visiting the restaurant itself for an immediate handout, and have taught their cygnets to do the same. The odd enquiring tap on the window turned into an aggressive series of raps. Far from waiting for guests to throw them crumbs, the swans started to actively harass them. Plus swan muck. Lots of it. On the patio. On the greens. Not nice. 'You'd think we had a herd of velociraptors coming to visit us rather than a few birds,' John said. 'Swans poo big time.' So the past week has been swan school time. The new diversion is to see the two swans, plus cygnets, solemnly following a golf cart, laden with crumbs, round to the other side of the lake to a feeding place away from golfers and diners. Big signs are in evidence. Do Not Feed The Swans. If only I could get Fizz to read, Do Not Eat The Ducks, how much simpler life would be.

11th

The partridge eggs saved from a nest disturbed by a stray dog, have hatched in my incubator. Partridge egg hatching is quite something. The partridge chick makes a semi-circular incision in one end of the shell and emerges with the shell virtually intact. You can literally close the lid on the empty egg after the hatch and make a whole egg again. Nine eggs hatched, seven chicks survived. One managed to get under the incubating tray (they are like bumble bees) and drown itself in the humidifying tray, and another partridge chick had splayed legs and never thrived. The others are doing well and John is adding to their numbers with twenty newly hatched partridge chicks from a game farm so that he has a decent size covey to go outside in late summer. Summer. Summer? I tell you those chicks are lucky to have hatched out in a nice warm incubator. The day they hatched brought yet another downpour. The chicks would barely have survived in the wild. Our intention is not for these English partridges to be put down for shooting but to increase indigenous numbers. We can still see several of the adult English partridges John released last year, but sadly no coveys of chicks.

'If he thinks that bit of wire is going to keep me in my place,
he'd better think again.'

12th

This morning John and I spent an hour going round the cattle and sheep in the fields. The lambs are standing with their backs hunched against the rain. Ewes and lambs literally shake themselves like dogs to dry their fleeces. Conditions are miserable and John is vexed that the lambs are not thriving as they should do at this time of year. As several are due to go to market on Monday, the proof will be in what the buyers are prepared to pay. However, even more miserable in the rain than the sheep are the cows. A calf born yesterday snuggled up to its mum to dodge the rain. A sodden introduction to life. However, the status of top miserable farm dweller clearly goes to John. He is desperate. The cows have once more broken down the electric fence that runs beside the fence that separates stock from a wheat field and needs mending. The ground that he had dug out for a fresh stretch of yard to be concreted is now full of water and he has had to cancel the delivery of cement. Finishing haymaking remains a distant dream. Barley is starting to turn and the thought of combine and tractors travelling in such soggy fields is a nightmare. And the forecast? More rain.

13th

There is a twin calf in the yard, which we have been nurturing for several months. It refused to suckle, will only drink milk from a bucket and has steadfastly refused to be weaned. John has threatened it with the hunt kennels on more than one occasion. Perhaps it had a wake-up call. This morning it has eaten a bucket of coarse mix.

14th

A neighbour who had cut a field of grass for hay the night before a torrential rainstorm covered his field in water, found to his amazement five days later when the water receded that not a blade of grass was left. 'I don't know what I thought would happen,' he said, 'but I thought there might be just a blade or two of grass left to make something of.' We have abandoned haymaking for the moment. It is just not feasible, and instead John is letting the grazing to a neighbour who needs the extra grass for his cattle. Instead of swathing the rape as we usually do and allowing it to dry off on the rape stubbles, John has had a contractor in to spray it off. Then we shall use a specialist contractor to combine the crop, as John does not want to risk getting our combine bogged down. The happiest members of our farm are the ducks and geese. The little pond in the paddock at the back of the house had almost dried up and the ducks were being forced to dabble in puddles and mud. But now they are floating and paddling gracefully in three foot of water. They are in duck ecstasy. They might not be so happy if they realised that several of their number are at prime weight for the roasting tin. Paddle on, ducky.

15th

Today I very nearly lost a finger on my right hand, through sheer neglect. On my right hand I wear my mother's wedding, engagement and eternity rings. I treasure the fact that they had graced her hand. Last weekend I was helping with some muck spreading. The muck attracts a fair few flying insects in the cab and somehow I got bitten several times on my arms and just under the rings on my right hand. How an insect got to deliver a bite there I do not know, but the next day my finger started to itch. Over the next few days I scratched away and made a half-hearted attempt to remove the rings as my finger looked a little swollen. 'It will go down,' I thought, and rubbed a little lavender oil in. But it didn't and began to feel chafed and raw under the rings. I twisted the stones round to the back of my finger to allow some air to the bite area as it was starting to weep, and drove up to Bryony's house to help her out with some babysitting. By the time I got there my finger was throbbing, very painful and the rings barely visible, with the flesh swollen over them. I was roundly told off. My son-in-law Chris, a surgeon, tried to get the rings off by threading a ribbon under them, winding the ribbon tightly and then attempting to pull the rings over the top. That just succeeded in my experiencing excruciating pain and my finger going an ever deeper shade of purple. 'We're off to Accident and Emergency,' Bryony said. 'The rings are going to have be cut off, otherwise you are going to lose that finger, the blood is not circulating.' My Mum's rings. Cut them off. I did not want to think about it. But I had to. And in truth I was a very spoiled patient as Bryony had done a six-month stint in A and E when a house doctor, and is someone the nurses had not forgotten. I was whisked in and a mini wheeled saw cut the rings off my finger. Tonight my finger is still a funny colour and the indentations clearly visible. 'Remember,' Bryony said, 'if you get bitten by a clegg again anywhere near your finger, get your rings off straight away.' I certainly shall. Kid gloves for all jobs from now on. And they never did get to go out. What a hopeless babysitter.

16th

The changeable weather for harvest has put an air of uncertainty over several events we have been invited to late summer. A shoot barbecue, a fiftieth birthday party and two civil partnerships. New events for us. One is my cousin's, who has been with her partner for many years, and has suddenly decided to 'go for it', as she said, and ensure that 'our affairs are tidied up and there will be no problems if anything happened to either of us'. It will be a super family affair. The other civil partnership celebration is nearer home and will definitely be all singing and dancing if his father's recent sixtieth birthday celebration is anything to go by. So at least, whatever the weather holds, we have some sparkle, sequins and glamour assured for the summer. And that's just my outfit.

17th

Happy days are here again . . . it is just amazing how the whole mood of the farm can lift once the sun comes out and the combine roars out of the yard and trundles off to the fields, intent on gulping down a crop of corn. I came back from Bryony's with my poorly finger and the roads were choked with tractor and trailers carting home tottering loads of barley. At one time there must have been about fifty vehicles behind a lumbering John Deere and its trailer, but I never begrudged an extra second of my time, as I was just delighted that the agricultural vehicles were on the move again. As soon as the tractor could safely do so, he pulled over and let the line of traffic by. I do not think the toots he received were of thanks from most vehicles, more of an 'about time too' response.

18th

Joy of joys, the welcome spell of hot dry weather and the fact that some of the barley and rape are now harvested has meant that John could try and get a crop of hay off a grass field specifically grown for forage. Cut yesterday and turned today, it will bale tomorrow. Miraculous. And even better, John went into the wheat fields this afternoon and the crop that he did not think would be ready for another fortnight, could be ready for the combine by the end of the week. He bit some of the corn and it is rock hard. But best not to get over confident. Disaster could still strike, as it did to a farm not so many miles away this weekend. It is on land belonging to a very big cooperative farming several thousand, indeed many thousand acres. John has been going very steady, very steady indeed with the combine when in the barley and rape, and will have to do so this weekend as the ground is still very sticky. He keeps moving and emptying the tank at the end of each pass so that there is no surplus weight at all in the machine. Therefore the sight of three tractors yoked together to pull out a £300,000 Class Lexon machine from peatland is a dire warning of the worst that the land can do to the highest-tech machinery.

19th

Some people's loves bring them flowers. Mine brings me mushrooms. But it does tell me that each morning, as John walks the fields to check on the cows and sheep before breakfast, he is thinking of me. There is always at this time of year, weather permitting, a heap of fresh field mushrooms on the kitchen table ready to fry in butter and serve up on toast for my first meal of the day. Lovely. What truer sign of devotion. My sign of devotion is to make sure that if I ever dare to go out and leave my husband alone at lunchtime (which is more frequently than he likes), I ensure he has a meal ready for 12 noon sharp. To this end, the bottom oven on the cooker is a boon. So into this slow oven, if I leave very early, goes either a frozen duck or pheasant, pork or lamb chops, braising steak or similar. Then a small bag of salad potatoes. A boon for wives whose husbands only require potatoes as their sole veg. Slurp of wine or stock or yesterday's gravy (what a slob, you are thinking), and that's it. It is reassuring to hear that I share my vice of ditching John on occasional lunchtimes with other farmers' wives, who also adopt similar long-distance culinary skills. But although you would think that life has been made very simple for such fortunate men, they still need instructing on exactly what it is they are supposed to collect and eat when their wives have gone to all the trouble of bunging it into a dish for them. For example. Off for the day went a neighbour's wife. Note on the table propped up against the salt pot. 'Lunch in bottom of Aga, cake in tin, warm apple pie up for pudding if you want one.' On her return she was chastised by her husband for 'the plain do' she had left for him. He had been very disappointed by the standard of the day's catering arrangements. 'Greasy and chewy and no flavour to speak of,' he said. As you can imagine, in no uncertain terms he was advised that in future he could cook his own lunch as, as far as his wife was concerned, she had poured love and devotion and a casserole into that dish to be cooked in the bottom of the cooker. Later in the evening she reached into the bottom of the Aga to retrieve the meat she had left on slow cook for the dogs. Minced entrails and offal that she bought weekly from the butcher and cooked up for the dogs' delectation. That night the dogs dined on a delicious, braised steak hotpot with all the trimmings. Her husband? A bottle of indigestion tablets.

20th

I have been thrilled at the increasing independence of a little flock of bantam chicks in the yard; all sixteen of them. Amazed that this Mother Bantam had brought so many chicks off. A flighty, indeed vicious bird, she stuck close to her nest, never budging even when you got close up to where she was sitting. Her motto was clearly that if I do not move a feather nor even blink, they won't know I'm there. Survival tactics, I presume. Then this morning I found a dead chick in the run as I went to let the mini flock out. No sign of trauma, just lying there stiff, head thrown back, claws clenched. This afternoon two more dead chicks in the yard and tonight another one dead in the pen. Chief suspects Pip and Fizz, who have been known to take a flyer round the yard with chicks in their mouth, cannot have done the dirty deeds as they have been with me all day.

21st

Disaster. Mummy Bantie lying dead in the middle of the yard and five more chick corpses nearby. We are flummoxed. A fox would have taken the corpses away to eat them. The dogs all accounted for in their movements. Especially since the start of the deaths. I shooed the remaining seven chicks into their pen, difficult, as without their mum to take the lead, the chicks just kept scattering hither and thither. John had a sudden thought as to the cause. 'I put some rat poison under those corrugated sheets in the empty bull yard,' he said. 'I thought they would be safe there as the dogs don't go in, the foldyards are empty and the poison was hidden away. Anyway, just go and check, will you, and see if it has all gone.' The rats, it turned out, had pulled the poison bait out from under the sheets and scattered it around. Little was left, but from chicken droppings around, my poultry must have got in through the bull yards and eaten the bait. The chickens just hop over the gates and get in where the dogs cannot. I swept away the poison bait that was left. Since then two more chicks have died but the remaining five seem fine. It was a lovely sight to see Mum and sixteen chicks around the yard. She was so proud and protective of them. Now they are just little heaps in the muck spreader. But wait. There is hope. I have just come in from the big shed and glimpsed a reddy brown bundle, half concealed amongst some old straw bales. The bundle was another of my bantams sat very tight on a clutch of eggs. Life's full circle starts again.

22nd

The recent anniversary of the death of my mother-in-law Rose is always an occasion for much trawling of family memories to recall the full and creative life that she led. Born into a farming family on a tenanted farm, her childhood, teenage years and early twenties centred on Salton Grange, North Yorkshire, where her family moved to when she was ten years old. An optimistic venture in the '20s, when to purchase land was an even bigger gamble than it is now. From five years old she walked along country lanes for two or three miles to attend the village school in Normanby. Cocoa for lunch was heated on the little tortoise stove that doubled up to keep the whole school warm. She left school at fourteen to help out at home. Denied the opportunity to go to grammar school because her father did not see the value of education for girls, the Land Army represented an unforeseen chance for independence. Later, romance beckoned and she married Bill, the herdsman at the farm where she worked. But her youth on the family farm, participation in village activities such as the cricket team, Sunday school, pantomimes, chapel, whist drives, singing, delivering eggs and butter for her mother, all left an abiding memory of a happy and satisfying life. Similarly, the Land Army gave her the self-esteem of a job well done and friends made for life. She often spoke of working in all weathers, driving tractors, clearing dikes, hoeing fields, tending livestock and the pride she took in supporting the war effort. But marriage and motherhood were her greatest fulfilment. 'My mother was never idle,' John said. 'I never saw her just sitting. She was either cooking, baking, sewing, knitting, gardening, tending calves, rearing poultry, flower arranging and, perhaps the skill that she was best known for, corn dolly making.' And just as her own family had made the move from tenanted farm to farm ownership, she pushed her sons into doing the same. Supporting them all the way. John's father had been a farm manager until John left agricultural college, and then the whole family took the plunge so that Rose could attain her dream of her boys being on their own farm again. 'The first year was dreadful,' she often recalled. 'We only had nine Ayrshire cows to milk and one of them died two days after we got it home. The hay rotted in the field as it was so wet. Our machinery was so old it kept breaking down.' But she got them through. Settled, her creative skills flourished. Always on call to decorate a chapel with flowers, put up a stall at a country show to demonstrate corn dollies, read poetry in Yorkshire dialect. An uncle who she had cared for left her a small cottage in Wrelton. She returned

those brand new smells and there is the added bonus of a sneaky crisp, biscuit or sandwich. Sometimes the problem is actually getting them to move more than two inches from our sides if the afternoon snack is especially appealing. They forget about all the interesting hedge backs and focus instead on that unexplored bun.

25th

With time allowed off for good behaviour, and the combine parked up until needed again, we have had a day out at a local agricultural show. Despite all the obstacles placed in their way by DEFRA and the government, farmers do a fantastic job in maintaining the countryside and its way of life. The livestock on show were magnificent. Jessica, our granddaughter, who was with us, particularly liked the little black Soay sheep from the Hebrides, which needed a top on their pen to stop them jumping out. We shall not be getting any, I was assured. She can just get soppy over Suffolks and Texels. John, however, was very nostalgic about the Ayrshires. I like the Belgian Blues. They waddle into the show ring rolling their double-muscled bottoms enticingly. I must practise that walk. With a similar-shaped rear end – fat, not muscle, I am afraid – I am sure I could improve on my present style of perambulation. Plus, a rosette, strategically placed, would help to hide some of it.

26th

For over a year we have stored my daughter's camper van under the barn. Or in front of the barn. In front of the house. Beside the house. In front of the grain shed. In the grain shed. It has done more mileage around the farm than it has done on the road. It was only ever taken for one family holiday in the past two years, and then brought quickly back to the farm as the roof leaked when it rained. At times of family gatherings it has proved particularly useful as an extra bedroom for hardy visitors and an intriguing playroom for grandchildren. But as an actual camper van going to a camper van sites? I don't think so. Last week it was due its MOT test. Left as usual to the last minute by daughter Bryony with an agonised phone call home for me to arrange it. Not easy as the camper van is classed a Section 5 vehicle (whatever that means) and our local garage could not help. I eventually sorted it out and then left it for Chris, my son-in-law, to get the thing there, predicting that he might have some difficulty, since the battery was as flat as a pancake even after being left for several days on charge. With all the comings and goings of everyday farm life, we sometimes only meet at mealtimes and bedtimes. Conversation is limited because of the need to 'get on' or go to sleep. Social niceties get strained and messages mixed and lost, despite my foolproof systems. As it happens, I was in London for a day and the messages and reminders I left John were about taking in the wool bags, the time for the appointment with the representative from FABBL (a scheme that accredits the farm with high welfare standards), the crop consultant's report on his walkabout and his spray recommendations, which fields needed the hay turning in and what I had left him to eat. All important stuff. Clean forgot about the camper van. And failed to remember to tell anyone about my new secret hiding place for car and assorted vehicle keys that was a result of a letter from the police about thefts in the area. Apparently the nature of the theft is not to rob the house, but to steal vehicle keys. The letter ended with a strong recommendation that keys should be kept in a secure place. Very secure, as it turned out. When Chris turned up to take the camper van in, neither John or Chris could find any of the sets, despite an exhaustive search. As the keys also contained the release for the immobiliser, they were stuck. And so was the camper van. Being busy and occupied elsewhere, and knowing John would not be available to answer any calls, I did not switch my phone on until coming home to let him know what time I was due back. Eighteen missed messages. Ah. They were worried about me. I should have let them know that I was fine in the big city. Not a bit of it. Not one enquiry as to my well-being. Where are the . . . keys? Where are the ***** . . . keys???? For Gawd's sake, where are the ***** . . . !!!!!! keys? Now if they'd asked me nicely . . .

27th

'I've gone against every bit of advice I received with this crop of barley,' John said as we sat and had our drinkings at tea time by the combine, 'and its turned out fine. Firstly I grew it from farm-saved seed, which even though we had custom cleaned and tested for germination, still worked out a lot cheaper than certified seed. Then I let the sheep graze on it for a fortnight last winter when the crop was looking a bit proud. It's an old-fashioned practice but I like it because I am old fashioned. Finally I didn't apply the final fungicide at ear emergence, which the crop consultant advised, but I did not agree with. And look. It is a good crop. True there's some volunteer wheat from the previous crop, but as it's for feeding back to the bullocks and isn't going off the farm, it will be ideal.' We pondered the wisdom of this and the savings made. Which was a good job, as after my day in London and all the little stop-offs at cafés, bars, handbag, toy and shoe shops, every economy is very welcome over the next week or so until I get the housekeeping back in order.

28th

Our swallow chicks are now seasoned travellers. A few weeks ago when we found their nest in our trailer, we were able to make use of a friend's trailer to transport cattle to market, but yesterday, with two pens of lambs to go in, the trailer was not available to us. So the chicks had to take to the road. Mum was not impressed. As soon as the trailer was returned to its normal parking place, she was straight back on the nest, chattering angrily. The journey had not taken too long and everything in the nest seems back to normal.

29th

The new home for the swallows keeps presenting problems. John pressure washed the trailer out but took care not to disturb the nest. Just washed the muck away. But next week it will be needed to take some fat stock into market and he is trying to work out a way of keeping the cattle away from that corner of the trailer so that their heads do not knock the nest down. Breaking news, however. Problem sorted. We can borrow our friend's trailer again for a week, and by then the swallows could be well on their way to quitting the nest. Housing crisis on this farm resolved. Time will tell. It is just unfortunate timing that the swallows and us need the trailer at the same time.

30th

Something different tonight. Clipping an alpaca. Oscar, the alpaca, has a coat so long and thick, he looks as if he was cut off at the knees. Additionally, Oscar's friend, allegedly a sheep, but visually an ambulating mound of wool only distinguishable as a sheep because of its eyes and bleat, could also do with a short back and sides. As Oscar has never been clipped before and is not trained to a halter, there was no perceivable way of bringing him quietly to the clipping machine that John had hung from a tree in his owner's paddock. Eventually, by fair means and foul, Oscar went under the clippers. Three of us had to get hold of odd bits of him. He uttered very strange high-pitched squeaking at first (never heard by his owners before), but otherwise lay quite quietly whilst his coat fell off around him. Crunch time was letting go. 'I'll be last one to get up,' Paul his owner said, bravely volunteering for a face full of green goo, as alpacas are renowned for the noxious nature of their spit. Not a problem. Oscar sprang to his feet, gave us one last baleful glance and disappeared off to the other side of his paddock, never to be caught again.

31st

We can combine again. Geoff and I are bringing corn trailers home as they fill, and tipping straight into the big grain shed for sale later. Very satisfying. This particular barley is a very clean sample from a different field to the one harvested several days ago. No volunteers here. John was advised to spray this crop for black grass last autumn. It knocked the barley back badly and it never really recovered. 'I shan't be doing that again,' he said. John agreed at the time that black grass might be a problem but feels it is more of an issue not to have the yield he expected. But that apart, he is very pleased to have the crop out of the field and in the grain shed.

August

1st

The poultry are feasting on the piles of scattered corn in the yard. John has been filling barley bins where the grain is stored over winter for the cattle. He backs a trailer of corn up to an old bath, raises the trailer to a steep gradient then opens a small tailgate to let the corn trickle out into the old bath. From there an augur takes the corn up into the bins. Jess is forbidden to approach the whole operation. The missing end of one of John's fingers is testimony to the inherent dangers of such an operation. As a little boy he investigated too closely when an augur appeared to stop running. Clogged corn removed, the augur ran again but took the top part of his finger with it.

2nd

The swallows who have nested in our cattle trailer will not be joining many more market trips. The fledglings are fully grown and will leave the nest in the next couple of days. Both Mum and Dad sit patiently on the telegraph wires waiting for the trailer to return home. This morning they both had beaks stuffed with insects and were straight in once the trailer was parked up.

3rd

Found John after lunch studying his ancient *The Observer Book of Butterflies*, awarded to him in 1963 for having 'the best wild flower collection' at Sunday school. The pages are well thumbed and have once more been able to identify a butterfly species accurately for him. In this case a speckled wood butterfly. 'I've seen three of these butterflies over the past week,' John said. 'I have never seen them on the farm before and was not sure of their identity. Come down this afternoon and see if you can see one.' Everything that the *Observer* said favoured the butterfly rang true. 'More abundant in wet seasons', and it has rained frequently here over the last month, and 'frequenting shady lanes', which the lane around the fields in that parcel of land is. There is a plantation of mixed hard woods and conifers that John planted about fifteen years ago and this must provide the leafy screen that the butterflies, blackish-brown in colour with large yellowish spots and one large white-pupilled black eye spot at the tip of the forewings, apparently relish. What is of interest to us is that the fields in that parcel all have the two-metre strip of unsown land around the edge of the fields. John has been distraught over the year at the increase in couch and other weeds in these strips of land, weeds he has spent years trying to eliminate, but which are now thriving under the new environmentally friendly entry schemes. Apparently the caterpillars of the species feed on couch, so this may be a reason for their sudden appearance on the farm. Flip me, the environmentalists may have a point.

4th

Sent to check on the progress of one of the few remaining British Friesian cows we have in the herd, to see if she had started calving. The suckler herd graze fields which are well inland, and I had to take the Land Rover through quite a series of muddy gateways to find them. There are only four Friesians in the herd, so they are easy to pick out amongst our Aberdeen Angus crosses. At first glance I could not find her at all, but then spotted a lone cow under a tree away from the main herd. A pair of legs and a bloody membrane created an unusual silhouette at her rear end. Any attempt by me to approach her to rip the membrane and allow the emerging calf to breathe, were frustrated by the cow simply getting up and trotting off. Not wishing to disturb her any more, I determined to get John out of his field on the other side of the farm to give the calf a pull. A combination of puddles, mud and speeds in excess of twenty-five miles an hour (top speed normally permitted) meant that the Land

Rover arrived in a spattered state at the field where John was power harrowing. As usual, I had to wait whilst he slowly traversed the field back to me (no point not continuing with the job in hand) and contain my impatience at our steady journey back to the cow. This time, with two of us on the job, we successfully got the calf out; however, both of us, clutching a slippery leg apiece, were needed to deliver it.

5th

Listened in to a feature on the radio on the rise in theft of working dogs. Apparently, well-trained dogs fetch high prices both for rounding up sheep and picking up on shoots. No worry there, then, about our current three. We can sleep in peace and be reassured that anyone who did have a moment's brainstorm and decided to steal them, would very quickly bring them back again. The trained dogs on this farm are of variable quality. Pip has an excellent nose but headstrong nature. She loves a full day's shooting, especially if there is lots of work in woods and retrieving from ponds and streams. Our Jack Russell Millie is totally untutored, but a storming ratter and mouser. I doubt whether anyone would get near enough to steal her. She can squeeze into the tiniest of places once she realises you want to catch her, and is only tempted out by premium cuts of meat, gourmet chocolates or a written guarantee that no-one expects her to do anything sensible like sit, come back, drop it or any other doggie trick. 'Obedience? I don't think so.' Our sheepdog Fizz is still a novice. It is amazing how quickly the sheep have rumbled this and challenge her at every opportunity.

6th

A trip to market is a great favourite with Jess. She enjoys the journey with John in the Land Rover and trailer when the cattle are taken in early morning, but then likes to go back and see how much they make. Today she was fascinated by the variety of body signals used by the buyers clustered round the main ring, to indicate to the auctioneer that they are in the bidding. 'Mamma, he's using his thumb,' she whispered as an apparently disinterested buyer twitched his thumb to raise the

'Eeeek! Who's been sleeping in our bed?'

price for a clean cow. 'Mamma, he's winking and he's nodding,' she informed me in dramatic whispers. Luckily, perched as we were on the top row of benches in the auditorium that makes up a sale ring, no-one could hear her over the mooing cattle and auctioneer's patter. I enjoyed the nifty movements of the man in with the bulls. Not all of the bulls amble docilely around whilst their fate and price is sealed. Some are determined to have a go at that fellow who is giving them a swift prod to keep moving. Some of them nearly have him as well, much to Jessica's delight. Lunch at the market is an undiscovered foodie's delight. Sumptuous roasts of sirloin of beef and pork loin. Top treat for Jess, and many farmers it appeared, chocolate fairy cakes. Jess went back three times for extras but was beaten to the last one by a burly farmer with three little buns balanced on the side of his over-brimming plate. A nod to those bulging rural waistlines, however, is the introduction of a salad bar. So to the pile of carved beef, roast potatoes, Yorkshire pudding and chocolate buns, a side plate of lettuce, tomatoes and cucumbers creates an eclectic guilt-free meal. 'Yes, I had salad for lunch, dear. What are we eating tonight?'

7th

Worked with John for half an hour yesterday trying to bring the sheep into the corral in order to check the flock out for maggots. The muggy weather is encouraging fly strike and John is finding two or three sheep a week are suffering despite the protective pour-on he doused them with a few weeks ago.

8th

Reminiscing with visiting friends about a previous August when we were in the midst of a foot and mouth scare. I was determined to be prepared for any extra biosecurity measures we had to take. At first we had no official notification about what we had to do, although to be fair, there was not a recognised infrastructure at that time for contacting all farmers quickly. We had Internet at our farm, but not broadband as we were too far from any server, and I was wary of giving any agency the opportunity to insist that all contact with us came via e-mails. John is a total Luddite when it comes to computers, and to leave all contact in my hands would give him an acute panic attack. I remembered during the previous foot and mouth outbreak being advised by a chemist that the most effective disinfectant for the virus was a solution of citric acid. Lemonade powder, no less. It is used as a mild disinfectant, and as foot and mouth is a relatively fragile, although highly infectious virus, a dilute solution of citric acid powder is as good as any proprietary disinfectant. The only trouble is that it is impossible to get hold of in any quantity from chemists, as it is also a highly desirable commodity to drug addicts, who use it in some way to melt down their drugs. So I went on the Internet and found a company dealing in food products who were able to supply me with as much of the stuff as I wanted. I bet the delivery man thought he was visiting a farmhouse full of crack heads.

9th

You risk concussion walking through our orchard to feed the hens. The apple trees are laden with fruit. We could join other folk with bountiful harvests and put a wheelbarrow full of windfalls at the farm entrance for passers-by, but some thoughtful soul nicked the wheelbarrow last year, so instead we doled out carrier bags of fruit to visitors. I let the banties out of their run at midday, by which time they should have organised themselves sufficiently to lay the family a few eggs. This does sometimes lead to a rogue hen sloping off to lay a few eggs in a forbidden place, but the resultant chicks, of which we currently have seven little fluffy bundles, are always an added bonus. The bantams' run is overshadowed by a Victoria plum tree and the hens have developed an absolute passion for ripe plums. The phrase 'dropping in your lap like a ripe plum' must have originated from Newton himself, as I consider that you are as likely to be hit by a plum as an apple when under one of the trees when the fruits ripen. They just drop off without warning. Synchronised bombing.

10th

Millie's skill and kudos as a rat killer is famed. She gets beside herself with excitement and ready to pounce, should a rat or mouse move a whisker whenever old bales are shifted, stacks of sacks moved or a heap of pallets relocated. We recently transferred all our remaining young bantams into the main hen run. A few of them would not go into the hen house at night and in exasperation I left them out. Big mistake. The next morning they were dead and John thought a rat had had them. But that was the rat's big mistake, as Millie found their nest under the hen house and has dispatched the lot. Fortunately the bantams that are left now all go in the hut at night.

11th

The sound of John's slow progress with the hedge cutter along our fields surrounding the village has filled the last few days. He needs a job when there is no corn ready to cut. We left the Entry Level Scheme which limits farmers to cutting hedges every three years. It meant that when our hedges were cut, it virtually ruined our hedge cutter and left hedges in a dreadful state. They had to be flailed and smashed to cut back the mature wood and for months looked dreadful. It also necessitated very careful cleaning up on the road to save any damage to bicycle tyres. This year, with only a year's growth, the job has been faster, neater, less damaging to the hedges and retains a good habitat for birds and wildlife. We would have stayed in the scheme but could not get enough points without including our hedges. However, John is continuing with all the other aspects of environmental management as we did before, only now we are not getting paid for it.

12th

Unusually I am harvesting apples before the plums are ready to pick. Not all the apples, but a tree that provides good eaters is ready and I have a daily cull of the bigger cooking apples. My magic peeler, picked up from a charity shop for a pound, is set up on a table by the back door. Every time John and I sit down for a short break, I can peel a few more apples, pop them in the microwave, and hey presto, another bag of apple pie filling for the freezer. The gadget works on a screw principle. You secure the apple onto four prongs, wind a small handle and ratchet the apple through cutting blades that whip off the peel and remove the core. Magic. Best of all, my granddaughter Jessica loves to use it and can be usefully employed with a bucket of apples and the peeler.

13th

Off to market again, with Jess summing it up later as 'the most exciting day of my life'. She was away early with Pappa to take two heifers in. One a management slip-up. A heifer with horns. And a nasty, bullying heifer at that. She has become quite dangerous, as she knows that she can use her horns to get in first to fresh hay and the barley trough. Several months ago we sold another cow in the herd with horns. It had been missed when John dehorned the calves, then graduated into the suckler herd and became difficult to handle once she appreciated the superior power her horns gave her. Dressed in a boiler suit and clutching a shepherd's crook she had found under the barn, Jessica oozed confidence and agricultural know how. At market, several farmers had brought either their children or grandchildren in. School holidays. What better day out. All the children were captivated by the agility of the man in the ring with the cows. He certainly needs to be able to move smartly out of the way if a cow, or young bull, starts to feel frisky and throw its considerable weight around. Fortunately he has a little escape gap between the gate in for the cattle and the gate out. Jess and her new friends were most amused when bulls, for example, that should have gone through to be marked with the brand of the seller, turned round and came back into the ring. Trying to get the gate shut on two ample beef rumps took some strength on the part of the man in the ring.

14th

This morning we introduced Millie our Jack Russell to a spot of sheepdog training. She has taken to it like a natural. Fizz our young sheepdog still needs some support on the job. John wanted to check on all the ewes and lambs for any signs of blowfly and needed to get them into the corral. They are not keen on this aspect of sheep management, perhaps sensing it is a precursor to market or something nasty with a worm drench. This morning went like a dream. A scatty, yappy, nippy little Jack Russell clearly scared them to bits. 'Let's get into that corral as quickly as possible' was their collective thought. Job done.

15th

Our teenage guinea fowl are having a torrid time learning some road sense. From twenty original chicks let loose to wander around the yard, only fourteen remain. The rest knocked down by motorists. Many disregarding the signs to slow down through our tiny village as they use it as a rat run to get through to a main road. Despite signs at both ends of our three-mile lane that it is unsuitable for heavy vehicles, huge lorries from a packaging plant still lumber through. The road, which must have been built at a time when the average width of a vehicle was a Model T, is now gouged out on both sides.

16th

John is now a very worried man, as it is me who reads and prints off all the spray instructions that come through via e-mail after the crop consultant's visits. He is keen to impress this new spray rep, to whom he is giving a trial run, with the efficiency of our farming operation. Therefore it may be a big mistake to involve me if I am not likely to get to the bottom of a page of dilutions and weather conditions ruling an application of fungicide or growth inhibitor, before my mind flips off onto something else. Like checking eBay or Amazon for a bargain.

17th

We have a housing crisis. More to the point, appropriate homes for expectant mums. In this case six hens who have all decided to go broody at once. Perhaps not as keenly monitored as they should be, with other business such as harvest on our minds, they have occupied various nesting sites, not all suitable, around the farm buildings.

First I found three hens crammed into an old pet carrier that had been discarded in the meal shed, two in a sheep trough that had been stacked away since lambing and another in an abandoned dog kennel. Rehousing was required. After shuffling round housing stock, two are now sharing a large coop in the paddock, two in yet more ancient pet carriers in the hen house, one left in the dog kennel and the other taking pot luck on the straw. Broody hens who are just sitting about rather than busy laying eggs, means a severe diminution of my egg-laying gang. And I have found that a regular visitor to a profitable nest is Mr Roland Rat. Sucked-out egg shells, or eggs rolled out of the nest ready for consumption, are his frequent calling cards. So I have decided on a short sharp war on rodents via some strategic rat traps. Especially as Millie has just missed killing a rat as it escaped into the bull pen. She is wisely a little cautious about ratting under Daddy Bull's hooves. He does not take kindly to busy little Jack Russells.

18th

'Have you any stubble fields we can run the dogs on?' a friend asked. We have in fact. Both spring and winter barleys are now harvested and provide useful locations for Joan's pointers to hone their skills in preparation for their real jobs on the moors. Joan takes her dogs all over the country to field trials, but their star turns are when on the grouse moors. There they take part in grouse counts. The dogs are expected to cover the ground methodically, going back and forth in a quartering pattern in front of their handler, to locate the grouse. Once found and the dog (in this case Ivy) gone into a point, Joan will move forward and hope to catch sight of some juveniles, or cheepers, hiding in the heather around their parent. 'You have to get your eye in,' Joan said. 'Once you have spotted the blink of an eyelid, you adjust to what you are looking for and see the young birds.'

The same areas of the moors have been counted for years and the records go back accordingly. This enables the gamekeepers to estimate how many grouse there will be on the whole moor and plan how many shooting days the moor will carry. To be accurate, the counts need to be at the same time year after year and with the same number of dogs. 'It's dead man's boots,' Joan said, as to whether she gets invited onto a moor. 'We all tend to be very secretive to hang onto our patches.' Joan does not take part in any of the shooting days: she just loves to work her dogs, improve their skills and share their enthusiasm in the job they are born to. One of our fields she considers especially good for training, especially when the wind, a cheek wind she called it, blows towards them. Ivy found quite a few rabbits, but pleasingly for Joan, was not distracted by them. She needs to keep them working as the dogs can cover enormous distances on the moors, covering about 250 acres in each sample of moorland, and they have to be fit. Her too. Puts me to shame.

19th

Searching in the freezer for the Sunday roast reminded me that at the start of the summer John declared that we had to live out of the freezer so that it would be clear of game and fruit by the time autumn came. However, I do not seem to be getting anywhere fast. I rarely go to the butcher, as we live off a surfeit of game, ducks and chicken, with the occasional (very occasional) fish from one of John's 'away days'. The freezers were emptying, there was space, and then wham, gooseberries/plums/tomatoes and blackberries hit home. And apples yet to come. To John's disgust (he hates spicy food), I have developed an absolute passion for a tomato curry recipe (garlic, ginger, chillies, cumin, curry leaves, halved tomatoes, coconut cream, lemon and coriander leaves) and have filled any available gaps in the freezer with tubs of it for the winter. When the shooting season starts, I think I will have to get another freezer, or husband, as there does not seem to be enough room for both in the pantry.

20th

Back at market again with Jess, who has by now made a few friends amongst the other farmers' children and grandchildren attending the

Summer time, and the living is easy . . .

auction. After a time, they all seemed to gang up together, comparing whose cattle were whose. It was but a small step to discovering how exciting it was to climb up and down the seat around the ring. That, however, was smartly put a stop to. Sales rings can be dangerous places. Only last year at this market a bull made it over the restraining bars, and one of the buyers at the side of the ring had to be hospitalised as he was knocked out. Once our cows came in, there was no holding Jess. She willed the price up. Very gratifying. Pappa was certainly pleased later on when we took the sales ticket back to the farm. Farmers generally give luck money on the sale to the purchaser. At one time it was all cash and buyers were never without their roll of notes in their back pocket. Today it is included in the sale price and is all reckoned for by Her Majesty's Inland Revenue. Still, today, with an excellent price received for a pair of bolshy heifers, John reckoned he had found his own little source of luck money. Jess.

21st

The impact of large vehicles on country roads has indirectly been responsible for an avian tragedy. A pair of swallows have put their faith in us again and built another nest in the cattle trailer. Previously this year, two broods had been raised. Two broods that have taken a weekly ride to market whilst their parents waited nervously on the telephone wires for them to return and for John to park the trailer back in the same place. Then they fly straight back in to resume their interrupted parenting tasks. Several weeks ago yet another three eggs were laid and Mrs Swallow settled in to raise another brood. Disaster struck, however, yesterday when a bridge in a nearby village was being repaired. The medieval packhorse bridge did not respond well to a battering from a huge artic lorry that should have had more sense than to try and negotiate it. In direct contravention to all the signs and opportunities for a diversionary route. When the bridge reopened, speed ramps had been installed immediately prior to the bridge. John set off for market with cows and swallow eggs. He checked at market and the eggs were fine. On his return journey, the trailer, being that much lighter without its load of stock, bounced hard over the speed ramps. 'I just didn't think about the consequences of that bump to the trailer,' John said. Sadly the three eggs lay smashed, bounced right out of their nest.

22nd

John is going to drill rape again this summer, after a definite decision never to grow it again two years ago. The thought is swilling round amongst farmers that rape has a potential as a fuel crop. We have had a delivery of seed rape and are hoping that the price will pick up next year at harvest time. One of our friends is looking into the possibilities of buying a crusher and burning the crop as a heating fuel. Who knows? The Chancellor will probably slap a tax on if he thinks that someone has discovered an untaxed fuel source, despite all the so-called encouragement for environmentally friendly alternative fuel sources. So to move the job on, John came into the kitchen to dust the flour and sugar out of my kitchen scales and weigh out a small bag of rape seed. He needs a test amount to judge against the bigger quantity required to sow, say, a ten-acre field. The rapeseed, which is tiny, is mixed in with fertiliser so that the drill can be recalibrated correctly for an accurate seed sowing. But we shall probably use a contractor to actually do that job.

23rd

Wet weather means that Jessica, who is staying with us, is confined to the house. It is too wet to play in the garden, so she has discovered the joys of baking, which is why my scales are always full of sugar and flour. Children love nothing better than stirring and tasting different cake, scone and pastry mixtures. At the end of each session the kitchen floor is sprinkled liberally with hundreds and thousands, sugar strands, Smarties, dolly mixtures and jelly tots. The dogs love helping to clear up and are keen to help dispose of surplus, uneaten fairy cakes.

The combine remains parked up under some trees away from the road, whilst we wait for the wheat to dry out again after more torrential downpours. I had been helping lead the corn. The last field has not got much further than simply being opened up. It is a matter of following the combine round (keeping a safe distance in case John has to stop and back up and to avoid the dust from all the chaff) so that John can empty the tank of corn into the trailer and keep going.

Needing to cook a piece of ham for harvest pack-ups, I came across a piece my late mother-in-law Rose had written on the annual pig kill. I thought I would copy it out for readers to think and possibly reminisce about. These are her exact words: they clearly show the difference today in me buying my ham and Rose having to really work for hers.

> *After Xmas 'pig killing' time came. The local killer came. We had the copper boiling. We hated hearing the squealing of the pig when it was being dragged to the slaughter. It was scalded in a tub, scraped clean and hung on a cambrill in the meal shed. Next day it was cut up into hams and sides, etc. Lots of fat to cut up and render. Usually we got at least two stone of lard. Pies were made, sausage meat, and hasslet. Scraps were the favourite but a fry was sent to all the neighbours. The hams and sides were salted down for three weeks. Then washed and brought into the kitchen. They were dried out for three weeks then put into muslin bags and stored away from flies and vermin. We boiled a ham for the Anniversary Dinner, the rest was used throughout the year. I hated pan boiling.*

24th

All it needed was for the weather to take up and the sun to shine with some intensity, for every combine in the country to roar into action. The harvest is on again, and in our case, nearly finished. Tractors in and out the yard. Golden tips of corn delighted and then infuriated the hens and guinea fowl, as they found themselves banished to the hen run so they do not foul the grain.

Our old combine has behaved beautifully. She needed some new belts to keep her running smoothly and regular doses of grease gun cartridges to ease her aching joints. But when required, she has rattled into action. Not all the tackle has come through unscathed. A nasty clunk in the gearbox of one tractor and rather ominous diagnostic work by a visiting mechanic has sounded the death knell for the tractor running the corn drier. A replacement is coming. Profits from the harvest already spent before the money is in the bank.

Although most of the corn has stood up well to the ravages of wind and rain earlier on in the season, the yield is down as there has been insufficient sunshine to swell the ears of wheat. As yet I have not heard any national figures for harvest, but although our corn has come through disease free and is needing relatively little drying, weights are certainly lower than previous years. But the pantry is full for the cows' winter feed. Until John can see bins full of barley, silage clamp full, glistening black heaps of haylage bales and rows of golden green hay bundles, he cannot relax. The corn harvest is jam on the bread.

A contractor has now been booked to drill the rape. The rotation will put some fertility back into the soil. The contractor has a new Sumo drill that does the job in one sweep. Discs at the front to cut the trash and stubble, legs that go under the soil to loosen and allow for drainage and coulters that go deep into the soil where the moisture is to plant the seed. All John will have to do is roll the seed in and make sure that enough slug pellets go on to kill off the thousands of voracious molluscs that can devastate a crop by eating it faster than it can grow. Investigating less toxic baits such as metaldehyde, which can be harmful to domestic and wild animals, is leading farmers to look at iron phosphate-based baits as an alternative slug control. Unfortunately, stamping down hard on them is not a practical solution, even with John's size 12 boots.

25th

Geoff always comes in to help John at busy times and to look after the stock if we go away. Currently he has been juggling the twin jobs of tractoring corn back from the fields and putting loads through the dryer. As the corn dries, an amount of spilled cracked grains spill out from the edges of the dryer. This produces a fine coating (especially on my windows and washing) of dust and seeds in the vicinity. There is always a crowd of bantams, ducks (when they get out) and guinea fowl around the dryer. Plus, as Geoff spotted, a budgie. Geoff came into the house clutching the irate, irritated, pecky little bird. 'Have you got a bird cage?' he asked. A what? Why should I have one? I thought. But my granddaughter Jessica knew better. A relic from my hippy-dippy days in Morocco, a white and blue Tunisian birdcage languished in a loft room. She brought it down in triumph. Samuel, for that is now his name, hopped in, swung on the swing and started to chatter away happily. Whatever next?

26th

At home the farmhouse windows facing the farmyard are grimed with dust from the corn dryer. That is my excuse anyway and I am sticking to it. I hate cleaning windows at the best of times and am grateful for the genuine get-out clause of corn drying to salve my conscience about being so lazy. Gradually the harvest is coming home and the big shed filling up with golden heaps of corn. None has been sold yet. Unusual for us, as John would normally sell forward, but this year he plans to wait it out to see what world prices move to. It is a gamble, but then it always is. One friend who felt he had missed out last backend when there was no market for his hay, absolutely cleaned up when spring/summer was late. Everyone had had to keep their stock inside for longer, and there was an intense demand for hay.

27th

Today saw us selling lambs again. The take-up in the weather has proved beneficial to their condition and John felt we had enough lambs ready to fill a trailer for market. We cannot have been the only farmers holding back. The market has been persistent in phoning to ask if we have any lambs to sell, as very few were booked in. Probably been a large number of lambs in today as everyone will have hoped for a good price after those calls. And because of that, prices will be down accordingly. Nothing like being an optimist. John is still uncertain as to whether to keep our Charollais tups. He has not been happy with the conformation of the lambs this year, although the weather has not helped them thrive. Perhaps it is unfair to make a judgement, given the appallingly wet spring and early summer we had. When we changed to Texel tups from Suffolks he was the same. He just takes time to adjust to something different, and the lambs we have sold did well.

28th

Against all the normal odds that face farming, we finished harvest. Everywhere you look are bare fields and large round bales of straw. Fantastic, especially as wheat and straw are such a good price. Even better, we had no major breakdowns with the combine. Almost unheard of. It has gone back into the shed with a chestful of medals for long service and good conduct. But we are behind with making hay. We have had a go today but some uncharitable rain has so far put a literal damper on getting baled. Hopefully it will not be too long.

29th

Approaching combining and haymaking is tackled in different ways by our neighbours. One only employs contractors who come in with the latest kit, but at a time which suits them, rather than their client. After all, they may have three or four farmers all ready to go at the same time and only one machine to go out. Then we have another friend who has just invested in a mega secondhand combine that still cost thousands. Huge (to us who have only a 14ft header) 30ft header and all the gear one could wish for in satellite tracking, etc., etc. But there has been a problem. And it has taken three call-outs and three sets of laptops to sort out that the reason the corn was all dropping out the bottom of the combine was because the stone trap was not working properly. Our stone trap, which is located behind the combine bed and collects any stones that are picked up by the rotating blades and feeder, can be emptied by John operating a lever that ejects the stones. Alternatively, it can be emptied manually. This mega combine had an automatic ejector, but unfortunately was automatically ejecting the corn as well as stones. So for this season, and the next few I imagine, we will stick with our combine's relative Stone Age technology that does not have a problem with real stones. John can, with occasional assistance, service the machine himself. As we have had the combine for many, many years from virtually new, he also knows most of its little idiosyncrasies. The ones he doesn't are discovered, and comprehensively linked to the machine's illegitimate parentage and . . . uselessness.

30th

The combination of wet weather and occasional sunshine has also bred an amazing horde of biting insects. A friend who used our downstairs loo last night, emerged frantically scratching his bottom, where he swore he had been bitten by a large mosquito lurking under the toilet seat. Just be thankful it was only your bum he bit, I told him as I rushed to spray the toilet with insect killer. It did mean that we spent the rest of the day checking the sheep for any sign of fly bite and maggots whilst we had them in a corral to worm the lambs.

31st

Decision time on the herd make-up next year. A number of old cows are going to go, and ten heifers that John was fattening up for the beef market are now to be served by the bull and come into the suckler herd. The eleventh heifer, however, will not join her sisters in the field. She had again somehow slipped through the net and had not been dehorned when young. Now she sports some rather wicked looking headgear and has unfortunately also quickly learned to bully the other heifers so she can be first into the barley trough. One of the older suckler cows also has horns and was a real nuisance over winter when at the silage face. She knew the other cows would get out of the way if she gave them a swift jab, and although no damage was caused, John was especially fearful that one of the calves might be harmed. She too is bound for market once her calf is weaned.

September

1st

We have been so lucky. Pressed on and harvested all the remaining wheat. In the end John was working till nearly midnight, with failed lights on the combine, just to make sure all the crops were under cover and out of the field before the rain, once more, fell and drowned everything. Some of our neighbours who use our equipment to test the moisture of their wheat tut-tutted when John started to combine. 'I'd wait a bit,' one said. 'The weather is bound to take up.' Well, it didn't. Well, not much, but fortunately the windows of opportunity that we worked in were dry. Normally, at this time in September, we would be starting to work the land and get ready for drilling next year's crop. This year, however, the land is still too wet to even think about it. When I walked the dogs yesterday evening as we went for our daily blackberry-gathering expedition, great puddles still stretched across the fields. Fortunately our corn did not come in too wet and has not required a lot of drying. The yield has been good as well, so with some of the corn sold forward at a reasonably strong price, the first part of the harvest payback is under way. But, and there is always a but, the merchants, as usual, are trying to talk the price down. That won't stop everyone saying the price of bread is too high. They always do at this time of the year.

2nd

Today I felt our bantam hen's chicks could manage the big wide world of the foldyard without the protection of their wire pen and with the guardianship of their fierce mum. There are quite a number of hazards the chicks have to face. Half-grown hungry kittens, enthusiastic dogs keen to retrieve anything with feathers, and George, son of one of our previous Labradors, Meg, on one of his many visits while his owners go on holiday. George is a dog who has accustomed himself well to a changing lifestyle. When at home, a solitary pet, he has the run of a range of classic cars and even the possibility of going aloft in his owners' plane. At the farm he has to settle for a ride in a twenty-year-old Land Rover with our motley gang. From his yelps of joy as he jumps out of the Bentley and into the back of our battered vehicle, I think I know which one he prefers. It has been raining hard today and all the dogs prefer the Land Rover to their kennels in such weather. They lie side by side, in the back with the door open, noses just tipped over the edge, surveying the downpour. The rain has freshened the grass and will, we hope, germinate the barley and wheat seed. The sheep in particular had nearly eaten up. We were driven to desperate measures when the tups and a motley assortment of old ewes and lambs that live in the paddock behind our house, had been left with barely a bite between them and needed supplementary feeding each day. They were virtually strangling themselves by trying to reach through the wire netting surrounding the area at the back of our house, to grab a mouthful of lush grass from our overgrown lawn. This garden was stolen from the paddock because we needed a safe area for our grandchildren to play when they visited the farm. With no visitors this weekend and therefore no need of a grandchild-restricted area, never mind a livestock one, the fence has been pulled back behind the house, and the sheep flocked in. I thought the sheep would ignore the play equipment we have in the garden. Not so. Within minutes, the slide on the climbing frame was being investigated. To the extent that two of the bigger lambs were to be seen curiously gazing out from the castle structure on the climbing frame. A quick spring down onto the ground, a trot up the slide. Hey presto. A real 'King of the Castle' game. We shooed them out at night time and counted the cost of the incursion in a host of sheep droppings all over the patio and lawn. Well, it will fertilise the grass, if not the paving stones.

3rd

Brought in a specialist tyre company this morning to pump the front tyres of our biggest four-wheel-drive tractor full of water. When this extra traction is combined with a full set of weights on the front of the machine, John hopes to have gained enough traction to start mole ploughing, a method using a bullet-shaped plough that drags through the ground to create a channel to let water drain away. This field is currently very wet, and without extra help, the tractor might just skid on top of the clay soil, churning up the field and making it almost impossible to make a decent job of ploughing, even when the land dries up. A contractor is coming in to help with the ploughing. The horsepower on their vehicle is greater than ours, and they pull a five-furrow plough. We pull a four-furrow implement with less oomph in our big tractor. The plan is for John to start mole ploughing the fields ahead of the plough. The 'tunnel' created by the mole plough supports the main drains in the field, allowing water to drain off faster and helping to aerate the soil. We are also waiting for another contractor to come in and clear a dike running alongside one of the big blocks of land that backs onto a main drainage board dike. The only equipment we have on the farm to clear out dikes is a diking shovel. Not mechanically driven. Man powered. John has cleaned the sludge out as best he can with the spade but it needs a proper clean-out and relevelling to get water away from the field more effectively. He actually enjoys diking and has a style I liken to demented grave digging. All you see as John gets deeper into the dike is clods of muck and old vegetation sailing into the air over the edge of the ditch. But I have not yet heard any soliloquies, Hamlet style. Forty acres of adjoining land next to this dike is still covered with straw waiting to be baled. John sold the straw to a neighbouring dairy farmer for baling over a fortnight ago, and he has not been able to get on because much of the field is water logged. It was a miracle the wheat was harvested before it rained. Hopefully, relevelling the dike will get surface water flowing again, and once the straw is cleared, the land work can start there. On the plus side, even though much of our land work is on hold, we had the good fortune to sell some corn forward and get it away. Our combine might be getting on in years, but without it we would have had another wait for a contractor and, with the huge build-up in demand, been even further behind. The combine is actually going out on loan this week to a friend who has not been able to get hold of anyone to come in and harvest for them. And we have a dryer. Over the last week John has had several requests to buy it, although the bills for oil that it uses are astronomical. Still, it is cheaper than sending corn to dry at the merchant's.

4th

Contractors upgrading our lane are enchanted with all the farm animals. The tups especially welcome their leftover sandwiches. Should build up their strength for their big autumn encounter with the sheep. Tups, not contractors. What were you thinking? This weekend we will be weaning all the lambs, and any noises in the night will be coming from the remaining lambs kicking up a huge fuss after being taken from their mums. The mums meanwhile rarely make a fuss for long once free of being butted and suckled by their bullying offspring. Roll on romance is all they care about. Twenty of the lambs are already fit for market as they are a good weight. The lambs we sent in last week were actually too heavy, but they got a good price all the same. Several cull ewes also made the trip. One or two had problems with their bag after summer mastitis and others had made the big mistake of being too independent minded. Not a good career decision for a ewe. Actually it is more logical than that. After making a management decision last year when lamb prices were so low that we almost went out of sheep altogether, John has been so impressed by the prices we are getting for lambs at market, that our flock numbers are to rise again. He plans to put the tups in with the ewes at an earlier date. Historically, with us, the tups are put to the ewes on Bonfire Night. Tastefully referred to as the Big Gang Bang. Last year they went in at the end of October and it worked well this year, with most of our lambs fit for market at a time when there was a good demand. Therefore weaning the lambs at an earlier date will give the ewes a chance to be in good fettle for tupping. So on Friday I am booked for a big day out at a sheep sale to buy some gimmers to boost flock numbers and rejuvenate the flock. I can see it all. Every other sheep farmer in the area will have thought the same thing and prices will rocket. Guaranteed a grumbly husband all the way home.

5th

On the land, two days of sunshine saw every combine in the area that had not had a chance to get its wheat harvested, on the go. John started ploughing in one field and the contractor we had asked to come in went into another. Steve the contractor effortlessly chugged up and down the field, admittedly on the best land on the farm, and had it done in just over a day. John took over two to do the same-size field. Both of those fields had been mole ploughed and so the water had got away, but two of the biggest fields on the farm are still waiting to be cleared of straw and so no work can get started on those until the straw has been baled. In one field, baling had got started by the merchant who wanted it, but he left the bales in flat piles of eight, and subsequent rain soddened the straw so much that the bales are virtually ruined. And still in the field. Nothing at all has happened in another, and until then, John cannot get started there at all. Luckily we got hold of some seed barley, so as soon as the ploughed land has dried up enough to get the combination drill on, at least one field can be sown. The other ploughed field will be going in with field beans, but they can wait until later and there is still plenty of other land to start mole ploughing. When ploughing, Steve's job was easier because he had five furrows on his tractor. Although our big tractor normally pulls four furrows, John decided to drop one off to put less strain on the engine. That was the idea anyway at the start of the day. Four hours later, John sweating and cursing all the way, the back furrows reluctantly parted company with their companions. 'These bolts have never been off since I bought this plough ten years ago,' John swore. 'They're rusted in solid.' At least I think that's what he said. Sounded more like '***** bolts. They won't ***** move. The ***** things.' Not for delicate ears.

6th

The shed is full of straw. Big round bales tower under the roof of the shed. John managed to get them all home in a frantic day of travelling back and forth. The hens are getting vertigo just deciding where to fly up to find that secret nest. Fortunately they abandon the idea once they have fluttered back down to the ground after failed frenzied attempts to get a foothold on the sheer cliffs of the stacks of bales. If they did manage to ascend to the top and hatch a brood, I cannot see how they would get the chicks down. They would be lost down a straw chasm. Guinea fowl keet wars are in full swing. As each brood starts to reach maturity, they become more feisty with the older keets, who then see it as their role to keep the young 'uns in order. And then the bantie foster mums join in too. It is Armageddon out there. Plus potential keetnapping. A bantie with four guinea fowl keets is extremely envious of another hen who has charge of sixteen keets in her pen. Mrs No. 4 perches with her little brood on top of Mrs No. 16's pen and hurls bantie abuse at her rival. Oh, the tranquillity of rural life. Another part of the shed's interior resembles a tightly packed box of bricks. Here it is full almost up to the eaves with mini Heston bales. They measure approximately 8ft long and are 2ft wide and deep and tower over you when picking a narrow passage to negotiate to reach the back paddock and hen house. The dogs, whose kennels were previously at the front of the shed and could observe all the goings-on in the yard, are now stuck right at the back and rather overwhelmed by the towers of straw. 'You'll be lovely and warm in the winter,' I tell them. But I don't think they appreciate that, as their view of all the comings and goings is now very restricted at night. Fortunately they spend all day in the yard, house porch or back of the Land Rover, so they are not really put out. And just think of those cosy nights to come.

7th

Returned tonight from a sheep fair with a trailer load of Mule shearlings to join the flock. Born about eighteen months ago, the shearlings are already big sheep. Mules are a cross between a Swaledale ewe and Blue Leicester tup. That produces a good mother with plenty of milk who, when running with our Texel and Suffolk tups, gives us a good crop of lambs. John was delighted at the prices he paid, but recognised that this meant a poorer return for the breeders. Several pens of gimmers and shearlings were withdrawn when the prices did not reach the expected premiums. At one stage we felt quite panicky that the pens we had our eyes on would not get to go through the ring, but eventually they did. Nonetheless, several other pens that John was interested in went back home. So much effort goes into the presentation of these sheep. Some owners dip their sheep prior to the sale in a coloured dip to brighten them for the sale. Others wash their sheep's heads and trim the wool round their necks for a cosmetic makeover. If any tups are for sale, the owners trim and 'square' them so that the backs appear flattened to give an illusion of breadth in the animal. Once home with the flock, the new sheep tend to stick together for a few weeks. When you go round the sheep in the morning, the newcomers stand in a group as if still uncertain of the others. It will change.

8th

Been a disturbing week with police, farm thefts and threats of violence in the neighbourhood. Just when you think you live in a quiet rural backwater where nothing ever happens, things do. There are dodgy characters frequently turning up in our yard. Mostly friends but just occasionally folk you know are up to no good. Best seen off as quickly and tersely as possible. Preferably whilst trying to restrain an apparently ferocious dog who looks set to tear them to pieces but who in actuality just wants to check if they have any chocolate on them. With agricultural and motor vehicles and anything not nailed down being taken, our security has been stepped up. But this weekend was real police interceptor stuff, with a neighbour's vehicle being rammed as the intruders tried to escape and eventually being hemmed in by farmers summoned by phone to catch up and block in the villains. And then wait for the police to turn up and arrest them. Villains, not farmers. It all leads to a very edgy night's sleep. Every bark or flicker of security light at night has John up and out of bed. He had gone out to the latest incident with a neighbour, as at the time the round-robin security call-up came he was out ploughing and had to be picked up to add some muscle to the team.

9th

Clouds of crane flies rise up before us as John and I walk the newly sown grasses on the field behind our wood. 'I'd much rather them be here than in our bedroom at night,' I commented to John. I seem to spend a good half hour before bedtime swatting Daddy Long Legs, the crane fly's common name, who have been drawn to our bedside lights through the open windows. Just when I think I have massacred every last one, another one appears, bent on a suicide mission on the lightbulb, or a swifter end from my fly swat. I would not mind so much if they minded their own business and ignored us, but they also seem to enjoy alighting in my hair, crash landing on my face or skidding over my shoulders. And that's after lights out. 'In another way, I'd prefer them in the bedroom than on the grasses,' John said. 'I'll have to spray for leather jackets soon, because the crane flies will be laying eggs in the soil and the emerging leather jackets will just strip this new grass bare.' Our friend who has a golf course has just had to do the same thing, as grass for the new greens is proving far too tasty for the myriad leather jackets. After spraying with insecticide, the greens looked more like a battlefield than a golf course.

10th

'I've got that ewe's number,' John said between gritted teeth, malevolently gazing at an innocent-looking sheep grazing with her lambs in the home paddock. Not a pretty sight, you will envisage: teeth clenched, glaring eyes. An improvement though on the manic expression that has been the most recent feature of his physiognomy as he chases said sheep down the lanes round the farm, out of neighbours' gardens, and at one time, their garage. This particular ewe, who was bought in with a penful of shearlings the previous autumn, has a hankering for pastures new. Wherever she may be. I have lost count of the number of people who have helpfully called at the back door to tell us that we had lambs out on the road and was only thankful that no accident occurred. To cars or people, that is. A painful glancing blow from a car might have served the ewe right and taught her a lesson. Not likely, however. You could not say she is brainless, as she evidently has a laser detector for a brain, that can seek out the weakest point in any hedge and push through it. This has been compounded by the fact that our roadside verges have been grazed by a number of travellers' horses, which have eaten out the backs of the hedges and reduced their stock-proofing abilities. To prevent any more escapes, John has reinforced the hedges with a roll of hedge back wire netting. It is only a couple of feet high, but fits into the bottom of the hedge and stops up the gaps. But, just to make sure, he brought the ewe home to the house paddock where she could graze alongside the tups. Close proximity to all those male hormones is not to her liking, however, and when the men from the electricity board came to trim back branches off trees that were threatening the electricity wires, she saw her chance. The men failed to clear up the branches they had cut down, and conveniently left them across barbed wire stretched across the top of the field fence, providing a handy scrabbling passage across the barbed wire and out onto the road. So drastic action has been taken. Her two lambs have gone to join fifty of the smallest lambs from the flock that have been segregated and weaned from the main flock, to graze in a hay field that has plenty of grass for them. They have all been wormed, dagged out and had the wool from their back legs shorn off. This is because with the very lush grass in the field, they would soon make a total clarty mess of their rear ends, and be very tempting targets for flies, and thus maggots. The other bigger lambs have been left on their mums, as John is starting to take a weekly draw off the flock for market of about twenty lambs at a time. The weaned lambs will initially lose ground, but the lambs that are still having the occasional suckle continue to put on weight. Mrs Ewe is now in splendid isolation from the flock and in with the cows and calves, whose field is, as much as humanely possible, totally escape proof. Mr Bull does not have a lot of interest in her womanly, woolly ways, so she is safe from harassment for the moment. However, not so long now until tupping time, when John hopes her hormones will take over and she will welcome a rampant ram. We'll see. She is probably compiling an escape plan even as I write . . .

11th

The big field that John was hoping to let out for grass, and then started to think might have to go down to beans as nothing was happening, is suddenly on the agenda again for grass. John had determined that the contract was not going to be taken up. He planned to go in the next day with the mole plough to lift the land prior to ploughing. And then the farmer who had indicated he was putting it down to grass but had previously made no move to act on the agreement . . . did. Rolled into the field in a big 200-plus horsepower tractor with a new Trio machine on the back. This is a machine with a combination of tines/legs that lift the soil, then a crumbler that knocks the clods out and then discs that really slice everything up. This Trio made mincemeat of the field in just a day and it will only need to be passed over with a combination drill full of grass seed to be finished. 'It would have taken me a fortnight to get that field ready,' John said. Just shows what can be done with big machines and really up-to-date tackle.

12th

I remember being told long ago that the sound of a baby's cry is pitched at a certain level to make sure that it is attended to promptly. The urgency of the cry is impossible to ignore. My new guinea fowl chicks have learnt the same trick. They are bionic. Keep getting out of the tiniest gaps in their pen and then make the most almighty peep peeping row to make sure that I, not the broody hen who hatched them and is stuck inside, race across the yard to pop them back into warmth and safety. From no luck at all at the beginning of the season with hatching guinea fowl, we have now got three clutches of keets and a fourth imminent. I love having guinea fowl around the farm. They are great characters. Brilliant watchdogs (except of course they are not dogs), they lay fantastic eggs and finally taste delicious. Their one drawback to us, but fail-safe mechanism for them, is when it comes to dispatch time, you have a difficult time catching them. Currently I know where the ten adults who are my main laying flock have their nest. I don't always and even now I have perhaps not found their main nest. Guinea fowl tend to all lay in the same nest, but I think a few are laying away. I am gathering up quite a few eggs for our use every day but do not expect to much longer. The season lasts from end of March until late September, so we are on borrowed time. Guinea fowl prefer a big patch of nettles (of which we have a lot), and my arms are regularly stung as I filch the daily treasure trove. Popular myth is that if guinea fowl see you taking their eggs, they will move the nest, but so far, they have not. My routine for egg collection is leaving it until I return from taking John his afternoon drinkings at about five o'clock. By then the guinea fowl are scattered in a distant field and nowhere near their nest. I drive close to the nest in the Land Rover and so disguise my approach. It's all very covert. I should have been a spy. The other reason I use the Land Rover is that that way I know where the dogs are and they don't spot where the nest is. Two dogs are safely shut in the back, but Millie, our Jack Russell, does not deign to travel in the rear. She lurks under the Land Rover until the others are in and then waits for you to open the driver's door. She scales the side of the driver's seat and takes up her position on the passenger side, paws balanced on the front shelf, on the lookout for rabbits. If you fail to have shut the driver window and she does spot a bunny, she is straight across your lap and out the window. Makes for exciting driving off road.

13th

Motherly love has just earned John a bad back and trapped nerve in his leg. This week the routine tests for tuberculosis are due to take place and the vet has notified us that he will be on the farm tomorrow. We are to have the herd in the corral, all numbered and correct with ear tags in place. Except that one had just ripped its tag out yesterday morning. John had spotted it on his walk round the herd and knew he had to get it put back in straight away, or risk compromising his cross compliance. Cows (and sheep) get their ear tags torn out in a variety of ways, and the office boys and girls of DEFRA, who are so keen that everything is neatly numbered, have no idea how difficult and dangerous it can be to get a suckler cow into a crush to stick a large painful object into its ear. Cows just do not go for it. Especially when it has happened more than once. Slipping and sliding in the mud and trying to dodge the cow, which was convinced that some desperate harm was due to come to her offspring if she was parted from it for just a minute, John fell and wrenched his back. 'I felt this dreadful jarring in my lower spine and then this excruciating pain in my leg.' Eventually, despite the agony, he got the cow in the crush, tagged her up, and then limped home, grey with pain. Tonight he has been to a physiotherapist and dosed up with painkillers. A lot of TLC has been prescribed.

14th

The dogs and I are out every night on a mission to get scratched, stung and prickled whilst brambling. The blackberries are luscious this year and I eat as many as I put in my basket. It is a relaxing end to what has been a busy day. The herd has just had its routine brucellosis test. John had collected the cattle in the corral area where the crush and walkway can be sited. The cattle are used to coming into this collecting area, as they have to walk through to pass from one grazing field to another, but it is when the gates are shut at both ends that the fun starts. There is always one cow that causes trouble. In this case an old girl who had seen this carry-on before and was going to make sure she slipped out before anyone had the chance to shave some hair off her neck and give her a quick jab for a reactor test. Every time a cow was let out into the adjoining field from the crush after her jab, she was pushing and shoving to get through the gate. Due to John's back injury yesterday, I was in charge of shutting and opening the gate and preventing mass breakouts. The young vet who was carrying out the test sweated buckets. He was clad in a rather fearsome protective set of garments, suitable for working in a plague zone where he might come into contact with airborne infectious spores. I exaggerate, of course, but he was certainly wearing enough rubberwear to keep any fetishist happy. As the cow numbers dwindled and even the bull had been through for his jab, Mrs Houdini was still prancing around out of reach and trying to push her way to freedom. Silly girl, though. She thought she had spotted an alternative route out of the corral down the walkway. She had. Straight into the crush. The vet will be back later in the week to see if any of the herd has reacted, and if they have, it will be very bad news. But the herd is closed and as far as we know there is no badger transmission of the disease on the farm. Fingers crossed and more painkillers for John.

15th

A small miracle has occurred. The guinea fowl eggs I gave up for duds, yet still out of sheer cussedness decided to put in the incubator and chance it, are hatching. At this very minute little cracks in the eggs are spreading out and if I listen carefully, faint cheep cheeps can be heard. The story goes that one of my Speckledy hens went into broody mode. She insisted on hogging a prime nest in the hen house, the main one that the guinea fowls favoured, and generally upsetting the whole status quo and pecking order in the fowl world. We fell into a daily ritual in which I would throw her off the nest and as soon as my back was decently turned, she would return. Eventually, just over five weeks ago, I decided to let her sit a clutch of eggs in a place of my choosing. A nice hen des res in an old pet carrier (very useful things for broody hens) in a quiet place in the barn. She hated it. Refused to sit. Cackled and carried on, kicked the eggs about. Back to the hen house. Broody again. Back to the des res. Same carry-on. By now she was tempting chicken casserole time, but in what I thought was a cunning move I let her sit a clutch of eggs in the hen house, but marked all of the dozen guinea fowl eggs that I put under her. On a daily basis I lifted her up and removed any eggs that other hens and guinea fowl laid under her. I had great hopes for the hen. Unfounded. Nothing hatched at all on the due date. I gave her extra time. The guinea fowl clearly decided it was a bad place to be and have abandoned the hen hut. Still nothing. Searching on the Internet, I found a man who had day-old chicks and contacted him. No day-old hen chicks, but he had six-day-old guinea fowl chicks. Result. The hen hated them. Trampled one to death. We put them in with some week-old ducklings. They trampled another one. Next into their own run with water and feed. And instantly drowned one. Now three chicks (and one is distinctly dodgy) shelter under a heat lamp and the hen is out on the street. But as a last chance I put the guinea fowl eggs in the incubator. 'Switch it off and throw them out,' John said. 'They won't be any good now.' But once more I am right. As usual.

16th

Back in June John rescued a nest of partridge eggs that had been disturbed by a stray dog in one of our fields. We successfully hatched the eggs off in the incubator and returned the chicks to the place where their nest had originally been. Albeit in a release pen to protect them from the large number of hungry foxes we seem to have acquired in this area and which represent the main threat to the chicks' survival. One of the numerous reps who turn up in the yard is a Game Conservancy volunteer. When he heard what we were doing with the partridge chicks, and that we were not returning them simply to take a pot shot at them over winter, he mentioned that the covey might well be adopted by a barren pair of adult partridges. And he was right. We have a proud adoptive Mum and Dad shepherding their covey of juveniles around. It is a lovely sight to see all the covey whirring over the hedges when disturbed. They have been living in one of the many beetle banks established around our arable fields. Because it has taken so long to harvest the last field of wheat, and much of the crop has started to shed, the Partridge Family (can't help it) have taken to living in amongst the standing corn. Subsequently when we actually got into the field yesterday to cut the corn, we were treated to numerous sightings of the covey. As it happens each midsummer, John orders about twenty-five grey partridges to put down in a small wooded area on the farm we call Jack's Plantation. The wood stands at the hub of several fields and provides a warm, sheltered environment for wildlife over winter, especially birds. The wood was named after our black Labrador of the time, Jack, three gundogs ago. How time flies. Again these birds are not meant for shooting, just for the pleasure of seeing them on the farm and hoping they form the nucleus of a breeding colony. Some stay, most wander off, but around the farm we have seen several thriving coveys this summer. John releases the partridges into a holding pen, and after a few weeks, when they have accustomed themselves to the sounds, smells, etc. of the area, lets about half of them out, whilst retaining the feeder within the pen. Plus the rest of their friends, to hold their interest. The released birds this year are particularly wild and flighty and at first John thought we did not stand a chance of holding any of them. But he now feels confident to

'Dive for cover, guys. He's planning another shoot!'

release the rest of the birds and then hope they will stay near the feeder, and perhaps the covey with the adult partridges. It does provide him with the excuse to go out at night checking for marauding foxes. This seems to have suddenly become a popular night-time activity in the area with fields all empty of crops. You would think a host of UFOs was descending on the locality with lights criss-crossing the land from lampers and their powerful torches and mounted headlights on the top of pick-up trucks.

17th

A pile of field beans on the grain shed floor spells out the last of the harvest. John had brought in a contractor today rather than use and abuse our own combine. Harvesting field beans can be a tough job, and not worth risking an expensive repair job on our own machine at the very end of the season. There has been a lot of tackle at work today on the farm, as contractors were also in to bale the last of the wheat straw. John got drilled up on another field of corn, Geoff worked behind the straw contractors to bring the bales home, the giant combine remorselessly gathered in the beans in front and spewed out the chopped-up stalks behind, and I was back-up for leading beans. All systems go.

18th

The upturn in the weather has enabled ploughing and drilling to move quickly. The field John is currently working in has been grass for hay and grazing for seven or eight years and should produce a good wheat crop next year. We pulled in contractors with a big reversible six-furrow plough behind a stonking great tractor to get the job done quickly for us, as the shooting season looms and no time can be wasted. Every time I ask a favour, I am solemnly lectured on how much work John is looking at. Every time another invitation drops tantalisingly from the phone, however, I suddenly hear that said hard-working farmer is amazingly free on the day in question. John followed the contractor with his power harrow, breaking the soil down for a good seed bed whilst it was still friable after the ploughing had buried all the grass and rubbish left after he sprayed the field off and disced it. The soil was fractured right down to the depth of the ploughing and it looked like sugar cubes. 'Frost mould,' the contractor said. Apparently the freezing and then defrosting of the soil affects the soil composition. He said he had seen it before in autumn following a very hard frost the previous winter. Whatever, the seed bed and soil look good.

The contractor we use has worked very hard to build his own business and we try to give him work whenever we can. At first we did not think he could get to us until midweek, and John was chafing at the bit to get on with drilling up. Then Martin, the contractor, rang. 'I can come today,' he said. 'Can you tell me which side he wants to start on in the field?' This is because even though it was some years ago that the field was last ploughed, there would still be the remains of a furrow and he would need to start from there to turn the soil back the other way and prevent it building up into a ridge. I couldn't tell him what John wanted because I couldn't find John. Despite my buying him a mobile phone, he consistently leaves it on the office desk and disappears without it. I spent half an hour chasing around fields and could not see him anywhere. Thick mist did not help and whenever I got out of the Land Rover and tried to listen, the continuous yelping of enthusiastic dogs who thought I had taken them out for a walk did not help. 'You'll just have to use your professional judgement,' I eventually told Martin. 'It's his own fault if it gets ploughed the wrong way. He should either let me know where he is going or take his phone with him.' 'Did I get you into trouble?' Martin apparently asked an unrepentant John later in the morning when they eventually met up. 'No more than usual,' was the reply. And the phone is still on the desk now.

19th

Several loads of wheat have already been sold but the other big grain shed is full. John has ordered a new grain trailer and I wasn't even consulted. He seems to have gone a little light-headed this year, what with draining fields as well. But we still have the same twenty-year-old Land Rover. I can remember writing an article about how modern it seemed with its radio and tape player. Both no longer working. If finances ever do permit the unwanted extravagance of a new vehicle for John, we may keep the current Land Rover for limited use, a taxation class where it is used solely for agricultural purposes and is only used on public roads to go between areas of land owned by the same person and within a defined distance. That would suit us just fine. Till then, the Land Rover we have has to keep going.

20th

At the end of June I raided, with accomplices, our walnut tree for immature walnuts to pickle. This was seen as a heinous crime, but as I pointed out to John, the squirrels would be bound to take their share in the autumn. I was merely pre-empting the theft, and I would at least have the benefit of eating some. They are now pickled to perfection. Delicious. But the squirrels are gathering to raid the now almost mature walnut crop. Cue dramatic music. What they have discovered is a very cunning approach strategy. Some aged squirrel must have advised against the usual mad dash from the big willow tree across open ground and recommended a concealed dash through the hedge, up behind the duck hut, onto the duck hut roof, finishing with a leap straight into the walnut tree branches. It is virtually foolproof and John is still trying to work out a safe angle of shot to stop the thieves in their tracks/leap/scuttle. Currently the squirrels are winning and the walnut harvest is diminishing. What a good job, I tell John, that I took some for pickling earlier. No consolation for his losses, I am afraid.

21st

I am plummed up. I have spent all day cooking and freezing plums, making pies, crumbles and chutney. I commented to John on the lack of wasps in the orchard and the perfection of the fruit on the trees. Similarly the grapes in the porch are magnificent, sweet and plump, and again no ravages by wasps. I had set a number of pop-bottle wasp traps in the fruit trees, but even they had very few victims drowned in the syrup. The mystery was solved when John came to spread the muck heap. He had hired a big muck spreader for the day to get rid of the giant muck heap that had been there since the foldyards were cleaned out at the end of winter. 'There were at least five nests in the heap,' John said. 'And I haven't seen a wasp on the farm since I destroyed the nests when I spread the muck. Mind you, I had to keep the windows on the tractor tight shut. The wasps weren't best pleased.'

22nd

We've just received a letter from the National Grid telling us that they want to come onto our land to inspect two of their pylons. They have the right to do this, but are responsible for any damage they may cause, however inadvertently. What is interesting in the letter is the addition of a line or two about biosecurity to pre-empt any re-emergence of the foot and mouth outbreak. They state, quite rightly, that they wish to observe any precautions we take. Those farms that encourage public access must continually be alert to biosecurity. I have considered it diversification, but any ideas I have floated past John get short shrift. What with all these health spas and keep-fit classes, we could offer a very nice line in mucking out sheds, speed walking a field whilst roguing it for wild oats, or power pulling noxious weeds such as ragwort in the two-metre strips around an arable field. Lifting the weights on the front of the tractor or carrying a four-stone bag of corn up and down the granary steps would soon emphasise an office worker's six pack. And we could reutilise our old sheep-dipping trough by offering a line in mud baths. Haylage wraps might be a superior offering to seaweed, and silage might have beneficial properties for the skin. Or maybe not. And then there is the livestock. The agricultural equivalent of a zoo. Bring anyone into the farmyard who is not used to being close up and familiar with animals and they just coo over a scrawny old bantam, go all Beatrix Potter over the ducks and geese, totally unrealistic about the perceived anthropomorphic qualities of cows and sheep, and fail totally to make the connection between that nice juicy steak and the bullock 'giving them a kiss' through the foldyard gates. We could at this moment add the zest of danger to a farm trip. One of our tups is turning out to be rather aggressive, especially as tupping time approaches. He has honed his gladiatorial skills on fights over possession of the apple peelings. Because I am addicted to stuffing as many apples into the freezer as space will permit, a mass of apple peelings and cores are constantly being thrown into the tups' paddock. The fights are incredible. We could pitch a visitor against the tup for the honour of an apple. Perhaps even provide them with a sack of apple peelings; the smell alone would be enough to tip our tup into a frenzy.

23rd

Tragedy. One extra beak we won't have to feed this winter. Bertie, the budgie that we bought to keep Samuel company. Samuel is the budgie we found in the yard. He has committed budgicide. Repeated swift jabs to poor Bertie's head. The aviary we bought Bertie from assured me that two male budgies would be companionable. Little did they know we harboured a psychopathic budgie. Or as one friend said after surveying the corpse of Bertie and hearing the triumphant chattering of Samuel as he tucked into a fresh tray of budgie seed . . . a cereal killer.

24th

After searching around I have once more located the nest of my errant guinea fowl. Only to find four of the more mature guinea fowl all perched precariously on top of a huge pile of eggs. After raiding the nest for some of the eggs, I have left them to have a go at hatching some keets out. They look very vulnerable sat in the middle of a large nettle patch and would provide a very tasty mouthful for a fox. So for once I am encouraging the night-time excursions of the lampers.

25th

The dry weather has been a huge bonus for landwork. Last week John finished off a roadside field (important to get them right, as they are in public view) that last year never even got to the point of being ploughed. It lay fallow all winter because of the wet autumn conditions. Another field was power harrowed yesterday and ready for drilling, and several others are fit to go. To rotate grazing and crop production, a current year's barley field is now already covered in a green dusting of emergent

'There's only room for one bird in this budgie cage . . .
and it's going to be me!'

grass as it goes back for the sheep and cattle to use. And today's job is to spray off a grass field that will go down to wheat. Much of the block of land across from the farm is down to permanent pasture for stock, but other fields away from the farmhouse and yards are constantly being jiggled about to make sure that none of the land goes stale and unproductive. For example, the field that has just been power harrowed harvested beans this year. Beans are a leguminous crop and enrich the soil. The plan is, and the bags of seed wheat in the yard proclaim, that next year the field will be wheat.

26th

As we speed into autumn John is starting to provide extra feed for the cattle outside. A neighbour asked him to 'tidy up' a grass field and let him have the hay he made. It was only a small field but the bales are providing a useful back-up for the stock. Plus I do not think there is any spare space to store them under the big barns. It is a very comforting feeling to see that bulging silage clamp, gleaming bales of straw and hay and overflowing barley bins. A nice full pantry for winter feeding. At least John won't have to resort to the measures that it is reported farmers in Uttar Pradesh, India have been led to. There, acute crop failures had left farmers with no feed for animals, no money to buy replacement seed and nothing to live on. So their wives were being sold to money lenders to settle debts. 'Don't worry, love,' John said to me after I read the article out to him in shocked tones. 'I won't. They'd never be able to afford you.'

27th

Our latest guinea fowl chicks (keets) are now housed in the big foldyard. Their pen is squeezed in, as most of the space is taken up with big bales of hay and straw and the pile of field beans. After the keets' first few weeks in the grain shed, it must be a frightening experience to suddenly be exposed to noisy dogs, lowing cattle and raucous bigger guinea fowl. The confusion (collective term) of guinea fowl hens is still broody and sat in a nettle patch bravely trying to hatch out an enormous pile of eggs between them. As fast as I try to make the pile more manageable, more guinea fowl hens lay underneath. To add insult to injury, a neighbour who had kindly removed a branch from a tree that had been broken in the high winds and was overhanging the lane, dropped the offending branch virtually smack on top of the nest. The hens clattered off the nest, cackling and creating as if all of us were intent on murdering them, but they have finally returned to the nest and the branch may actually be doing them a favour as they are now almost concealed from view, and sheltered from any excesses of the weather. The Aylesbury ducks we reared are now well on, eating an enormous quantity of grain. Our first clutch of guinea fowl, hatched in May, are almost mature enough for the table, but I like to see them so much around the yard, I doubt if they are going to make it onto a plate. I have developed a real soft spot for these quirky little birds. They eat bugs and pests, do not scrat like the hens, cheep and squawk away and make the most marvellous guard dogs for the farm ever. No-one or thing comes through the gate, near the hen house, into the yard without them starting panicking at the top of their decibel range. Fantastic. In the greenhouse and orchard I am now overwhelmed by produce. I am not much of a gardener but can manage a grow bag. Friends and relatives go away bowed down under the weight of tomatoes, plums, apples, peppers and chillies. The season of mists and mellow fruitfulness is currently translating into a time of pans of plums and apples and chilli and tomato sauce, but not all at the same time, bubbling away on top of or in the cooker prior to frosty immersion in the freezer. Probably, knowing me, never to be seen again until I am looking for something else. I am always retrieving interesting, shrivelled and frostbitten bags with mysterious contents from several years back. This year's vow? To write on the bag/container exactly what it is that I am freezing. I have it off to a fine art with pies. A friend gave me a set of alphabet pastry cutters. Now pies display whether they are plum, apple, mince, chicken, etc., and John is not left to eat a meat and potato pie for pudding, when he was expecting something fruity instead.

29th

The crane fly problem persists on the grasses. After consulting the experts, John has found that he has to wait until next spring before he can spray for leather jackets. Fair enough. You do have to give them time to hatch out after the crane flies have laid their eggs. Apparently until then the leather jackets do not pose any significant problem to newly sown pasture. They eat the roots of the grass and can pose a very expensive threat to grass. A neighbour lost an entire field of new grass to leatherjackets. He had to bear the cost of not only reseeding the field, but also waiting until the crop grew again, and paying for silage crop for winter feed that he had hoped would be home grown. Hope the experts know what they are doing. However, John has not been frustrated in his desire to spray something this week that threatens his crops or pasture. He has just returned from spraying the newly sown barley field for black grass. The job had to be completed now (and I mean now) before the barley emerged. The field was sown at the end of last week, and as it rained last night, the task was on the top of the emergency must-do list. Black grass is becoming a real problem and would compete with the barley, and smother it, if it was not dealt with at this early stage of the crop's growth. As it would also reduce the crop's yield, seed before the barley was due to be combined and thus perpetuate the problem, the black grass had to go. No question. Moving the sheep to fresh grass yesterday re-emphasised the extent of the Daddy Long Legs plague: clouds of them erupted into the air as we moved the ewes to new grasses as part of the annual preparation for tupping time. Still some time off before their romantic encounters with our four tups, the ewes are in recovery mode from motherhood after weaning the last of the lambs a week or two ago. It kept all of the village awake for the night as John put the lambs in the house paddock and took the ewes over to the furthermost grass field on the farm on the night they were weaned. We just put our heads under the pillow and willed the lambs to shut up. They did eventually, at around three in the morning. It has been quite a long time since we actually walked the flock through our village, and a new experience for a young couple who have bought one of the few roadside cottages. From sale to conversion, the cottage has been transformed from a ramshackle two up /two down, to a very smart executive country residence, complete with detached garage and conservatory. But no gate or fencing fronting their property. I'm sure they appreciated the hasty trim and munch that the ewes delivered to their lawn and borders. When I do catch up with them (they are part of the band of village/city commuters who are moving in), I will explain how a natural lawn cut is so much more environmentally friendly than a petrol-driven lawn mower. Sheep emissions good. Petrol fumes bad.

30th

John is now back into the rhythm of mole ploughing, discing, ploughing, power harrowing and drilling. He is having a few problems today calibrating the drill in order to sow the correct rate of grass seed on a field that is going back for grazing as part of the crop rotation and grass management. A vital little metering device has fallen off the drill and so we are busy trying to convert kilograms to pounds, hectares to acres and then divide it all up by the number of passes he has made over the field power harrowing. After the first pass with the drill, he realised he was going to put too much seed on and not have enough left for the job. Now, after my mathematical skills have had a go at the problem, we think the seed is going to be spread too thinly and we'll have some left over. Where is a genius when you need one?

October

1st

John is replacing part of an old barn roof where the barley bins are kept. Each bin holds up to forty tons and is feed for the bullocks, heifers and young stock when they are housed inside. We had a problem last year when the snow blew under the old roof tiles and settled on the top of the open bins. Once the snow melted, the moisture and the heat from the herd who are in the foldyard next to the shed, germinated the top layer of barley. A bit of a waste and not what John wanted at all. The pantiles on the roof just rested on wooden laths. Over the years many of these had rotted and this had added to the weatherproofing issue with the roof. A few years ago Geoff had repaired half of the roof, but now it was John's turn to take up his ladders and get up there to finish the job off. I feel most uneasy about him working on the roof, but he has been very careful and systematic about the job. He has built himself a cushion of big bales around the base of the building so that he has something substantial to rest his ladders against, and, if necessary, break any falls. To do the job properly he is felting the underside of the roof so that even if the snow gets under this winter, the felt will keep the roof watertight.

2nd

A good piece of official news has arrived. The periodic blood test that the cattle had several weeks ago, has had a negative response to brucellosis. We can date the tests back to the recurrence of the problems that John has with his knee. It was when he was gathering the cattle up to go into the crush for the vet, that a cow caught his knee, then later when he slipped in some mud when gathering up the sheep, he went over on it again. As this is the same knee he had to have operated on for a torn cartilage, it is a worrying development. Mindful of the fact that John was limping badly and that the knee injury was partially down to the vet's reluctance to get up close and personal to the cows, the vet suggested that the check of the cows on their reaction to the test could be done without gathering them all up again into the corral. Instead the front of the Land Rover was chosen as the seat of operations. Literally. He sat with his binoculars and checked off each cow for any suspicion of a reaction to the test, in the shape of a raised lump. John checked them off against their ear number tags; job done. No positive reactions. No knee strain. This afternoon, however, he is putting his knee at risk again. We still have a lot of hoggs (this year's lambs) to get ready for market. The warm weather, sunshine and rain means the grass keeps growing. And what goes in at the lambs' front end, must come out at the rear. Usually very sloppy and mucky. The worry at this time of year is not flies and any risk of maggots, but just to get them looking nice and tidy for market. Although as we wormed them as well, they cannot go to market for at least a fortnight. As devoted wife, I have been helping John, so both of us are a nice shade of luminous green. Front and back. But despite threats, I am unwormed.

3rd

Today saw us on the first shoot. Very unseasonable in bright sunshine. We had friends and assorted members of our family staying. On the shoot I was required to wave a feedbag flag as I walked in a line with the other beaters. My style is more of a flap than a waggle, whooshing my flag through the air in order to keep the ducks flying. I have to admit to very mixed feelings here. These ducks were my babies. John and I had reared them from a day old, attended to their every quack, kept them well fed and watered, and now everyone was shooting at them. My flag wave was more of a limp-wristed flutter and flop than the majestic slicing of the airwaves that was going on all around me. 'I think I've let too many of the ducks get past me,' my neighbour wailed. 'Good,' I thought. More to get away. 'Don't worry, they don't want too many shot on the first day,' I lied. 'That was the best thing to do.' But my philanthropy to all things feathered was not taken as far as it could have been this week. A friend whose business is centred on egg production for medical purposes such as 'flu vaccines, was having his annual turn round and cull of hens. The hens live in huge barns and I had asked previously that when the time for new stock was taking place, could I reprieve some of the old hens and bring them back to the farm for a free-range life? But now the time had come, I did not have enough room in our hen house for them. Our very own chick production explosion amongst the bantams meant there was no space in the hut, and no practical alternative.

4th

Farm work up to date as much as is possible, John and I went into town for a meeting with 'The Bank Manager'. Because of changes taking place within our farming partnership, and sales of land and property, John and I needed to set up a new account. Now, John has been a customer of his bank for many years; his entire farming life. They needed photographic and documentary proof that he was who he was. He actually had to take in his passport and driving licence. 'How do I know you are who you say you are?' John asked the bank manager. 'You fellows change every five minutes.' Embarrassed laugh from banker. Who then proceeded to laboriously complete a form on his computer, tapping away with one finger for the next twenty minutes. Virtually in silence. The form could have been filled in manually in about two. This all taking place in a 'flagship' branch that had cost seven million to refurbish and appeared to be staffed by meeters and greeters with important-looking files under their arms. 'We would prefer it if our customers took advantage of our automated services,' we were told, i.e. 'Don't come and actually bother us in person.' They even gave us one of those little tickets such as you get at the supermarket deli counter to make sure we took our turn at the appropriate place and time. 'What do you think?' I asked as we left. John replied, 'When I joined this bank the manager sat down and talked to me about the business and was really interested. That chap hasn't a clue what we are doing and doesn't seem to want to know, apart from making sure there is security for the overdraft facility. What did you think?' My answer? Some of that seven million could have been spent on a typing course.

5th

The last brood of guinea fowl is hatching out in the incubator. We have hatched out thirty-seven guinea fowl chicks this year, some under broody bantams, so their future on the farm seems assured. There is still the original flock of ten who lay the eggs that I snaffle for either culinary or hatching purposes. People in the village regard them as pets and the older birds have a clear scrounging routine to their day. The guinea fowl will stop laying soon, as their egg-laying season runs from spring until early autumn. The first clutches I set to hatch had very little success, but the fertility of the eggs must have improved, as several clutches I have given to friends did. In fact I cleaned the incubator out and sent it off with a friend, plus fourteen guinea fowl eggs, for her to try a last hatch of the season. My friend already has a few guinea fowl from some of our eggs that she set under a broody hen in May, but these will be a last hatch of the year. The concept of keeping guinea fowl for the table is easier in theory than in practice. Once they have abandoned their broody hen or (as has happened in most cases) she has abandoned them, they take to perching high up in the barn and are very flighty and unapproachable. We have had to resort to subterfuge and trickery to get the fowl into pens, but I think this lot might need even more dastardly tactics. All that is a long way off, though. Currently they are fluttering around the yard, chirruping away, stealing the hearts of all who see them. Only one problem for them in life. They do, when mature, taste very, very good.

6th

The plan is to give the corral a day or two to dry up, as sunshine is forecast. Sunshine? What is that? So the next campaign is to wage war on slugs. Despite one top dressing of slug pellets, a new generation is already attacking the freshly emergent rape. Last night, before it was totally dark, John went over a field he is power harrowing for wheat to scatter another load of pellets before drilling the corn, and to top dress the rape. This morning slug Armageddon. Slug pellets have to be applied with care, as metaldehyde, an active component, can be lethal to hedgehogs in large quantities. We use a low dosage, ensure it does not enter a water course and only apply when necessary. Difficult balance to maintain, but the wet season, lower yields this year and predicted food shortages next year, focus your mind very sharply on producing the goods.

7th

All the fields drilled in early autumn look green all over now. John has had one or two disagreements with crows and rooks, but that fight seems to have entered a lull. It is still war on with the squirrels though. I think we get one nut for their two, but gradually our nut haul is increasing. There are two string bags of nuts hanging from hooks in the kitchen to dry out. Can't say I am too thrilled by them, as when they dry out they can shed quite a bit of dust and debris. But the walnuts will be a delicious treat at Christmas. Our old stock bull, our big boy and Daddy to most of the cows and beef stock in the herd for the last few years, is looking lonely and forlorn in one of the bull pens. Tomorrow he goes to market. Hopefully someone will buy him to use as we did as a stock bull. As he is older, however, he may go for stewing meat and I feel so guilty. Know I shouldn't – after all, farming is a business – but he has been a super bull, lovely temperament, and we shall both be sorry to see him go.

At home the three gangs of guinea fowl keets are now a big gang of one. The adults, ten of them, range far and wide in the village, but the keets, twenty-six in all, hang around together. Ten younger keets remain under a heat lamp. I hatched them out in an incubator, but it will be a while before we let them loose to roam. Meanwhile the older keets are everywhere. No decorum. In the grain shed, if they get half a chance, scratting around on top of the straw stack and hay bales, investigating flower troughs and the ducks' hut. They were even pecking at the old bull's feet this morning, so perhaps he is not so lonely and forlorn after all. He has twenty-six little friends to keep him company.

8th

One of my favourite cartoonists was Henry Brewis, a Northumberland farmer. He used to do a brilliant depiction of a frustrated sheep farmer. Crook thrown in the air. Sheepdog scuttling for cover. Sheep in all directions. Expletives deleted filling the air. And so it was this morning. The initial plan, simplicity itself, was to gather the lambs into a set of pens rigged up in the corner of the field. Pick out those gimmers marked to go in with the ewes with the tups, and bring the others home for market. What could be easier? Well, for a start the lambs, without their worldly wise mums, haven't got a clue when it comes to being bossed about by dog or shepherd. Total demoralisation for us followed when a couple of passing walkers offered to come in and help. 'We've been watching for a while,' they sniggered (yes, sniggered), 'and wondered if you wanted a hand.' 'Thanks,' John said. 'We'll manage.' Manage? I was on my knees, but after we had put Fizz back in the Land Rover so she could watch (still only just out of puppyhood) and not learn tricks we had mastered, such as splitting the flock whenever they got within a sniff of the pens, we did eventually corner the little darlings and triumphantly shut them in the pen.

9th

Yesterday morning, after taking the old stock bull in, John spotted a dead ewe in the field. She was still warm. Fresh meat. Prior to foot and mouth we could pay the hunt kennels to take her away. Now it's 'Sorry, mate. Can't do.' Frantic search then for that piece of paper with the number of an animal research programme that would collect newly deceased sheep carcasses for scrapie, a disease that scientists are investigating for a link to BSE. Half an hour later of finding items I had been looking for ages, I eventually turned up the number and put in a call to the research department. 'Are you in the scheme?' they asked. No idea. We had been a year or two ago. 'Are you still?' they asked. 'Not a clue,' we replied. An hour later and it turned out that the scheme was finished, but they gave us a number for another research scheme that collected carcasses. At least the scientists are doing well out of all this.

'If you ring up early enough in the day, they might be able to fit you in,' we were told. 'Depends if they have collected enough, as they only want fresh carcasses.' Vaguely sinister (is there a Frankenstein cow out there?) but turned out to be really helpful. 'Did we have the ear tag number?' they asked. Miraculously yes; John had taken it out of the sheep's lug hole and laid it reverently by the phone, which was now burning with a white-hot heat. Amazing. They were with us by lunchtime and relieved us of our corpse. Brilliant. Something works in this whole farce.

10th

Apparently there is huge concern amongst environmentalists about the amount of methane that cows are producing, and the impact it is having on the greenhouse effect and the environment. The methane mentioned was delicately referred to recently on the radio as that which cows 'burped'. No official worries then about the methane that is produced from their other end. Botty burps, as my granddaughter is proud to refer to them. Scientists are looking to control cows' flatulence through additives. Charcoal, I expect. Wonder if it will send the milk a funny colour? But what about sheep and goats? They are also ruminants, and when put in a global perspective, I expect the combined wind passed by all the cows, sheep and goats in the United Kingdom is as faint as the whisper of a baby's breath when compared to the gale force of the beef herds in South America and on the plains of Africa. I expect wildebeest are ruminants as well. I bet they pass a fair bit of wind when a lion is chasing them. Helps them to get jet propelled. But, as usual, the poor old British farmer is to be made the scapegoat for every environmental ill. I can see it all. Not only will we have to be putting an ear tag in their lugs, but now a plug in their rear ends, or, failing that, a gasometer to be attached to their tails to measure the amount of methane they produce. I see, however, a light, maybe methane fuelled, at the end of the tunnel. There is now a gas pipeline from Norway, as it is envisaged that we shall soon be net importers of gas. We have slumped from producing 95% of the gas we use from our North Sea fields, to needing to import 95% of our needs, from Norway's gas fields. Attempts to rely on alternative fuel sources are foundering. Neighbours have just grubbed up a willow coppice planted to fuel a neighbouring power station. We considered it briefly, but only briefly. They went ahead and have had their first harvest. Disaster. The cost of harvesting the willow and chipping and drying it to provide fuel for the power station, outweighed the cost of the return they received for the crop. After much heart searching they decided to abandon the scheme and plant conventional crops, but needed to drag out the willow roots before the field could be ploughed again. The willow had the last laugh. When dragging out the roots, they found they were lethal to the tractor tyres and had to get a crawler in to do the job. Even more expense. What is needed is an imaginative approach to harvesting the methane gas that is being produced for free from our dairy and beef herds. It could produce a tremendous revival in farming fortunes. We could have the chair of the NFU on OPEC (if it still exists). Our scientists must be able to come up with a solution. Never mind one big pipeline under the sea. It could be either lots of little pipelines trailing from cows' bottoms or, as mentioned before, some kind of plug fitted into their backsides, and then let the cows rip when they get into a specially constructed methane container. A whole new Big Bang theory.

11th

Disaster has struck. One cow dead and another seriously ill. The dead cow is a fit one. Nine years old. Healthy calf. No reason to worry about her. And then, next minute, she is laid dead in the field. I contacted the hunt to see if they could collect her from the farm. No. They were no longer able to collect fallen stock, it had to be brought to them. So we took the forklift out into the field, lifted her into the back of a trailer and took her down to the kennels. When they realised she was over two years old, they would not touch her. So it was back to the farm and on the phone to DEFRA. Who are sending a licensed dealer to collect her. But no-one knows when. So there we are with one dead cow still in the yard and John goes to check the herd to discover another cow apparently on its last legs. Both cows have been grazing in a field that is bordered by a lot of oak trees. Have you seen how many acorns are on oak trees this year? Thousands. And have you seen how many acorns are littering the ground around the oak trees? Thousands and thousands.

I listened to a radio programme last week about the concern the New Forest authorities had about acorns. In large numbers they are lethal to the ponies and horses of the New Forest, and so the authorities are bringing in pigs to attempt to truffle up the surplus acorns before the ponies and horses get to them and make themselves ill or die. 'Do you think it's the acorns?' I asked John. But that theory was dismissed out of hand. John was beginning to think it is a shortage of minerals, as this cow is staggering. Not BSE-type staggers. But mineral deficiency-type staggers. 'I haven't topped the minerals up this week,' he said, 'and as the grass is still so lush with the warm weather and the rain, everything is going straight through them and they might have become mineral deficient.' To ensure the well-being of the cow, we called in the vet. He recommended a mineral jab, but administering the jab had its own difficulties. Due to the deficiency, the cow had become very aggressive, and actually got its head down to butt John, who is not moving as well as he usually does because of his knee injury. 'I put the vet in the crush first,' John said. 'I thought that was the safest place. Then when the cow got her head down to try and have a go at me, I slipped a halter over her head and tied her to a post. Then we injected her.'

12th

Invited to attend a harvest supper and harvest festival celebration in a friend's local village hall and church. A good congregation filled the church. However, reflecting on the decline in numbers of worshippers, this congregation, many of them farmers, was drawn from a number of parishes. The church looked beautiful. Flowers and fruit filled the windows and surrounded the pulpit. A real country gathering. Altogether a combination of three vicars and a lay preacher led the service. Hymns were traditional and themed to harvest time, with the sermon based on the history of the hymn 'We plough the fields and scatter the good seed on the land'. Did you know the hymn was originally from North Germany and was called the Peasant Song? Neither did I. Nor I think did anyone else. It was originally seventeen verses long but the translation condensed it down to twelve, and now only three verses, plus the refrain, are sung. Up till this point I think the vicar had us all nodding along, enjoying the enlightenment. Then he chose to contrast the traditional farming methods illustrated in the eighteenth-century hymn to those of modern farming with John Betjeman's parody: 'We spray the fields and scatter the poison on the ground'. Quite lost my sympathy then. What a pity he didn't quote the lovely poem about the church mouse who simply loves harvest festivals, as 'for me the only feast of all, is Autumn's Harvest festival'. In the poem the mouse stuffs himself with the ears of corn around the font and scrambles up the pulpit stair to 'gnaw the marrows hanging there'. Maybe, though, the vicar did know the poem and chose to ignore it because his congregation had to be drawn from such a wide area. As the church mouse reflects, 'It's strange to me, how very full a church can be, with people I don't see at all, except at Harvest festival.'

13th

As darkness falls, the bawling from the yards and across the fields quietly subsides. Today John has started to wean some of the winter-born calves who have been out with their mums for the summer. Those cows will calve again early in the New Year and so it is time for them to stop suckling these calves and get fit for their next progeny. To separate calves and cows, John came up with his usual cunning plan. The herd have been coming to feed on a big bale of barley straw in a ring feeder in the corral. When a fresh bale goes in, the herd all congregate. It is a relatively simple matter to close the corral off and divert some the calves down the race and into the back of the Land Rover trailer. That is the theory. It never goes quite as easily as that, but today we brought fifteen calves home, all well grown, and they have gone into one of the fattening yards.

But they did not all stay there. Late afternoon the crescendo of bawling was suddenly stilled with an almighty crash. They had broken down the yard gate and escaped into another yard. Luckily for us, that was in yet another enclosed yard, so apart from trampling down some feedbags, they have not done much damage. Rather excitable, though, to get back in. They might still be called calves, but they are half grown and could cause you some damage if you got in their way. As it is, they raced around for a time and then we shooed them back in and strapped the gate shut.

14th

Escaping stock is not only our problem. A close friend, Dave, recently bought a couple of young bullocks from market and secured them for the night in a yard within a yard. Yesterday morning he went to check on his purchases. They had gone. Cleared off silently in the night. As he was chasing around the farm and locality, a neighbour stopped him to say one of the bullocks had got into a field of his cows. Using the charms of a seductive matron, the neighbour had persuaded the bullock to follow her home, and she now had the bullock penned in. So that one was easily caught and brought home, but where had the other one gone? Sightings flooded in and Dave conscientiously checked all reports out. Near their village is an old packhorse bridge and there had even been a credible sighting of the animal going over the bridge when the lights turned to green. And then coming back again. This critter knew its highway code, apparently. At the end of a frantic day with no joy finding the lost beast, Dave and his family decided they had done all they could and would resume the search this morning. Got up and went in to check that the first bullock was still securely in the yard, within another yard. So it was. Plus the happy wanderer. How? We are still pondering the question over coffee.

15th

Sleeping with ear plugs in again tonight. Well, not really. But the neighbours in our village might want to if they sleep lightly. We do not, as we are usually whacked by the time we turn in and asleep immediately. More calves weaned today, so that currently there are thirty recently, to their minds, orphaned calves in the foldyard next to the house. What a racket. Their mums out in the fields cannot hear them as we have made sure that they cannot access the fields closest to home. When we used to milk, it was a regular occurrence for one of the dairy cows, whose calf had been taken away at about three days old, to turn up in the farmyard after crashing through a hedge to get to her baby. Weaning remains a mucky business as we continue to bring the cows and calves into the corral inland in order to separate mums from offspring. They are still tempted by the offer of unlimited silage just through the corral gates. Cows can resist anything except temptation. Or silage. Despite tonnes of stone being laid down each year in the corral, it sinks without trace when trampled on by about a hundred cattle, aided especially by this season's downpours. We were up to our welly tops in mud. Slurp, slurp, slurp at every step.

Almost all last year's bullocks have now been sold, so the foldyards were empty, except for a truly orphaned calf and a very slow developer. But now they are filling up rapidly. The cows themselves will not come home for at least another month, but we are bringing the young bull home today as he definitely needs feeding up. He has lost ground over the summer. After a literally shaky start, as he had an abscess in his hoof, he has fulfilled his role and purpose in life admirably. Now he can have the rest of the autumn and early winter to recuperate and recover.

16th

At a very young age, Jessica, our granddaughter, has already been hired and fired from her first job. A dismal employment record in place. Mind you, she did not have the most tolerant of employers. John, or to her, Pappa. And she was given, as I state in my role of defending attorney, a disproportionate amount of responsibility at a very early stage in her now aborted career. It is her holiday half term and the job description, given over breakfast, was to help her grandfather feed the lambs. Suitable clothing was provided – a boiler suit and wellies – and transport: front seat of the Land Rover. Training provision was, as far as I can tell, sketchy. As a result, instead of spreading the feed out along the bottoms of two troughs in the field, Jess tipped the whole lot up in a big pile in one. Therefore, instead of lambs being able to spread themselves out around four sides of the trough to feed, an unholy scrumdown took place. As John was stood with her the whole time, Jess was never in any danger of being knocked over, but John said she was overwhelmed with the speed at which the lambs appeared from the farthest edges of a field once they spotted a bag full of grub. 'They learn it off their mothers,' he said. It reminded me of one of Henry Brewis's cartoons where one farmer remarked to another, as they saw a burglar with his swag bag crushed beneath a flock of sheep, about the folly of carrying any sort of sack through a sheep field. Ditto Father Christmas. Our sheep will even follow an empty sack, much to the amusement of some neighbours who were helping us to move some sheep last week. After all, sheep have not got X-ray vision, and as long as the paper sack rattles enticingly, you are a ewe's best friend. Till she knocks you over and discovers the truth.

John has been grateful for all the help we can give him over this past week. With a break in the wet and dismal weather, he has been flat out to get as much land as possible drilled. Plans change daily. At one moment we are going to wait till the spring, in the next, a window of opportunity is to be seized to get another field drilled this autumn. As a result he has been getting up at four o'clock to get out onto the land and not coming home until darkness falls. Several times I have taken him his lunch down the fields, as he prefers to work through rather than lose the traditional hour taken for lunch and a quick snooze. Not that that hour is peaceful. Reps, merchants and chancers all know that half past twelve to one is a good time to catch a farmer indoors. And that in their dozy, post-luncheon daze, they might agree to something that in a more wakeful hour they would not normally give the time of day to.

17th

'I need a hand to get those remaining lambs collected up,' John said. My heart sank. These were the lambs destined for market. The lambs we had separated out last week are in with the flock to be tupped. All these remaining lambs could run like the wind and not one of them was responsive to threats or directions from either dog or farmer. Or the farmer's wife. 'We'll just walk them quietly into the collecting pen,' John added. Oh really? One look at us as we entered the field and the flock scattered. Game on. Every time we brought them closer to where they could be funnelled into the collecting area via a set of wooden pens and thence into the trailer, they broke away. Once more the invective and fury of John's language questioning the legal parentage of the lambs assaulted my delicate ears. You could hear the derisive baas from the flock. 'I'll sort them out,' John decided. 'I'm going to round them up with the Land Rover. They'll be tired of the job before I am.' Never mind filming sheepdog trials, the BBC should have a new programme of Land Rover trials. Cowboys on horses have nothing on John in a Land Rover. Bouncing over the field, screaming reverse gears, wheel spin. A motorised rodeo. Eventually the lambs gave in and we manoeuvred them into the collecting area. It was high fives all the way.

18th

Recently there has been an explosion of rats in the farm buildings. Millie, our Jack Russell, is a seasoned rat killer, but a number had gone to earth in the combine and are inaccessible to her. What annoys me most of all, however, is the rats' invasion of my apple hoard. In addition to freezing apples for pies and crumbles, I have squirrelled away apples in a purpose-built store that John created for me out of wooden pallets. When I came to add an additional layer this afternoon, I discovered that rats had already eaten into the top layer of fruit and I would have to do some repicking and replace all of the apples I had stored. Fortunately there are still apples on the trees. I give away as many as friends are willing to take, but most of them have had a good apple harvest too. The fruit kept exceptionally well last year, whether because of the cold, the store construction or unblemished fruit I don't know, but I had apples until well into April.

19th

John is gradually retreating into his silent, moody, thoughtful, worried mode that is a sign the days are drawing in and there is still a lot of work looking at him, so it's good for him to get away for a day. We are increasingly taking the line of bringing in specialist contractors to do specific jobs. For example, with a field that has been down to grass for five years and is going back into the rotation for wheat: their ploughs are bigger, their tractors more powerful, and they can get the job done in half the time and without risk to our machinery.

'Wheeeeeee. Tell me if you're feeling dizzy!'

20th

A day out to a ploughing championship. A trip down Memory Lane for John with the vintage machines, and a short break for me. I was amazed how many people we met who we knew. At one stage John despaired of ever getting round the vast area devoted to match ploughing, as we appeared to be drifting from one set of friends and acquaintances to the next. Fortunately I got stood next to a very knowledgeable lady when I was watching the working horses. She possessed a wealth of information on the tack that the horses were wearing and kept pointing out all the points that the judges would be looking for when judging the final piece of ploughed land. 'See how he is keeping the horses moving as he lifts the plough out at the end of the furrow,' she said. 'He is keeping everything taut so that the horses do not get their legs over the traces as they turn. He must make sure the swingle tree' (I am sure that's what she called it) 'remains straight so that the chain does not tangle round their legs and cause them to kick out.'

The horses were magnificent. So intelligent. Their ears constantly twitching as they listened for verbal instructions and able to keep totally immobile as the ploughman adjusted the 'boats' and angle of the plough before they set off. A beautiful pair of Suffolk Punches had apparently been saved from the French meat market. They were the lucky two from six hundred horses destined to be butchered. I know we send cattle and sheep to market, but horses seem different. They are so attuned to people, it just seems awful to slaughter them for human consumption. Most of the horses glittered in their brasses. John's mother possessed many and they were hung all over the walls of her little cottage at the farm. To see them actually being used for purpose is to see them brought to life. Elsewhere vast behemoths of machines moved at high speed over the land, ploughing or discing. Onlookers smartly stepped out of the way as the machines bore down on them and I marvelled at the light touch of health and safety standards in our increasingly bureaucratised world. It was the same with the steam-driven plough. Travelling between two steam engines, a plough consisting of a man sitting on it to balance it and another to steer it, whipped across the line dragged by a steel hawser, which if it had snapped, could quickly decapitate most of the closely packed observers. 'I used to drive one of those tractors in the early seventies,' John said, drooling over an immaculate David Brown Selectamatic. 'I used to keep a broom handle by my side to try and knock down the seagulls that followed. Working in an open cab might be cooler but you are exposed to the elements and seagull muck.' The sight of a Doe working with two tractor engines yoked together to provide 160 horsepower almost proved too much in terms of nostalgia. 'The farmer we bought our land off used to drive one of those,' John said, 'and our land is so heavy that one got stuck in the autumn and stayed there until the next spring.'

21st

We are making arrangements for the herd to come home. The calves that were weaned a week ago have settled. No more bawling day and night. Logistically the biggest problem facing us is how to inject all the expectant mums for rotavirus. This disease is recognised as a common cause of infectious calf scour and created havoc in our herd a couple of years ago. We lost several calves with the condition. The ones that recovered never thrived. Calves derive immunity from the colostrum in the milk from their mums in the first days of life if the cows have been vaccinated against rotavirus. The time is coming to carry out this procedure. Normally we could arrange to gather the cows in the corral and push them through one at a time into the crush so that they are secure when jabbed. It is a different job vaccinating a suckler cow to a dairy one. When we milked, the cows patiently waited their turn (all sorted out amongst themselves from top cow to bottom of the pile) to come into the parlour. Once in and attached to the milking cluster, they got their heads into the feed hopper and were oblivious to what was happening until they had finished their dairy nuts. Jabs, swabs, artificial insemination, whatever; not a problem. But suckler cows are not used to being handled on a daily basis. Wild is the best way to describe them. The weather has precluded the use of the outside corral. Both of us have lost wellies in the morass and mud in there. Trying to chase anything is like wading through glue. So a cunning plan has formed involving once more the use of the gate system we bought earlier in the year. The idea is first to get the cows home. Simples. By means of the haylage enticement method, we intend to get them closer and closer to the last field gate until it is only a short belt across the road and into the farmyard. Then to gather the cows in the heifers' yard and only to allow them out one at a time, through the aforementioned gate system, into a mini duck trap set-up that leads into the crush. This will be cunningly hidden behind the corner of the yard so that in theory (note, in theory) each cow does not see the crush until the last minute. Then, either they will walk in (unlikely) or back off. Here is the cunning bit. John will be hidden behind the corner with needle and vaccine all prepped. Either they walk into the crush and get jabbed in there, or back off and get jabbed in the bum from the rear anyway. Can't wait to see if it works and how many times John and I will be vaccinated. And it all has to be repeated again as well. So, no problems with the runs for us this winter.

22nd

Outside my office window I can see the Mule shearlings, bought today at a sheep sale, settling in for the night. We have turned them out in the house paddock as they have to be kept away from the main flock for several days to ensure traceability in the event of a disease notification. 'I thought we were cutting down on sheep numbers,' I said to John as we drove to the sale. 'Well, they're starting to make really good money again,' he said. It was true. The price we paid for them was exactly twice as much as the last lot of Mule shearlings we bought in two years ago. Prices have soared. Dealers put a bottom, minimum acceptable price, in the whole sale even for the oldest sheep, as the killing price for any sheep has rocketed. Could not have been a better day for holding the sale. Cold and crisp. Bright blue sky. No rain. Still my feet were frozen by the time we went back to the Land Rover and flask of hot coffee. Everyone, in their various shades and layers of green and brown attire, looked cold. The huddle around the sales ring kept you warm in your body but couldn't prevent your toes from gradual frostbite. Coming back, John decided we would go the scenic route and visit the farm that used to belong to his grandparents. But we took the wrong turning. After taking directions from a wayside farmer, we confidently headed down a dead end lane. And then had to reverse back with trailer and sheep in tow until we found a place to turn round. 'You've gan the wrang way,' our helpful friend, who had by now caught us up, commented. He was planning to visit the sale, it turned out, and had not realised that it had got so late that folk like us were by now leaving the event. He knew John's uncle and was soon able to put us on the right road after a long chat about sheep prices and the difficulty of making any money at all in farming.

23rd

The devil flies are still attacking the sheep. This morning John came in for assistance to catch a ewe that has maggots in its shoulder. Incredibly, she must have originally had maggots in her foot, and then because ewes sleep with their legs tucked up (this one, in any case), the maggots have crawled into the fleece on her shoulder and wriggled through into her flesh. 'I thought she had a poorly foot,' I said in desperation. 'She has,' John replied. 'You'd have to run a lot faster if she was fit.'

24th

An image-conscious shearling made a frantic leap at the press photographer perched on a set of portable steps just outside the confines of the sales ring. The photographer fell off his steps into the crowd and then directed his lens at the less image-conscious auctioneer, who decided to straighten up his tie before facing the local paparazzi. John and I were attending yet another sheep sale to try to get another tup for the flock. Two of our tups are showing signs of age, broken mouthed at the corner (lost a tooth) rather than full mouths (all their teeth). However, their tackle is still in full working order, so we will take advantage of that for the main flock of ewes, but plan to use a new, and the youngest, tup on the shearlings and gimmers. That is, young sheep who have not had a crop of lambs yet. We had to bide our time for the sheep sale whilst small and large farm implements were sold off. The crowd followed the auctioneers round the field where tractors, a combine, ploughs, muck spreader, pig troughs, trailers and even a set of old lawnmowers were up for grabs. Just as we thought they were coming to the sheep, they headed back into the buildings to auction off some hay and straw. By the time they all wended their way to the sheep pens, the niftier farmers had already positioned themselves close up to the sales ring. And us. Not so much nifty, but because we were not interested in any other of the items, we had grabbed pole positions for the sheep sale. We had spotted a fine Texel tup in a pen. Not that he took much spotting. There were only four tups for sale. There had been a much larger sheep sale the previous week, but John is not keen on buying show specimens. He feels they often get dressed up and primped up for a sale where there are prizes being given, and the tups/bulls/sheep go off downhill once they are put out in the field to work. We were looking for a good working tup, and thought we had found one. The auctioneer knew most of his buyers. Remarked on the wild nights out he's had in the 'sin cities' of the area. He must lead a sheltered life. But he knew his sheep, and pattered out a constant stream of praise for the stockmen who had brought them to the ring. After a brisk set of bidding, the tup was ours to bring home. He is at this moment in close confines with the other tups, so that they do not knock all bells out of each other when they get put out in a field together. Release a strange tup into a paddock with a settled clique, and they will swiftly set about trying to kill each other. Death by charging. By tomorrow morning he will be close, personal and fraternal with the other tups. We hope.

25th

An excited friend rang to say she has bought herself a small flock of goats. Did I have any tips on looking after them? Well, I might, but my advice would certainly not be of the expert variety. I had a fling with keeping goats twenty-five years ago and vowed never again. My little flock of goats were distantly related to Houdini and preferred the veg patch, the roses, flower troughs, perennial borders; anything except the field they were in and the grass they were supposed to eat. 'Let's get out' was their motto. The kids were delightful, but even though I had numerous testimonies that young kid meat is tasty, low in cholesterol, etc., John and the children would not eat it. My attempts to milk the nannies were abysmal. And then once I, and they, did get the hang of it, none of the family would drink the milk either. I had carton upon carton of it in the freezer until in desperation I gave it all away to friends whose child had a cow's milk allergy. Finally I gave my little herd away to a traveller family who had expressed an interest in the goats for their own use. They took a far stricter approach to limiting their grazing opportunities and planned to tether them on the wayside with no hope of escape. Plus they seemed to have no inhibitions over the kid meat. Perhaps I should have persevered. We are close to a successful goat farm which supplies milk for goat's milk yoghurt and cheese, far more popular now than it was then. Goat's meat is acceptable and indigenous to the wide range of cultures in our increasingly diverse national community. I wished my friend luck. She'll need it.

26th

Pip has taken any encouragement to come into the house and dry herself out on a comfortable sofa as a goal to aspire to at all other times of the day. Leave the back door open an inch and she is in, sliding along on her tummy until she has slipped under the radar that is John's watchful gaze and slithered through the kitchen door into the snug and onto the sofa. It is the very least she deserves after all her efforts picking up on the shooting field.

27th

The twenty-five gimmer lambs that John has selected from this year's lambing to keep in the flock are ready and waiting to be served by a new young tup. I could swear there is a distinct smell of perfume and powder emanating from their field. John does not want to put them to our old tups for obvious reasons. They are their daughters. The ewes, both our old ones and about twenty bought in at market, will meet up with their paramours, our old tups, on the same day, so as to coordinate lambing time. At least that is the theory. It is to be hoped that the young 'uns will know what to do without any examples being set by their elders. As John says, 'I'm not providing any demonstrations.' The weather could not be better. The grass has kept growing and gimmers, tups and ewes are all looking fit. Only one lamb is causing us concern. It has swayback and John is treating it for a mineral deficiency after getting veterinary advice. The lamb looks quite distressing. We brought all the stock lambs home last week to give them a health check and this particular lamb just kept turning and wobbling on its legs, to the point where it was on the verge of collapse. John picked it up and put it in the back of the Land Rover, as it would have been cruel to walk it home. It is in the paddock by the house now with another lamb for company and hopefully will respond to its treatment. Jessica, our granddaughter, who is with us, is fascinated by the lamb's wobbly gait. She keeps a close eye on it through the kitchen window and runs to tell me every time it falls over.

28th

To try and give Jessica an early warning on the dangers of drink, I have been telling her that perhaps the wobbly lamb has been having too many sips from Pappa's drinks cupboard. Jessica loves exploring all the nooks and crannies in the house and soon found where he keeps his stock of drink. John's office is groaning under the weight of bramble whisky and sloe gin that he has made and is stockpiling for the winter months. These drinks are especially welcome on shooting days and not unwelcome at any other time, especially later in the evening when you are just winding down from an arduous day. Whilst there is a very good crop of sloes this year, we struggled to find many decent blackberries. Luckily a friend had picked too many and we have swapped eight pound of brambles for eight pounds of walnuts. The walnuts have been prolific, even if we are having to share them with the squirrels. So once more the Lowther Farm booze operation swings into action. Gin, whisky, sloes, brambles, and sugar slosh around my kitchen and hopefully at a later stage, down our throats. We just can't stop making the stuff. Or sampling it. Another deliciousz drink ishz raspberry gin to the shame recshipe asz for brambleshz. Excushzhze me while I shzlide gently off my shzeat and shzlump into an alcofrolicolic dazhze. Hic.

29th

Operation Jab, to again vaccinate all the cows in calf against rotavirus, went successfully. Only one cow managed to escape the cunningly laid trap of gates and crush, and she was jabbed in her rear end once she had her head into the silage and was oblivious to all else except a good feed. The syringes caused more problems than anything else as the needles kept breaking. We ended up using four syringes by the end of the session. No qualms here about sharing needles. What was good enough for one cow, was good enough for the next, unless they happened to snap off in the cow's rump. And now, along with the miserable weather, as the clocks have gone back, we are getting dark, dreary evenings. John says it is going to be a long winter. We have definitely finished land work as everything is too wet to continue. Friends who have eighty acres of potatoes still to lift are despairing if they will ever get them this year and there are still fields that will never get their corn harvested this autumn, or sown for next year. At home I doubt we will get any more broody hens this year, but the last broody one I set with eggs has just brought off eight bantam chicks. Tiny bundles of yellow feathers. Early evenings have made me reorganise the hens and bring in all the little poultry groups of varying age and maturity to spend some time incarcerated in the hen run. It has meant a sudden increase in the number of eggs we get. Instead of the hens laying in inaccessible nests on the hay and straw bales, they are actually having to lay their eggs in nest boxes in the hen hut. A novel experience for most of them. I have even discovered a nest of guinea fowl eggs at a time of year I had expected them to stop laying. This year is all to pot. Do not be lulled into a false sense of torpor and tranquillity in the countryside, however. Our young stock bull may be having a quieter time of it tucked up cosily with the bullocks and no cows to bother or excite him, but soon it will be all go in the sheep fields.

30th

We have just introduced the tups into the ewes so that the autumn's romancing could get going. One of the tups is getting quite elderly and is normally very steady and slow on his legs. For the past month they have all been eating themselves into cider-induced stupors prior to their star turns. The paddock they are in borders our orchard and the tups are quick off the mark if they see any fallen fruit before I get to it. When our old horse Rupert was alive, this was his domain, and he cleared any apples off branches that overhung the paddock. Now the tups get the lot. Let's hope drink does not impair their performance. As the old tup tottered along the lane after his buddies, a whiff of hormones must have drifted past his nostrils. What a change. Smartened himself up immediately. Almost rocketed into the field along with his mates and set to on the first ewe he could find willing to entertain his carnal desires. I must admit he looks weary again now, but as John says, 'He's still working.'

31st

Suffered a reaction today from walking through the sunflower crop when I was invited to go beating on a friend's shoot. The sunflowers have been planted as a game cover and winter feed for pheasants. 'Tap the sunflowers as you go through,' we were asked by our team leader. I did. And not only that, but as Pip was still on a lead at the start of each drive, she also tangled herself round every other sunflower and we ended up dragging along half a dozen plants with us. The air was thick with sunflower pollen. At the end of the day I collapsed with what I thought was the well-earned fatigue from dragging myself, soaking wet from the occasional downpour, through brambles, woods and dense undercover. My chest was tight and I felt 'fluey. Had my cynical jibes about bird 'flu come to haunt me? Was this the ducks' revenge? The first case of avian 'flu in England brought on by deceased ducks. I dissolved a couple of aspirins in whisky and lemon and flopped on the sofa with an old film, old farmer and a wet Labrador. Boy did I moan. 'It's your fault,' I lambasted John. 'You didn't put a spare dry coat in for me. You didn't pack any waterproofs. You took my hat.' I could of course have done all those things myself, but I was in charge of refreshments and John, in theory, is in charge of all other resources. Plus it is balm to the soul to have a good moan every now and then. Especially after Pip and I had done so well picking up and working towards giving John, as a guest gun, a day to remember. It took me twenty-four hours to recover. That is how I knew it wasn't a cold, or 'flu. Suddenly the symptoms lifted, and from talking to another friend on the shoot, who takes antihistamines as a precaution, I realised it was the sunflowers wot were the culprits.

November

1st

Many of the lanes surrounding our village are lined with oak trees. They are all dropping acorns by the thousand and attracting a veritable plague of wood pigeons and large numbers of pheasants. Two of my friends have had their car headlights dashed by pigeons rising from the ground at the last minute and taking flight directly across the path of their vehicles. Disastrous for both pigeon and headlights, and all our neighbours are commenting on the pigeon numbers, as they have never seen so many before. We have a friend who spends his weekends pigeon shooting for farmers to try to keep the numbers down on growing crops. He will have his work cut out this autumn unless the birds move on to another area.

John intends to shoot at least one pigeon though. He has had our granddaughter Jessica's help recently when he is plucking pheasants for the freezer. She enjoys the task but rips the skin as it is a skilled task and is difficult for little fingers to pull out all the tail feathers. But plucking a pigeon is a different job. Very simple. In fact the feathers come away so easily that many dogs are wary of retrieving pigeons as they dislike getting a mouthful of feathers for their pains. I think we should have more than one to go at. Pigeon pie. Delicious. And nice and fat from the acorns. A bountiful harvest indeed.

2nd

'Save me the duck livers,' I had asked John when I knew he had five ducks to pluck after an evening duck shooting. Last year he had enlarged a muddy old pond and although John only intends to visit it a few times, it is proving a good provider for a roast lunch. He had spent the hour before tea out in the meal shed, stood over an old dustbin, denuding the ducks of their lovely plumage. Now he had brought them in to draw the giblets before dressing them in a snug freezer bag. As I peeled a pan of potatoes for lunch the next day, I could smell the burnt feathers as John singed the down off the ducks with our ancient Gaz stove, a veteran of many camping trips. Potatoes in the pan, I fetched out the cooking brandy and made ready to make myself a sumptuous spread of duck liver pate. I spooned a generous lump of butter into a pan and went to fetch my main ingredients from the utility room where John was working. 'Could I have the livers please?' I said. A grin spread over John's face. 'They're in there,' he pointed, indicating a gory mess of giblets, entrails, duck's head and feet. 'If you really want them, you'll have to fish them out. I forgot to keep them separate.' I should have known. Men cannot multi-task. I suppose the answer is, if I had really wanted the livers, I should have drawn the ducks myself, but John makes such a professional job of it whilst any birds I dress look as though they have met with an even nastier accident than they did.

The next job will be to find room in the freezer for the ducks. One is destined for lunch but the others are in for the cryogenic treatment and despite my best intentions to empty the freezer before the start of the shooting season, a glut of blackberries, plums and apples means that every cubic inch is full of frozen fruit. Even eggs from when the hens went into overlay. I don't know how they will thaw out but I had read somewhere that you can freeze eggs if you separate the yolks from the whites. We shall see at defrosting time.

The dogs could be very egg bound.

3rd

To cope with the anticipated rush on freezer space when the geese and Aylesbury ducks meet their maker, I bought a spare freezer today. At vast expense. Twenty pounds. It has been shunted into the old milking parlour ready for action and I just hope it works. It has not been switched on yet, but according to the young lad at the community warehouse where I bought it, it was freezing well after switch-on. 'There's no lights showing,' he said, 'so I'll knock you something off for that, but I swear to you it works.' It better had.

It would be one big cook-in if six geese and twenty ducks all went soggy on me at once. The warehouse is a fascinating place, raising money for local charities, organisations, schools and individuals. I prefer to take all our unwanted goods there rather than give everything to a vast international organisation. The drawback is that as often as I take several dustbin bags full of toys that the grandchildren have grown bored with, clothes we no longer need, the remains of a cupboard tidy, I still come home with 'just the thing I have been wanting for ages', which someone else has decided that they don't.

In this case a freezer.

4th

What a good job we moved the lambs when we did last week. To survive in the field as it is now they would have had to develop fins and webbed feet. There is only the tiniest area of grass that is not submerged in water. In a strange twist, I have been looking for dowsing rods for John in order that he can locate a source of water underground. When we were digging out the big pond many years ago, we used dowsing rods to locate a spring that fed the pond.

An ageing hippy turned up with his pieces of copper wire, marching up and down the field, waiting for them to cross at the strategic point.

I must admit I was sceptical. The dowser confidently claimed when the rods crossed over a specific point in the field, that here was an underground spring. Dig down and we would strike water. We dug and did not, but mysteriously the pond, scraped out by a digger from a muddy and wet part of the field, did fill up, and has never dried up or lost its level. Even in times of severe drought. But we mocked too soon. And the next year a huge sinkhole appeared in the ground just where he said he could sense running water. He was right. We had not dug down far enough. There must have been running water because some source was filling the pond. We never have found out from where. It just was. I started my search for the rods on eBay, and was amazed at the variety of uses and claims made for them. Scientific studies have concluded that dowsing is no better statistically than chance, but John is a firm believer in the rods' effectiveness in finding water, and in this particular case wants a set in order to locate a particular drainage pipe. My researches have seen claims for the rods in establishing the feng shui of an area and balancing the energies to assure health and well-being. This could be really useful on a farm to make sure that the cows have a well-aligned energy field in the foldyard. Also, it seems, the efficacy of the rods would be assured if we bought a set from water witches who had laid the rods on special Cornish stones, and they could be used to discover graveyards. And ghosts. Now where did I bury those phantom sheep?

All this of course seems pretty irrelevant given the drowned state of the field John wants to locate the drain in. John assures me that the rods react to magnetic fields, and I honestly cannot believe that my rational husband believes in all this, but he does. So now we await the drying-up of the field in question before he can go out with his set of rods and walk over the area where he suspects the drain is located. Go out today and he would need a set of flippers and a snorkel.

5th

'This will be the first year I have ever known the cows to be out on Bonfire Night,' John said. Out, but staying in their fields, we hope. Although our village is only tiny, more of a hamlet than a village, three families already have brushwood and rubbish piled high in their gardens ready for the big night. They all know that we have stock and feed inside in the barns but several of the families have ponies and all have dogs. So overall they are considerate and just put on a short show for their immediate family. The straw is not as vulnerable as it was in past years when we stacked everything under a Dutch barn, and many of the big bales are stored well inland in the fields they were harvested from. Still, it pays to check all the extinguishers are full and the hosepipes connected up. Although our Labrador is not at all bothered by loud bangs – indeed, if it is gunfire, positively revels in it – our sheepdog and Jack Russell are both very timid about gunshot, fireworks, thunder and lightning.

One year an old sheepdog of ours, Nell, became extremely distressed by fireworks in the village and was severely kicked when she took refuge in our foldyard with the cows. The following year we returned from a meal after a shoot when it was already dark and some pre-Bonfire Night fireworks had been set off. Nell was not in her kennel. We found her cowering in the poultry hut with some very irate chickens. That put them off lay for a week.

Years ago we always put the tups in with the ewes on Bonfire Night. Fireworks in the field as well as up in the sky. Lambing patterns change though, and the tups now go earlier to try to catch a better market when the lambs are fit.

6th

The man from the farm assurance scheme was with us today. We have been in a farm assurance scheme for beef and lamb for the last few years. Being farm assured means that the work we do to maintain high standards of food safety, animal health and welfare and environmental care on the farm is recognised as meeting agreed national standards of best practice. Any beef and lamb produced on our farm that then passes through an assured supply chain is also eligible to carry the Red Tractor logo. The inspection took the morning and started with the stock. As all the cattle are inside now, that was the easy part. The inspector needed to see where the herd was housed, bedded up, fed and their general welfare. The same with the sheep, only as they are all out in various fields, that took longer. Then on to the paperwork. Which fortunately, as John is meticulous about keeping records, rarely presents problems. Different matter if I was in charge: we'd never find anything. As with any inspection, the things that need to be recorded and notified grow with each year. We thought we were doing well providing a sharps box for safely disposing of any needles. What we didn't realise was that we also needed a broken needles policy. Luckily we weren't asked for it and by now I've drafted one. Also that any farm cats should be wormed regularly and their treatment recorded. I tell you, if we were able to hold onto one of our farm cats long enough to worm it, there would be a need to record in a farm accident book our treatment and the first aid received.

Our inspector was, I must say, very helpful. Thorough and rigorous, but also, as a farmer, possessing a good dose (recorded in his medical

'Love is in the air . . .'

records) of common sense. Even with John knowing exactly where most things are, there was still a fair bit of scurrying round to lay our hands on some obscure documents that, although not statutory, needed to be looked at and verified. We waved him off with a sigh of relief, but the most painful part of the inspection will come in the New Year with a demand for a three-figure sum to stay in the scheme. We chew it over each year. Should we or shouldn't we? Where the scheme benefits us is when stock is sold on to independent butchers. They like to display the names of individual farms they have bought beef from at market, and to emphasise that it meets farm assured standards for welfare and traceability. You just hope that the public appreciates it too.

One of the tups has managed to trap and upend himself in a dike so that he was on his back and unable to get up and onto his feet. It must have happened last night: if it had been any longer, he would not have survived. When sheep are on their back they cannot expel any gas from their rumen, the first of their four stomachs where their food is digested, fermented and produces gas. Sheep, with no sense of embarrassment, get rid of this gas with either a burp or by breaking wind. So refined. So, if poor old Mr Tup was on his back and could not burp or worse, his lungs would get crushed by the increasing amount of gas and he would suffocate. All we wanted was a flatulent, belching sheep for a full recovery. Interestingly, whilst the balance organs for humans are in the ear, in sheep it is the fluid, and in this case gas, in their stomachs. So we achieved the desired effect by suspending the tup from a forklift supported by a split fertiliser bag. The pressure on his tum produced the desired result, his circulation was restored, and we put a large warning notice and several clothes pegs in his vicinity for delicate noses.

7th

We have set out our stall to organise the farm office in the buildings we had converted for John's mum to live in. Since her death they have clogged up with the detritus of family life: old toys, old clothes, old furniture, stuff we can't bear to part with but should. In the midst of it we have the office computer and filing cabinets, but the idea now is to update it all for an efficient office set-up. My sister has a holiday home in Spain, which has been partially furnished with outcasts from the 'basura', or bin area. No-one has an individual dustbin. Instead there are communal collection points where everyone puts out stuff they don't want, although the real rubbish goes into large skips. You acquire quite a collecting bug and there is no shame in it at all. Genuine duff rubbish is in the skip anyway. If there is another potential life for a something you don't want, leave it for others, to see if they do. Very green. So a story John told me about a builder friend's experience when renovating an old farmhouse was very familiar.

Most of the kitchen fixtures and fittings had gone to fill a skip hired for the purpose. But the cast iron bath was one item too many for the weight permissible in the skip. To hire another skip was uneconomic as only this item needed to go. What to do? 'Let's lift the bath out and leave it on the front lawn,' the builder said. 'We'll see what happens to it.' Next morning the bath was still there. And the next. But by the next morning it had gone in the night. Disposal problem solved. Recycling achieved. Perhaps that's what I should do. Just pile all the stuff out in front of the farm and wait for someone to recycle it in the night.

8th

We're in the money. An early retirement beckons. Riches are ours. Scrap the overdraft. The annual cheque for the wayleave payment for electric poles on the farm has arrived. £1.62. I even struggled to pay it into the bank as a result of a payment set-up from years ago when the family bought the farm. The payment details his father and brother's name on the cheque as well as John's. As his father died over thirty years ago and we have now bought Geoff, John's brother, out, the lady behind the bank counter was unimpressed when I tried to pay the cheque into our account.

Normally we post this cheque directly to our bank and it gets paid in without fuss. This time John asked me to go into town to pick up the medication for the cows from the vet's, and I decided to call at the bank from which, occasionally, I draw some petty cash. I went to the wrong lady. The other bank clerk knew me and said it was OK, but this new lady was determined to do the job properly and it took half an hour to sort it out. Just imagine, it must cost nearly 50p to send the cheque, 50p for us to post it back to our bank, and I've no idea what it costs in man hours to write it at the electricity board end and then for our bank to pay into our account. Bet it's more than £1.62.

9th

Sometimes it really does seem as if your thoughts and words are being listened to by a higher being, and that you have to be very careful of making any provocative remark. Especially about how reliable your car is proving to be. Such hubris will immediately exact swift retribution. Such as said car suddenly losing power and any acceleration within thirty seconds of saying 'This car hasn't given us a minute's trouble all the time we have had it.' It was spooky. Luckily we were close to home and coasted round the corner and into the yard.

10th

It looks as though the tups, young and old, are successfully completing their allotted tasks with our flock of sheep.

Nearly every one of the ewes sports a coloured bottom, testimony to the ardour of the tups and the consent of the ewes. We only have to wait until spring to find out if the job really was well done. John plans to leave the tups in for a few more weeks, then take them out for a 'well-earned rest' just before Christmas. Talk about masculine bias. They have ten months off until next tupping time. Only requirement to eat, drink and lounge about. Fortunately the tups have come through without any apparent damage to life and limb. Just occasionally they literally go off their legs if lame and cannot work the flock as John intends them too. It always strikes me as odd, the incongruity of this damage affecting the tups' performance, but if you think about it (not too deeply, mind), it's all about achieving a perfect balance at a crucial time.

11th

A few teething problems with our youngest breeding sheep: the gimmers and shearlings. They are in a different field, with their new paramour Mr Texel, Tex for short. Apparently these young ladies were so overwhelmingly attractive to the tup in the next field, a distinctly lecherous specimen belonging to a neighbouring farmer, that he kept clambering over the fence on his side to share their delights with Tex. John caught Mr Over Sexed And Over Here, put him in the trailer and back through the gate into his own field. This morning he was back in with our ewes with a satisfied smile on his face. And another hole in the hedge. So we had to move the girls. About a third of the gimmers and shearlings have already been covered by Tex. Their bottoms send out a red beacon through the foggiest weather to tell the world what they have been up to. In fact Tex's raddle has had such a hammering from his close encounters with the ewes that the straps needed tightening up. It is strapped onto his chest by a harness that tightens over his back. That way when he covers the ewes, the raddle leaves its mark.

To catch Tex means quite a chase round the field as he is none too keen on being distracted from his true vocation. He is the biggest and strongest of all the tups and we sincerely hope that he proves more virile than the last Texel tup we had, who we seriously doubted for a time as having any interest at all in the ewes. At that time the tups spent most of the year with our old horse Rupert, and the Texel we had then seemed fonder of Rupert than any other four-legged friend. This particular tup would graze virtually directly under Rupert. You could hardly see daylight between them. We gave up bringing Rupert in for the night in the summer as both Rupert and the tup were very distressed to be parted. The relationship was literally at its most fruitful in the autumn. The field Rupert grazed bordered our orchard and he was in the habit of eating all of the apples within reach as soon as they became ripe. Reaching up to snatch an apple usually meant he dislodged another couple from the tree. Very handy if you happen to be the tup in closest proximity to him.

The tup was probably not so much disinterested as incapable from fermented cider in his stomach.

The other tups are all in with the main flock, and from the rainbow-coloured bottoms of the ewes they are in with, doing very nicely indeed. We use different-coloured raddles for the different tups. A sort of performance-management guide. Raddles are very useful. By changing the crayon in the raddle after the end of the first three-week cycle of the ewes, and noting which raddle belonged to which tup for that period, John can tell which ewes are going to be late lambing, or those ewes that may not have come into season at all. The abattoir beckons in that case. No room for any hangers-on around here. It's a results-only ethos that drives performance bonuses on this farm. The bonus being that you get to spend the next year in a field instead of a casserole.

12th

The main foldyard is now full of the weaned calves that were born early in the year. They will be moved when all of the herd comes in there tomorrow. Two hens that had reared guinea fowl keets and are still wandering around the yards with them, are seriously put out. Both had established nest niches in straw bales in the big yard. Now these bales have been scattered for bedding and the hens have to find new nest sites. What they do not realise is that tonight we are catching the pair of them and putting them back into the hen run. Usually our egg count is falling off by this time in the year, but because we have a number of bantams born in the early spring, we are still getting lots of eggs. Even the Aylesbury ducks that we hatched out in the spring are starting to lay. It's an egg bonanza.

13th

I think that the foxes in this area have bugged our house.

John and I were discussing the fitness of our small flock of Aylesbury ducks and had come to the decision to have a tasting of one the next night. A couple of friends were invited round for the grand feast and I had worked out my menu to accompany the guest of honour on the table. As we slept the sleep of the just (just plain exhausted, that is), I dimly recall agitated barking in the yard. Millie was fast asleep in the kitchen. She has always slept in and can be heard snoring away or yipping excitedly as she chases rabbits and rats in her sleep. So the only other guardians of the farm, Pip and Fizz, were in their kennels or beds and not free to physically challenge any intruders, although obviously alert to the trouble afoot.

What a dumb pair John and I were. Instead of just burying our heads under the pillow and wishing the dogs would shut up, as we did, we should have got up to investigate. Then we would have found our intruder, Mr Charles Fox, pre-empting our feast with his own. All that remained the next morning was a flurry of forlorn white feathers and a pen of very agitated ducklings that had suddenly woken up to the reality of farm life and that there is no such thing as a free bowl of barley and a fox-free pen. 'How on earth had he got in?' I asked. The pen has a drop-down hatch. It slides down between runners and is apparently secure. The fox had not only managed to lift the hatch, but to add insult to injury, lifted it clean off so that it had not dropped down behind him to trap him in the pen. I suppose we should be thankful for that. If he had been trapped inside, he would have killed all of the ducks and although we might have caught him red handed/jawed/pawed the next morning, there is every likelihood that he would have slipped past us before we realised the extent of the massacre.

14th

John has moved the main flock onto the winter barley. This year's barley has shot away, and the whole crop is standing too proud for its own good. The ewes are delighted with this luxurious fare, and the change in diet will be beneficial not only for the winter barley, but also to keep the ewes in prime breeding shape. They will be moved at the end of the week back onto grass. Our tups show no signs of losing interest in their allocated task. Even the newcomer, the tup lamb we have put in with the gimmers, this year's female lambs, has soon learned which end is which, what goes where and for why, very quickly. A precocious lad. To keep up the sheep's strength for all this going on, John had ordered a couple of buckets of minerals, which are apparently the sheep equivalent of Viagra. Guaranteed to keep up their strength and flush out the relevant breeding bits to increase fertility and passion. Please quash rumours that farmers are purchasing these for domestic use. Each bucket was supposed to last the ewes ten days. Ours got through the first bucket in a day. No wonder they have been so keen to participate. Apparently instead of the minerals being in a hard form, the cake has been too soft, and our ewes, and now the tups, have been eating the stuff out of the bucket instead of licking it.

15th

Tupping, technology and technique was the subject of a deep conversation tonight when we were at a post-shoot dinner. I was in a semi-comatose state after a day fighting through brambles, undergrowth and mud with the rest of the beaters on the shoot, but considerably livelier than some of the poor old pheasants and ducks who had also been there. A friend who lambs about three hundred ewes has come up with a cunning plan to a) ensure that his sons are home on college holidays to carry out the lambing and b) ensure that all the ewes lamb in a prescribed three-week cycle. To this end he bought a vasectomised tup, known in the trade as a teaser. Oh the cruel deception. This young Swaledale tup lamb, who had been nipped in the bud, so to speak, was then put in with the ewes for three weeks before tupping time to bring them all into season together.

Lambing is fast and furious on their farm, and all of it when his sons are at home, and he and his wife away somewhere warm and exotic. 'That young tup's a real goer,' was our friend's judgement on this emasculated tup. 'We'd only put him in a day and he had covered about forty of the ewes already, and on the next day he was ready for the next forty.' 'How can you be sure he's sterile?' was the key question. After all, our friend has a very nice flock of Suffolk crosses and will be using pedigree Texel tups for the real thing; the last things he will want are the progeny of a randy little Swaledale. 'I have my proof in a jar,' our friend said. A jar? Apparently when the vet vasectomises the tup, the important bits are kept for posterity, or at least until all need for proof has been met. Gruesome, eh? Can you imagine if surgeons did the same for any male of our species going for a snip job? I have heard of people hanging onto gallstones and tonsils as pickled reminders of their op, but perlease, not these.

16th

All the cattle are now home in the yard and only those cows who surprised us with late deliveries are left with calves at foot. The rest of the calves are all weaned. As is usual, we managed to persuade assorted friends and neighbours to help us get the herd home. With a posse of mates, everything is possible and the job looks easy. When there is only John and me, the cattle, I am sure, sense the gap in defences as they cross the road. This year, however, more problems were encountered in the field than on the lane. When John assembled his troops, about two thirds of the cattle were already standing at the gate. The old cows know what the job is. They recognise that they are being fed nearer and nearer to home and the smell of that enticing silage clamp is wafting across to them. But a few of the younger stock remain to be educated. When John went in to try and drive them out of the field, all the young 'uns turned and hared it back across the field into the corral. The rest of the cows following. Luckily John had shut the gates into adjoining fields and the herd got no further than the collecting area provided by the corral. He shut them in and allowed a few minutes to settle down. Then opened up and walked them slowly back across the field to the main gates. This time most cows came home without fuss, although they took a bit of persuading to walk out of the field and across the road. Needed time to eat the grass on the roadside verge and ogle passing cyclists. But nothing could persuade the last dozen cows to leave the field. Mooing and bawling, kicking their heels up, racing back across the field (gates fortunately shut into the inland grazing), but refusing to come home. We were about on our knees chasing these renegades round the field and eventually had to concede defeat for the morning. After lunch, the second plan was to tempt them with a big bale of silage – 'bound to work' – but it didn't. The only way in the end was tractor and trailer, bringing them home three at a time from the corral. Once in the yard, they were as settled as the rest of the herd. Why the fuss?

17th

At last all the cattle are settling in the yard. We have dragged it out as long as possible because of the warm autumn, but once rain and wet, windy conditions started with a vengeance, everything had to come home. Initially the noise from the foldyard was deafening. Mums and calves objecting strongly to anyone who would listen as to the injustice and insensitivity of farm management. Splitting families asunder with all the attendant trauma, etc., etc. With limited space to hold the cows and recently weaned calves, they are within earshot of each other and there is nothing to stop parent and child communicating. Vociferously. The cows are hopefully all in calf to the new bull. We intend to breed from the heifer calves born in the New Year and they are now all in a separate part of the yard to the bull calves. For fairly obvious reasons. I tell you, rampant teenage hormones have nothing on this lot. The heifer calves from the year before are in another yard. Once the main herd starts to calve, we shall remove the bull from their midst and introduce him to his new girlfriends. I am afraid the lot of the bull calves is to go to market. In some cultures it might be the males who draw the lucky straw; in cattle I think it is the female of the species.

18th

A basket of fresh field mushrooms sits on my kitchen worktop. Suddenly, in the midst of November, a field, permanent pasture for years, is covered in pale fungi. Delicious. And at this time of year quite a surprise. This field, having been grazed by the cows all summer, has occasionally yielded a mushroom or two but never this late in the year. The happy discovery came about as John is working close to that field to fill in a dike that is obsolete now from work on a drainage scheme. The dike always needed to be cleaned out every winter, as cattle paddled the sides in as they grazed the field. Now, to support the drainage scheme, this dike can be potted, stoned and filled in.

It's John's winter project. And the sort of job the dogs love John to be working on. They can accompany him in the Land Rover and have plenty of opportunities to either laze around in the back and watch the man at work, or sniff around and see what he is turning up as he digs.

19th

In the yards, a midnight excursion for some of the stock that had been weaned led to a lot of excitement and an excess of mooing. We woke to such a bellowing and bawling that at first we thought there had been a mass break-out. A peep out the bedroom window showed no cattle milling around outside so we left it till this morning to discover the cause of noise. Somehow the young weaned stock must have opened the gate from their yard and got into the main foldyard with the cows. The most recently weaned were back with Mum. They had had quite a reunion party.

20th

Moved the sheep again to yet another field of fresh grass. The first move was to be inland across several fields. Then a rest prior to walking them through the village. In fact the sheep ended up moving themselves. 'Shall I tie the gate shut?' I asked John. 'Don't bother,' he said. 'They'll be all right in here for an hour or so, they've plenty of grass to be going at.' We meant to alert neighbours with concerns about their front gardens so they could shut gates, take guard, come and watch, yell or boo. But in the meantime we would have our lunch. Just at the last mouthful the phone rang. The sheep had come home, through the gate, along the lane, nibbled at any remaining flowers and ended up in a neighbour's paddock. Very thoughtful of them. They had done all the hard work themselves, although we still do not know how many drivers they might have upset on the way.

21st

Just a few of this year's lambs left to go to market. They have reached about 100lb weight each, nearly a cwt, or 45 kilograms if we are being Euro correct. This is a good market weight, but John has judged they still want a bit more finish on them. By that he means more flesh on their backs. As there is not a lot of goodness left in the grass, John feeds the lambs some rolled barley every day. This also gives him an opportunity to make sure everything is OK and have a count-up of stock. One lamb was missing. The field that they are in is level and in the corner there is an inspection chamber for the drainage system. It stands just over a yard high, about 4ft in diameter, goes down approximately 8ft and has an open top. There is a concrete bottom to the chamber and two drains from a couple of fields drain into the chamber and then out, eventually into a dike. If there is a lot of rain, the water can back up and stand in the bottom, but usually it just runs through. Just before John decided to leave the field, as there was no sign of the lamb, a faint bleating sound drifted across to him. At first he thought it came from the hedge bottom, but when he went to look, no lamb. Next he thought maybe the lamb had got through to the next field. But no, it had not. As he walked the boundary of the field, he realised that the bleating was growing louder and that the source appeared to be the inspection chamber. Peering in, he found his lamb. Eight foot down and with four wet feet. As soon as the lamb spotted help, it stopped bleating. Now there is faith in your shepherd for you. But John said, 'I'd nothing to get it out with. As soon as I walked away, the lamb went frantic, so I decided to come back to the farm to get you and try to pull the lamb out.' Fortunately for me (I was busy idling away doing very little and enjoying it too), a friend was driving past the end of the field on his way for a morning's pigeon shooting. A neighbour has a field of emerging rape plants and the pigeons are feeding voraciously off them. After stopping for a chat (farmers are notorious gossips), our friend was organised to fetch a rope from the farm and give John a hand in the rescue attempt. He lassoed the lamb in the chamber, pulled it up far enough for John to get hold of is front legs and then together they hauled the lamb to safety and back to its friends.

22nd

The big tractor has been back and forth across the yard all morning loading corn ready to be picked up in the next day or so by a grain merchant. We find the easiest method is to fill the big trailer first and then tip it into an auger on the mobile corn dryer. The auger then takes the corn up into the dryer and fills it ready to shoot into the big articulated lorries as they draw up alongside. John then fills another trailer ready to repeat the process once the first load has been emptied. The bullocks, whose yard is close to the dryer, have been keen observers of all the comings and goings with the tractor. The weaning that created such a furore recently has been forgotten, absorbed into the day-to-day life of the herd. The calves that were separated from their mothers last week are all far more interested in when the next load of rolled barley is being tipped into their trough or if a big round bale of straw is to be rolled out. In fact, John has to be very careful, as the bullocks, and especially the bull, have soon latched onto the play factor of a big bale. Not to be encouraged when they are pushing at one end and you are trying to push it at the other. There is no contest. They win.

23rd

All the goings-on in the sheep field since the tups went in, seem to have increased the ewes' appetite. For food, of course. John has decided to move the flock further inland to a field that has not been grazed for many years. It is a small area of grass, about five or six acres, almost totally surrounded by trees and called the Shoulder of Mutton. Until the government dispensed with setaside, we had just left the field alone. John has no intention of ploughing it up, but as grazing off the meadow would do the wild flowers and grasses no harm at this time of year and probably some good, he outlined to me his strategy to take the sheep overland to pastures new. Lured by a bag of apparently tempting sheep nuts, and with the encouragement of our sheepdog at their heels, the ewes and tups were hustled out of their current field. Off for a fairly long walk that would take them over three fields to the Shoulder of Mutton. Here the environmentalists have done us a favour. Around every field that has been worked up you must leave a two-metre strip of unploughed land for a beetle bank/wild flower reserve/grassland refuge. 'They'll follow you along that,' John assured me. And he was right. I was convinced the sheep would spread out all over the fields and

'Ooohhh. You are naughty. But I like you!'

we would never get them into the fairly narrow opening of their fresh grazing, without a lot of chasing about. They followed like devoted dogs along the grass strip. Not a mite of trouble. Nibbling along the way and seduced by the rattle of the feedbag. If only everything was so simple.

24th

All around us other herds are leaving the fields for the big sheds over winter. One sight we shall miss near home is the sight of a big black Berkshire pig called, I believe, Sally, who likes to go out to meet her owner's herd at milking time. She has a keen eye and appetite for a bucket of milk with the calves after milking. Sally is also an epicure for acorns. She is currently roaming the verges under oak trees to hoover up any going whilst she waits for the herd to come in. John has also seen her pacing one of her owners on the quad bike as he goes down the fields to gather the herd up. 'She can get up a fair speed,' he said. Pigs might not fly round here, but they can certainly run.

25th

Up at the crack of dawn to get a trailer full of suckler calves ready for market. Jessica is staying with us and very excited to justify her farming boiler suit with a proper job: helping Pappa with the paperwork. Her role was to hold onto everything and make sure we did not forget the passports and every other piece of paper necessary to sell livestock. The calves sold well. Came in quietly, were a matched bunch and looked fit. I had seen a lot of buyers taking note of them when they were in their holding pens and there was a bit of competition when it came to sale time. We took Millie our Jack Russell with us in the Land Rover, but she was not impressed with the car park. Every time Jess and I went back to let her out for a wee, she just trembled and refused to relieve herself. Her bladder must have been bursting, but no way was she going to give in on alien territory.

We had noticed over the previous few days that Millie, usually an incontinent little terror, was turning into a very trustworthy little dog when it came to being clean in the house. No puddles to be seen. No little piles of poo. Although not too keen to go out now that it is turning wet and cold. But then this lunchtime I went into the front room at the very end of the farmhouse. Not used very frequently at all. Mystery of the successful house training solved. Millie has found her very own inside toilet. She is in disgrace.

26th

The first of the new calves has arrived to one of our young heifers. We exchanged bulls with a neighbour over last winter. Our heifers could not be served by this particular bull as all the heifers were his daughters. I am afraid it was rather downhill for him after his outing. Life off our own farm must have turned his head, as he was never as quiet and dependable again. Although sad to see him go, I was secretly relieved as he had become difficult to handle and I feared for John's safety.

27th

Another new arrival: a big red corn trailer. John ordered it when I was not looking and unable to veto or query the expenditure. The stick I would get if I spent that much money without asking. It makes our old trailer look very tatty and rusty. We shall keep the old one for cleaning out the yards, as nothing as common as muck will be allowed to sully the pristine interior of the new trailer for at least, oh, I would say, a week.

28th

A distinctly smelly Jack Russell is laid across my feet as I write this. Despite a dip in the bath, she still reeks of dead squirrel, a scent she finds irresistible and I find revolting. The squirrel was one of the nicely decomposed (to Millie) scavengers of our big walnut tree. There are, despite the squirrels' best attempts, several bags of walnuts hanging from the kitchen beams. We will crack them at Christmas. An old horse drinking trough in the yard, now planted up with herbs, has four sturdy little walnut trees grown from nuts harvested a couple of years ago. John will plant them out in the next week and no doubt plant a few more nuts in amongst the sage, oregano, mint, chives, rosemary and dill. No doubt, too, I will inadvertently dig them up in the spring and then hastily, and guiltily, rebury them.

29th

Spent a fruitless hour looking up the number of the Pied Piper. Must try the Hamelin telephone exchange. Just when we think we are getting on top of the rat problem, more of them appear. Last night we locked Millie in the big grain store to see if she could catch any of the rats that are currently haunting our dreams and the grain shed. In the best horror films Millie should have come out with all her hair white. In fact when we opened the doors in the morning she was fast asleep curled up on her blanket, not a bit the worse for her night's incarceration. Despite the corn shed being certified as rat proof, you can clearly see rat trails up the corn mountains. John even shot one rat whilst it was staring down at him from the top of a heap of wheat. At least he got a rat in his sights.

One of our friends returned home from a night out and decided to 'have a look round' before bedtime. Spotting a couple of rats scuttling across a foldyard, he let rip with his gun. And totally annihilated the alkathene pipe carrying his water supply. Bedtime was a long way off before he cleared up that mess. We may, however, actually be starting to make inroads into the rat problem with the help of some stray cats in the yard. For the last week we have glimpsed the whisk of black and white tails disappearing out of sight in the foldyards. Jolly good.

30th

Final rotavirus jab for all of the cows in calf. They had their first vaccination a month ago. The vet could give us no reason as to why rotavirus suddenly appeared in our closed herd. It could be as simple as a bird carrying droppings from an infected herd in the district. But we've got it in the herd now and the only way to deal with it is an annual vaccination. The vaccine is shockingly, staggeringly expensive. Therefore the important thing to do when injecting the cows this morning was 'Don't drop the bottle.' Needed extra hands to make sure that as the vaccine was drawn out, each bottle was in safe custody until the next animal was in the crush.

Then there was all the faff of taking numbers and recording the medication in our records. We haven't found an easy way to identify which animal has been dosed, as sprays do not show up on our black Aberdeen Angus-cross cows. Although I have suggested that with all the Christmas decorations in the shops, a squirt of artificial snow onto each of their backs would make an effective mark. And look festive too. It is noticeable how the temperament of our cows has changed over the years since we were an entirely dairy enterprise. The heifers coming through into the herd are all much wilder as they are not handled on a daily basis as the dairy cows were. Injecting the cows was therefore quite a fun-filled morning. None of that quiet amble into the crush. Took quite a bit of cunning and logistic planning to push several cows at a time into the run, thus giving them little room to manoeuvre, i.e. have a go at us, before entering the crush for that all-important jab.

2nd

Invited out for supper, we were delighted to share the evening with friends including a local vet and poultry farmer. Talk turned to the bird 'flu scare a few years ago and the range of precautions that were introduced. 'I had three sets of Wellington boots and overalls to change in and out of when I went into the hen house,' our friend Dave said. 'But the haulier who had just brought us all our new birds, continued to use the same dirty old pallets to load up the crates of hens with, that he used to go to all the other farms. We tried to take all the precautions we could with tyre washes for vehicles, but we could not control something like that.' There was lots of nodding in agreement and scary stories about how foot and mouth was spread around the country a few years ago. So we needed something a little lighter to talk about and our friendly vet supplied it. As part of his practice he attends to the welfare and good health of police and prison dogs. 'You are very conscious of keeping on the right side of these dogs when treating them. Especially the prison dogs, which are not as used to being out and about in the general community as much as ordinary police dogs. Their job is to protect personnel as much as hold down their target, and their personalities are very finely balanced between aggression and biddability. But the sniffer dogs,' he went on to say, 'are different again. They are very friendly and disarming and frequently trained not to alert targeted offenders to the nature of their task, for example when mingling with visitors going into prison.' The story continued that several weeks ago one of these dogs came in for its regular health check. As the surgery was busy, the dog and its handler had to spend some time out in the waiting room, and the dog, as usual, was keen to follow its normal habit of greeting and responding to affectionate pats and strokes. It was particularly zealous in wanting to sit close to one particular man with a small cat in a basket. Gazed up at him adoringly and wagged its tail enthusiastically. 'His handler was chuckling to himself when he came into the treatment room for me to check the dog over. I'm off duty now,' the prison officer said, 'and anyway I'm not a policeman, but the dog has sussed out that he's either carrying drugs, or has been recently smoking or taking them. He kept telling me what a lovely friendly dog it was and that normally he didn't care for dogs, but he could really take to this one.' If only he knew.

3rd

In the pantry we have/had an old-fashioned meat cupboard with wire sides to keep flies out. I think Pip was tuned in psychically to the recounting of the super sensitivity of dogs to smells. Despite the safe itself being recently moved after a previous attempt by Pip to burgle its contents, Pip must have scrabbled away at the wire and removed the remains of a roast leg of pork for her afternoon snack. On a different scale, John has come to terms with our other bushy-tailed thieves. We have had all the walnuts we need off the walnut tree in the paddock, about 46lb this year, and so any that are left are fair prey for the squirrels. He is not quite so magnanimous, however, about the squirrels out in a small plantation of deciduous and evergreen trees that he planted fifteen years ago. After an initial onslaught by voles, the trees became well established. John sorted out deer predation with 6ft high fences. But a fence is not a problem to a squirrel. Just a handy leg-up. What the squirrels are doing now is taking out the growing points of the young trees, the oaks in particular. So instead of growing straight and true, they are branching out or, in the worst-case scenario, dying off.

4th

Time for the seasonal argument over the Christmas tree. Agreeing on every aspect of domestic life would be a miraculous state of affairs in most marriages, and certainly not always a feature of ours. Particularly when the choice of tree presents even more of a contentious issue for discussion than normal family discourse. For many years we picked out a tree from Christmas trees that John had dug in amongst plantations of hard woods he has created around the farm. He must have planted several thousand trees over the years and they now provide a warm winter retreat and shelter for wildlife. However, the Christmas trees have now either grown too big to bring into the house or are too straggly after being crowded out and stunted by bigger trees around them. For the past year or so John has struggled to pick out anything suitable, even resorting to sticking several branches in a pot and trying to persuade me they all sprang from the same root. So today I decided to actually buy a tree. This decision was justified in my mind even further by a well-oiled confession by John (we had had friends round and an excess of bramble whisky) that the scraggy offering I had accepted last year in the spirit of not provoking yet another confrontation over a tree, had been rejected by a friend whose husband had tried the same trick out on her. Oh. The duplicity of men. Or farmers, anyway.

5th

At this time of year, cards often tell a story of the year gone past and news from home and abroad. One particular friend who has gone through several (and I mean several) marriages and subsequent divorces, seems to have come up with the best solution yet that I have heard of to solve the vicissitudes of single life. Clive fills his time with female company, sees the world and is fed, housed and clothed at no expense to himself. He has become a dance partner on a cruise ship. Perennially circling the world and rather hoping, I think, to meet that rich, single woman of his dreams. Such women, I am sure, would never consider the role of a farmer's wife. Not this week anyway. Nor many others probably, when I look back at the ups and downs of agricultural life over the last year. It can be idyllic, I know, but when you see for example the trail of straw and puddles currently decorating my kitchen and utility room, and the host of fresh scratches in the bottom of my sink from buckets being filled from the kitchen and not yard tap, I tell you, any woman would think twice.

6th

'Has anyone asked what I want for Christmas?' came the plaintive request from John. 'Because if they do, can you tell them I want some more mole traps.' Goodwill to all men, then, but definitely not to moles. Not when they are making such a mess of our newly drained field of wheat. Conditions are obviously just right for worms now – not too wet and

'For me? Too kind. I'll see you down below shortly.'

not too dry – and if they are right for worms, then they are just perfect for Mr Mole and all his mates. But what a Christmas present. I suppose we could make present opening quite a snappy session and preset the traps to go off just as the wrapping paper gets ripped away. Or even include a 'One we caught earlier' just to make the whole job as gruesome as possible. So, if you want some mole traps, buy some mole traps, is the official response to that request. I will consider an extra dog lead or two, especially as it is me who usually loses them, but I do think that Christmas needs to possess more awe and wonder than just being a time for exchanging gifts, and certainly not gifts as prosaic as a mole trap.

7th

The cows look comfortable, warm and dry in their winter quarters. Outside it may be icy, windy, raining, sleeting, snowing, hurricanes even; but who cares? Certainly not the cows. They have a ring feeder full of barley straw and a clamp brimming with delicious, juicy silage. Four calves born to the heifers are equally content and fussed over not only by their mums, but also all the other cows in the herd. When you go in to check up on things, the herd press round the calves, so that soon all that can be seen of them is four inquisitive little heads peering out from beneath a forest of black legs and very fat tums.

In another yard, several of the heifers are bulling. They are too young to be served by the bull as they were only born this year. Promiscuous lot. That has not stopped them bouncing around in their yard and pushing their gate open so that they have broken into the main foldyard. So now it is game on to get them all back in their own yard and well away from temptation.

It is rare for things to go to plan round here. It is now a major and time-consuming occupation to keep our cattle provided with drinking water. Frequently troughs and drinkers are frozen solid each morning, and even when eventually thawed out, they freeze up again as soon as it is night time and the temperature drops still further.

8th

The sheep have been moved again to fresh pastures. They know the routine well. Having eaten up in their present field they are only too eager to trot along the lane to fresh grass, following a tempting feedbag being rattled in front of them. It's the oldest guinea fowl and some of this year's bantams that I feel sorriest for. They have roosted all summer in the orchard. Luxuriant leaf growth has protected them from balmy summer showers and the first of the autumn's gusts. But now the trees are stripped of their leaves and at night the fowl all cling to the bare branches with only their feathers to keep them warm. I've tried to catch the bantams and shut them in the hen hut so that they get used to a dry hut at night, but they are having none of it. If I forget to catch them up, the bantams are back in those trees and out of my reach before I realise. They might not be able to fly, but they hop onto the lowest branches and then work their way to the top of the trees. I went out when the wind was really fierce last night to see if they were OK. However wildly the branches swayed, they clung on grimly. It is their choice.

9th

Reaching into the back of my car to retrieve my shopping, I noticed that the bag was curiously empty of several of the goods I had bought at the butcher's. Notably the sausages. I had been distracted when I arrived home and left the back of the car open. A fatal error with hungry dogs around. Recounting this tale to friends brought out a host of other stories. One remembered how her father had gone to pick up a pair of his racing pigeons that had been blown off course and landed at an unfamiliar pigeon cote. He was contacted because of the pigeons' identifying rings and set off the next day to pick the pair up. With him in his Land Rover he took his two shooting dogs. By the time he retrieved the pigeons it was getting late and he was invited in for a bite to eat. Returning to the Land Rover, he was horrified to find the back of the vehicle full of feathers. Pigeon variety. The dogs had decided if he had gone in for a snack, they deserved one too. And how handy to find a couple of tasty birds so thoughtfully provided for them at the end of a long day.

To bring this tale of arch criminals to an end, I must name my own granddaughter. We are going out tonight and my contribution is an apple pie, on the top of which I had cut out pastry letters that spelled Merry Xmas. My ancient set of alphabet cutters come in very useful here. I love to name pies and had aimed for Merry Xmas rather than Merry Christmas, as it required less space round the pie edge. But no longer. Mer Mas, it now says. We have a pastry thief in the house.

10th

My friend Tine has just called at the farm to ask a favour. 'Have you got any spare pheasant heads? I just need a couple of fresh ones from your next shoot.' 'No problem,' John answered. 'How many do you need?' He did not seem to find anything strange at all in the request and even went further into the exact requirements for the decapitated birds.

Now Tine, my friend who has this sinister interest in dead birds, is a woman who has to be doing. No slobbing around in front of the telly for her of an evening. If she's not cooking, knitting, baking, sewing, painting and decorating or organising her husband Pete (who needs it, it must be said), she is engaged in her latest craft pursuit. Currently, stick dressing.

John has had more than a passing interest in carving handles for his own crooks and walking sticks and there is even now a gruesome bag of sheep's horns and antlers hanging up in the meal shed. So he knew exactly what she required and why. In order to get the exact proportions of the handle correct, she had been advised to work from life (or in this case death). The heads would pop in and out of the freezer like Dracula rising up from his coffin. We await with interest the finished outcome. Next specimen could be a real still life. Pete.

11th

We continue to be visited by foxes every night who are seeking out any weaknesses in the chicken and duck hut defences. Recent snow makes it very easy to see where their nocturnal excursions have taken them to. If the fencing had not been recently renewed around the chicken run, I think we would have suffered serious poultry predation. As it is, I feel like feeding the chickens to the fox anyway as they have completely stopped laying in this weather. I am fed up with them as they are eating a vast quantity of grain every day and producing nothing. The pigeons love it. Go to the run and vast flocks rise up into the air from round the corn feeder. And what use is a pigeon? They do not lay any eggs for me.

I have to be vigilant in keeping the hen's water drinker flowing and not frozen solid. Out in the fields John has despaired of trying to keep the drinking trough water supply defrosted. He smashes through the ice on the top of the water and concentrates on providing plenty of hay and ewe nuts to keep the sheep well nourished. I expect the fallen hay around the racks is also providing a modicum of nourishment for passing hares and rabbits and maybe even some deer. Foraging for food is a hard task in this weather. A concern for the foldyards is the weight of snow and ice on the roofs. John has been up to check that ours are sound and is pleased that he renewed the pantiles on a barn roof that might have been vulnerable given the present conditions. Unhappily, the poultry shed at a friend's farm has suffered a collapsed roof. Fortunately it was not the shed that housed all their Christmas poultry, but it was the shed they did the plucking in. It's going to be a cold job unless the weather changes.

12th

John has just found more than moles in his fields. Leeches abound there too. Proper blood-sucking jobs. The kind that doctors in times gone by, and current times too, apply for blood-letting. The job that took John in there was to clean out the dike down one side of the field. The dike is not too deep and narrow and he has been able to do the job with a spade, rather than the digger. What he has turned over has been a wriggly mass of leeches. Or, as was suggested when I looked up the collective noun for leeches, a politician of leeches. Ouch. Apparently surgeons make use of leeches' ability to drink half a teaspoon of blood in less than fifteen minutes to drain congested blood from wounds, or in the case of plastic surgery, for reconstructive work. Bet that doesn't figure highly in cosmetic surgeons' public relations material. In times gone by, men would bathe in a ditch, trousers rolled up to their knees, legs smeared in pig's blood and collect the leeches that adhered themselves to their legs, for sale. Now I do appreciate that in all the years I have been married to John times have always allegedly been hard, but I do hope that this is not one money-making scheme he expects me to contribute to.

13th

The abominable feather man tapped at my kitchen window. John was in full geese- and duck-dressing mode and there was hardly an inch of him that did not sport gently fluttering down and feathers. It was a marathon session. Starting at seven in the morning and not finishing until about eight in the evening. Geese are sensitive souls. You cannot just do one or two for the table and come back and finish the rest a few weeks later. They would go off their food, pine and lose condition. I am afraid it's all or nothing. And that includes most of the ducks, which have been raised with the geese. More importantly, however, these ducks had reached a good time in their feather condition to pluck them. If they were or had been in moult, the new, pin feathers are difficult to pluck and the duck does not dress as well, and it would be mid- to end of January before they could be dressed again.

As a result of this mass slaughter, I am persona non grata with the neighbours. They get very attached to our poultry, and their Christmas spirits are dashed by the annual event. 'I can't bear to see John carrying the ducks and geese out of their huts,' one neighbour said, as she prepared her stuffing for a Barbary duck roast. 'They are such characters, I'll miss them,' said another, as she perused her recipe books for gooseberry sauce to go with roast goose. Our ducks and geese have had a great life: free range, protected (as much as possible) from predators, and lots of grass and barley to eat. Plus a pond for a dip.

John had certainly made his plucking shed comfortable. Sat on a bale of straw under a pig lamp, kept supplied with coffee and tea by the missus. Then allowed back in the farmhouse after a dust-off for his lunch and tea. Goose and duck down is unruly stuff, however. Everywhere I look, a white puff of down lifts into the air and floats onto another hiding place. It will take me days to vacuum it all up.

14th

Despite prevaricating for the last few weeks, I have eventually faced the inevitable and started to write my Christmas cards. I had even got to the stage of just shoving any cards we received into a drawer as I felt so guilty at receiving them. I needed an excuse for why I had not got pen to paper. So I am getting fingers to computer and drawing up names and addresses of all the lucky recipients of my smudged seasonal wishes. I'm not really such an obfuscating card writer. It is just that time gets nibbled away at such a huge speed. Whenever I have my days planned, something always prevents me completing my tasks. Plus I am extremely easily distracted. Attention span of a gnat, my mum always used to say. The idea was that today I would go to Bryony's house and help out at the tenth birthday party organised for my grandson Ollie. The plan was this. Take all the children and parents to one of these big play barns. Buy any dads and mums attending coffee and a newspaper and let them relax and chat. The children would whoop it up on bouncy castles, slides, rope nets, tunnels, etc., etc. Then feed them chicken nuggets, turkey twizzlers, pizza, fish fingers and chips. All good healthy stuff. Works a treat. For some unknown reason, John pleads farm management duties and avoids all such places and activities.

15th

Spent a night with granddaughter Jessica kicking me senseless in the bed she insists on sharing with me. Then I made breakfast, read books, nearly drowned in the bath with her washing my hair and got ready to come home to write my cards and cook a meal for friends. But where were my keys? A relaxed check turned into a more serious search: a tipping-out-bags session and a frantic turn-out of everything in sight. But two hours later, nothing remotely resembling a key, although my handbag had been left on the floor and found on its side with the zip open. Had I left it like that? Knowing me, yes. Ollie, the birthday boy, has a penchant for putting things in unusual places. Such as down toilets, bidets, out of letterboxes, in Wellington boots. But no. No keys hanging on the Christmas tree or anywhere else slightly illogical to us but highly logical to him. Crunch time. I rang John. Would he drive up with the spare set of keys and would Chris my son-in-law meet him on the motorway? To their credit, both agreed without demur.

Eventually I got home. I had messed everyone's day up and yet again would not have time to write those dratted cards. But tonight the phone rang. 'Guess what I have in my hand?' my daughter said. 'Where were they?' I replied, knowing the answer immediately. They were in the front of Jessica's Barbie camper van. Of course they were. Ollie loves to see cars start. Adored the camper van. Longs to turn the keys in the ignition. Why didn't we think of it? At least I know where the keys are now . . . but where is that Christmas list again?

16th

The dining room looks like a dining room again after closely resembling a morgue for several days. The slate floor, notoriously cold to toes, was just right for chilling off the geese and ducks in safety after they had been dressed ready for the freezer. Normally we leave poultry out to chill in the old milking parlour, but an unusual range of visitors had left John rather more security conscious than usual.

Just prior to Christmas there seemed to be a stream of decrepit old vans and pick-ups in the yard, asking if we had any scrap to sell. I can only assume that these folk have some problems with reading, as bold notices on both gates state that visitors can only come into the yard by appointment/arrangement and that we have CCTV coverage.

Notwithstanding the argument for domestic/business security, there is also the constant concern over biosecurity. If these old vans are travelling from one farm to another, they would be prime conduits for bringing disease in. They have a disconcerting habit of dropping off one of the passengers (there are always at least three crammed together on the front seats) at the farm entrance, who then wanders up to the farmhouse door via the buildings, whilst the driver tries to hold you in pleasant conversation and banter at the back door. They miss nothing. And the last van was far too interested in the geese and ducks freshly plucked and singed and hung in the meal shed.

17th

Extra effort is going into housework because of the Christmas clean-up. The house looks amazingly tidy, although I doubt it will stay the same once Ollie, Jessica and Sophie arrive.

My daughter Jo usually takes it into her head that the fridges need a good clean-out as well as the house. The subculture of the fridge makes a reluctant appearance once she starts her attack. Forensic evidence of my feckless approach to the dates given as 'best by'. 'Do you know how long you've had this yoghurt, Mother?' she cries out. 'Months. It was "best by" in October.' 'But it's sour milk to start with,' I counter. 'It's meant to have gone off in the first place.' Not acceptable as an excuse. She even made me throw away my little cans of tonic water, as they had gone out of date in August. 'But they're in tins,' I said. 'Explorers carried tinned stuff for years in the Arctic and Antarctic. They'll be fine.' The answer came in the form of the jangling of tonic water cans into my waste bin. No pity.

The last time she finished this task I was able to dump the oldest of the fridges (which was virtually only a cupboard and no longer chilled) and streamline the contents of the fridge into one. I have to admit the fridge smells better (it did have a rather unusual aroma), I know what I have got and I know it is all edible. But all the fun has gone out of opening things.

18th

Alarms fitted for her security when John's mother lived with us, have now been dusted off and new batteries put in place. Those dodgy visitors have made us very security conscious. You cannot move outside once the alarms are switched on, without a chime or piercing screech rending the air. The first night we hardly slept, as kittens and cats regularly broke the security beams. Set higher, only one alarm was set off at precisely the same time, 1.14 am on two subsequent mornings. The third night, John woke at 1 am and looked out to see the visitor. A fox. Sublimely unconcerned (presumably checking his watch), strolling through the yard, alert to any pickings. Not a sound from the dogs either. He must be a very regular visitor and no longer seen as a threat.

The one other item on the farm that has been under equally close security watch has been the gingerbread house that Jo-Jo, our daughter, has decorated for Jessica and Ollie. It has stood, a vision of fairytale wonder and hopeless temptation for anyone with a sweet tooth. Silver balls drip off the snowy roof. Jelly tots, Smarties, midget gems and fruit pastilles dot the garden. Dolly mixtures create a wandering path through the glittering garden. It is so pretty. So delicate. And ever so slightly at a tilt when the icing sugar cement did not quite hold the roof and walls straight. Two gingerbread characters stand rather drunkenly on guard. Too much Christmas pop, probably.

Their days, however, like those of the ducks and the geese, are numbered. It might break the odd tooth or two to dismantle the gingerbread house, but the gingerbread figures are far more vulnerable and have been promised to Jess and Ollie. Perhaps they have been the fox's ultimate prey. Remember the tale of the Gingerbread Man and of how the fox carried him to 'safety'? That's why he is stalking the yard. Waiting for the little men to make a run for it.

19th

My youngest granddaughter Sophie, whose birthday is on Christmas Day, has very specific tour arrangements of the farmyard when she comes to visit. Although slightly overawed by the cattle in the foldyard, we still have to peep though the yard gates and wait for the cows to come and blow down their noses at us. Sophie is both delighted and terrified at the same time. There are eggs of course to collect, chicks to hold, guinea fowl to upset and ducks to laugh at for their waddling gait.

20th

It is so wet everywhere. In our village we have a constant stream of neighbours asking for help with blocked drainpipes, culverts under lanes and just sheer quantities of water that should be getting away much faster than it is. Often it is a matter of rodding through, but it seems that not one other man in the village is capable. They stand and watch and praise John's manual skills, but demonstrate none of their own. The problem appears to be that the drainage authorities are not keeping the main drainage dikes clear. The authorities hold water back so as not to flood urban populations, failing to regularly dredge rivers to get water out to sea or clear undergrowth and vegetation from banks so as to speed up the water flow. The result is water backing up and leaving roads that are akin to ponds rather than tarmac. The plus side is, and I am an optimist at heart, the car and Land Rover are sparkly clean underneath. Our actual yard may be muddy and straw filled, but take the vehicles out onto the road, and it is better than a pressure washer car wash.

21st

John was out very early this morning with his gun. One clutch of bantams, hatched out in the summer and ready to lay next spring, have been killed by a marauding fox. Unfortunately for him, however, he came visiting in the snow. I appreciate that everything is hungry at this time of year, but he ate one or two and just killed the rest and left their bodies for a return snack. That, I am afraid, was his undoing. We had heard the dogs barking regularly at about three o'clock in the morning and knew from the alarm that he, or another fox, also visited at an earlier hour, but after seeing where his tracks led, this particular morning he was expected. End of visits.

John has been back out during the day, after more vermin. The rising water levels have driven a large number of rats into the buildings. Millie is beside herself with excitement for most of the day ratting. She is constantly in a filthy state because of digging holes and investigating under sheds. As her bed is under my desk, my nostrils are currently assailed by a putrid aroma of muck, drains and decay. Lovely. And to think, once I get sat down on a sofa, she will want to be on my lap. Perhaps before we get to the evening doze I ought to give her a quick shower and rub down.

22nd

A pair of mallards paddle ecstatically across the lake formed in our biggest barley field. Half an acre of water plus – an overflowing pond.

How can it be? Just last year John put some new drains in towards the main lateral. Even before that, we certainly hadn't had anywhere near this amount of water after any persistent rain. No, John thought, it had to be a collapsed main. This did not bode well. An extra winter job to try and find which part of the drainage system had fallen in a forty-acre field. And at Christmas time. But, starting with the principle that it would be best to check where the pipes drain into the main dikes and ditches around the field, John checked the main lateral first. Not a trickle of water coming out. So that narrowed the search down. Could still require an awful lot of spadework, however, to find where in the system the blockage was. First things first, however, and John had to check the outfall. Armed with a set of drain rods, he pushed the end of the rods, with a large screw on, into the pipe. Nothing with the first section, or second. Then, once he had attached the next length of rod, the rods met some resistance.

Something, not solid, but springy yet impervious, was blocking any further probing into the lateral. John is a big, strong man: 6ft 4in, 15 stone. We don't do metric. Heaving on the end of the rods, he forced through whatever was blocking the screw end of the rod and then pulled back. Stalemate. Another heave. Then another. Finally something began to give.

Last summer the drainage board cleared their main drainage system, which borders one side of this field. A huge willow tree had spread its roots across the ditch. The drainage board had done a good job pushing the tree, part of which was diseased and rotten, back off the ditch. But some of the roots must have kept their territory, because what John pulled out of the drain was a huge, fibrous mass of matted willow tree roots. 'As soon as I pulled the roots clear, the water just bubbled out,' John said. 'It came with such a force that it was hitting the other side of the ditch in a jet.' He was immensely satisfied with himself. I had to go down straight way to examine the roots and relive the root/drain saga. You could actually see the water level dropping in the field, and today, although the barley looks a bit stressed and yellow after nearly being drowned off, it will survive. And the pond is back to its normal level. The mallards aren't very happy, though. Last I heard, they were off to Copenhagen to refute all these claims that water levels are rising due to climate changes.

23rd

I have a new best friend. One who will never let me down. Always speaks gently to me and never ever gets cross if I go the wrong way or get my road direction skills muddled. You've guessed. I have a satellite navigation system. It's great. Perhaps I have phrased that wrong. It is not me who has sat nav, it is actually John. It is an early Christmas present, but as I do all the long-distance map reading, I see it more as mine.

I think by now he is well acquainted with his daily drives back and forth to the fields, can just about manage trips to market without directions and has no problem finding shoot locations. When we need to go somewhere different, however, I can be relied on to mix left with right or brightly inform him that we have just passed the road we were meant to go down. Mrs Sat Nav does none of that. Very precisely before a turning comes up she lets you know your distance and then reminds, not nags, on action required. If by chance you miss it, after a few seconds' realignment when she might prompt you again to make the turn, she will rethink, and redirect. Brilliant.

Not that I don't love maps. And just to be sure, I also print out a copy of routes I am taking. No need to be totally reliant on technology. It is just a little unnerving to launch into a journey with no idea in which direction you are heading, especially where motorways are involved. Not that sat navs always get things right. Friends staying with us a few weeks ago had driven across from Shropshire. They found their way to the farm via their sat nav. About ten minutes away they rang to tell us to put the kettle on. Twenty minutes passed and still no sign of them. Then came the phone call. Could John come and pull them out with the tractor. They had turned down a soggy green lane near the farm, which no-one ever uses but must have registered on the sat nav. And they were up to their axles in mud.

24th

John and I are working together here in companionable silence. Me at my computer. Him dressing a pile of plucked pheasants and ducks. Everyone else has gone out for last-minute Christmas purchases. Both of us pleased to be doing what we are doing, not envying each other's task and pleased it's not us doing the shopping.

John makes a brilliant job (as I never tire of telling him so that I do not get the chore) of dressing game and poultry. I have freezer bags ready to pop them in the chiller. Do not say that I do not play my part. But as the night draws in, and with family all safe and warm and ready to enjoy the festivities, I often think of one of my favourite poems at this time of year, 'The Oxen' by Thomas Hardy:

> *'Now they are all on their knees,'*
> *An elder said as we sat in a flock*
> *By the embers in hearth side ease.*

It somehow sums up the feel of this time of year for me, as we do those last-minute checks in the foldyard on Christmas Eve. All over the festivities, any dereliction of duties in farm and stock care is never even contemplated. The cattle, lowing away as usual, have to be checked at night before bedtime and the sheep visited several times during the day. Can't say we sat up with them round a fire, though.

> *We pictured the meek mild creatures where*
> *They dwelt in their strawy pen.*
> *Not did it occur to one of us there*
> *To doubt they were kneeling then.*

I am not sure whether I noticed the cows were all down on their knees, but a few are starting to look decidedly more matronly than usual, as calving is due from this time onwards. Which is another reason for delaying bedtime to trudge through the straw of the foldyard. But finally,

> *So fair a fancy few would weave*
> *In these years! Yet I feel,*
> *If someone said on Christmas Eve,*
> *'Come see the oxen kneel*
> *In the lonely Barton by yonder coomb*
> *Our childhood used to know,'*
> *I should go with him in the gloom,*
> *Hoping, it might be so.*

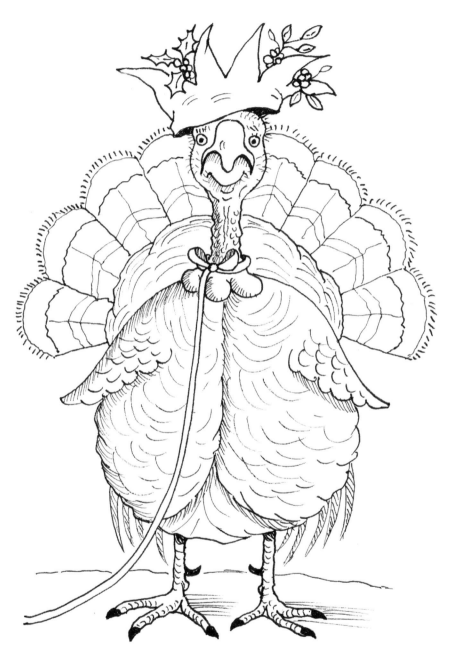

'So what's all this fuss about Christmas lunch, then . . .?'

25th

Christmas Day has flown by in a flurry of wrapping paper and food. Family and friends staying. More friends calling in for drinks and chat. And of course Sophie's second birthday to celebrate. She is convinced that the whole of the Christmas celebrations are laid on specifically for her, and that the Advent calendar's true focus is on 'my birthday, Mamma'.

Outside, the stock of course cannot be neglected and no-one can really relax on Christmas morning until all the jobs of feeding and bedding up have been completed. To be repeated in the evening. Jessica loves to help John with these jobs when she is here, especially collecting eggs for breakfast.

Meanwhile the dogs, especially Millie, greet all who come with equal enthusiasm. Millie has perfected a ping-pong style of welcome: bouncing off visitors to either their delight or horror. Depends where she has been on the farm as to whether they get covered in straw, mud or cow muck. Ideas as to how to persuade her to desist are welcome. But she is a brilliant ratter and mouser and for this John will forgive her anything.

However, it was unnerving when she started barking furiously at what appeared to be a random spot in the hall, only to find that a mouse-sized gap had been nibbled in the carpet and a drafty hole revealed under the floorboards. It upset me, but not nearly as much as a friend who visited a farm up in the hills for coffee and noticed a rat leap out of a cupboard, scamper across a table and jump onto a shelf, only to disappear behind some cans of beans. The farmer (a bachelor and likely to remain so) was totally unfazed. 'I saw him do that yesterday as well,' he commented. 'Perhaps I'd better get a trap or two.'

26th

The carpets on the landing and bedrooms hint, indeed strongly indicate, that a fly Armageddon has taken place. Upstairs reeks of fly spray. Little black corpses litter beds and floors. In the words of granddaughter Jess, 'It's gross, Mamma.' Gross indeed and a direct response to turning the heating up for seasonal cheer. And a combination of turning out little-used cupboards and leaving the attic doors open at the top of the stairs. The endless nooks and crannies that cluster flies hibernate in in an old Georgian farmhouse have suddenly warmed up and promised a false spring to all those dormant insects. Usually I am tactical with the heating. Downstairs fires, oil-fired cooker, underfloor bathroom heating and electric blankets, plus hopefully a hot farmer, usually suffice. But with children and visitors and Christmas, I let the heating have its head. Cue a fly invasion.

27th

Decided to take some time out with Jessica and Ollie to walk the dogs and feed the fish on the big pond. All went well at the pondside. Ollie and Jess looked real professionals in their green boiler suits with high-visibility stripes. Young farmers. The dogs were keen to chase the stale bread and teacakes into the water and to swim after balls thrown in by a very well-coordinated Ollie.

Things were going well. Ollie and Jess had an established pattern of getting a handful of bread or picking up a ball and standing well back from the edge of the pond for the throw. Ollie was brilliant. Went nowhere near the water. Then in a flash he slipped his hand, wet from the ball, out of mine, ran behind me straight to the water's edge, and jumped in. Just like that. He disappeared from view. The water is deep, dark, and he was too far from the bank to reach out and grab him.

A nightmare situation that gave me no choice but to jump in after him. Fortunately, he bobbed up, buoyed I imagine by trapped air in his boiler suit. As he went under again, with me this time, I grabbed him and struck out for the shore and John's outstretched hand. Scrabble, scrabble in the mud and we were out. Ollie never even cried. Just looked shocked. I felt it. I had put on two fleeces to keep warm and they were very heavy and sodden with water and my Wellington boots were full of evil, dark water. A hot bath beckoned.

28th

The water troughs in the foldyard have frozen up again and John needs hot water to defrost them, and what better way to find it than by trailing into the farmhouse. The grit mixture to melt ice, which John bought from a supplier, seems to consists of an equal mix of salt and mud. I have been thinking of giving up completely on trying to keep the floors clean. Compounding the mess is Ollie, whose sole ambition is to run a track of Thomas trains straight across the pathway of any passer-by. I have lost count of the number of times I have tripped over a stray engine or tender. Only to be muttered at darkly by Ollie for wrecking his set-up.

29th

It has been a busy month at home and on the road to try to keep in touch with the family and friends. Birthdays, school concerts, parties and productions have meant a lot of extra miles on the car's clock. Luckily a clash in birthday dates was narrowly avoided. At one point a few years ago I thought I would have grandchildren in different parts of the country expecting us to attend birthday parties on the same day.

30th

We are approaching the end of the year on a mysterious note. John has just returned from the pond, with the dogs, to tell me that the ducks and carp are being attacked and killed by an unknown predator. John has his suspicions, and it is not a fox. Rather mink or even an otter. They have been spotted in the vicinity. Several duck carcasses have been left by the pond with their breasts eaten out. Some carp, too, are on the side of the pond, with only the heads bitten off or just the ghostly glitter of fish scales remaining on the grass. Apparently an otter feeding trait. A fox would make the ducks stay on the water, but the few remaining ducks appear frightened to go onto the pond. Whatever is taking them, can swim well. It will be purely theoretical soon, as there are hardly any ducks or fish left. Those that have not flown off to safety will probably soon be eaten or killed by our unknown assailant. And the fish cannot fly away, they are trapped. So it is not looking like a Happy New Year for the ducks and carp.

31st

It is the last day of the year. Seems only a short time since we were getting ready for New Year's Eve twelve months ago. Where has the time gone? What does the New Year hold? Health and happiness and love for family and friends, I hope. And a good harvest, buoyant market price and no breakdowns will do for John. Happy New Year, everyone.